NAIS

Journal of the NATIVE AMERICAN *and* INDIGENOUS STUDIES ASSOCIATION

VOLUME 1.2

Fall 2014

NAIS (ISSN 2332-1261) is published two times a year in spring and fall by the University of Minnesota Press, 111 Third Avenue South, Suite 290, Minneapolis, MN 55401-2520. http://www.upress.umn.edu

Copyright 2014 by the Regents of the University of Minnesota

All rights reserved. With the exception of fair use, no part of this publication may be reproduced, stored in a retrieval system, or transmitted, in any form or by any means, electronic, mechanical, photocopying, recording, or otherwise, without a license or authorization from the Copyright Clearance Center (CCC), or the prior written permission of the University of Minnesota Press.

Postmaster: Send address changes to *NAIS*, University of Minnesota Press, 111 Third Avenue South, Suite 290, Minneapolis, MN 55401-2520.

Information about manuscript submissions can be found at naisa.org, or inquiries can be sent to journal@naisa.org.

Books and other materials for review should be addressed to NAIS Reviews, American Indian Studies, 1204 West Nevada Street, University of Illinois, Urbana, IL 61801.

Address subscription orders, changes of address, and business correspondence (including requests for permission and advertising orders) to *NAIS*, University of Minnesota Press, 111 Third Avenue South, Suite 290, Minneapolis, MN 55401-2520.

SUBSCRIPTIONS

- **Individual subscriptions to *NAIS*** are a benefit of membership in the Native American and Indigenous Studies Association. NAISA membership is $50 annually. To become a member, visit http://naisa.org/.
- **Institutional subscriptions to *NAIS*** are $100 inside the U.S., $105 outside the U.S. Checks should be made payable to the University of Minnesota Press and sent to *NAIS*, University of Minnesota Press, 111 Third Avenue South, Suite 290, Minneapolis, MN 55401-2520.
- **Back issues of *NAIS*** are $25 for individuals (plus $5 shipping for the first copy, $1 for each additional copy inside the U.S.A.; $9.50 shipping for the first copy, $5 for each additional copy, outside the U.S.A.).
- **Digital subscriptions to *NAIS* for institutions** are available online through the JSTOR Current Scholarship Program at http://www.jstor.org/r/umnpress.

JEAN M. O'BRIEN COEDITOR
    (*White Earth Ojibwe*) University of Minnesota
ROBERT WARRIOR COEDITOR
    (*Osage*) University of Illinois, Urbana–Champaign
KYLE MAYS MANAGING EDITOR
    (*Saginaw Chippewa*) University of Illinois, Urbana–Champaign
JAMESON R. SWEET MANAGING EDITOR
    (*Lakota/Dakota*) University of Minnesota

EDITORIAL BOARD

KIM ANDERSON
    (*Cree/Métis*)
    Wilfrid Laurier University

KATHLEEN BROWN-PÉREZ
    (*Brothertown Indian Nation*)
    University of Massachusetts, Amherst

LUIS CÁRCAMO-HUECHANTE
    (*Mapuche*)
    University of Texas and Comunidad de Historia Mapuche

VICENTE M. DIAZ
    (*Pohnpeian*)
    University of Illinois, Urbana–Champaign

CHAD HAMILL
    (*Spokan*)
    Northern Arizona University

JOLAN HSIEH
    (*Taiwanese Siraya*)
    National Dong Hwa University

SUZI HUTCHINGS
    (*Central Arrernte*)
    University of Adelaide

KELLY McDONOUGH
    (*White Earth Ojibwe Heritage*)
    University of Texas

MAY-BRITT ÖHMAN
    (*Lule/Forest Sámi*)
    Uppsala University

MWALIM PETERS
    (*Wampanoag*)
    University of Massachusetts, Dartmouth

JACKI THOMPSON RAND
    (*Choctaw Nation of Oklahoma*)
    University of Iowa

PHILLIP ROUND
    University of Iowa

MAUREEN TRUDELLE SCHWARZ
    Syracuse University

NOENOE K. SILVA
    (*Kanaka Maoli*)
    University of Hawai'i, Mānoa

ALICE TE PUNGA SOMERVILLE
    (*Māori*)
    University of Hawai'i, Mānoa

COLL THRUSH
    University of British Columbia

MAGGIE WALTER
    (*trawlwoolway pakana of the north eastern nation of Tasmania*)
    University of Tasmania

NAIS

Journal of the NATIVE AMERICAN *and* INDIGENOUS STUDIES ASSOCIATION

CONTENTS
VOLUME 1 • ISSUE 2

Fall 2014

Articles

MARK RIFKIN
1   The Silence of Ely S. Parker: The Emancipation Sublime and the Limits of Settler Memory

LAUREN GREWE
44   "To Bid His People Rise": Political Renewal and Spiritual Contests at Red Jacket's Reburial

JANICE CINDY GAUDET
69   Rethinking Participatory Research with Indigenous Peoples

MICHAEL SNYDER
89   Imagine Lennon as Choctaw Code Talker: Indigenized Beatles in LeAnne Howe's *Miko Kings*

Special Forum
Perspectives on the Israeli–Palestinian Conflict from Indigenous Studies

JEAN M. O'BRIEN AND ROBERT WARRIOR
105   Introduction: Indigeneity, Palestine, and Israel

ERIC CHEYFITZ
107   The Force of Exceptionalist Narratives in the Israeli–Palestinian Conflict

STEVEN SALAITA

125 Inter/Nationalism from the Holy Land to the New World: Encountering Palestine in American Indian Studies

ERIC CHEYFITZ

145 Response to Steven Salaita's "Inter/Nationalism from the Holy Land to the New World: Encountering Palestine in American Indian Studies"

STEVEN SALAITA

147 Response to Eric Cheyfitz's "The Force of Exceptionalist Narratives in the Israeli—Palestinian Conflict"

Notes from the Field

MALINDA TRILLER DORAN

149 Dickinson College Builds Carlisle Indian Industrial School Resource Center

JOEL T. HELFRICH

151 Cultural Survival in Action: Ola Cassadore Davis and the Struggle for *dził nchaa si'an* (Mount Graham)

Reviews

KELLY S. McDONOUGH

176 *Nahua and Maya Catholicisms: Texts and Religion in Colonial Central Mexico and Yucatan* by Mark Z. Christensen

MARIE SCHNITZLER

179 *Indigeneity: Collected Essays* edited by Guillermo Delgado-P. and John Brown Childs

EVAN J. HABKIRK

182 *Victims of Benevolence: The Dark Legacy of the Williams Lake Residential School* by Elizabeth Furniss

GINA STARBLANKET

184 *Mark My Words: Native Women Mapping Our Nations* by Mishuana Goeman

SETH SCHERMERHORN

187 *At the Border of Empires: The Tohono O'odham, Gender, and Assimilation, 1880—1934* by Andrae M. Marak and Laura Tuennerman

CAMIE AUGUSTUS
190 *Telling It to the Judge: Taking Native History to Court* by Arthur J. Ray

JESSICA BARDILL
192 *Native American DNA: Tribal Belonging and the False Promise of Genetic Science* by Kim TallBear

KATRINA PHILLIPS
195 *Indians and Wannabes: Native American Powwow Dancing in the Northeast and Beyond* by Ann M. Axtmann

KYLE T. MAYS
198 *Our Fires Still Burn: The Native American Experience* by Audrey Geyer

Articles

MARK RIFKIN

The Silence of Ely S. Parker: The Emancipation Sublime and the Limits of Settler Memory

I'M WATCHING *Lincoln* in a movie theater, and in the middle it cuts from a scene about the machinations of political operatives paid by the Lincoln administration to secure House votes for the Thirteenth Amendment to a scene of General Ulysses S. Grant in Virginia meeting with Confederate commissioners. One of the men in the frame appears to me to be Native. Later, at the end of the film in a scene set at the Appomattox courthouse, the site of General Robert E. Lee's surrender, that man returns, and I suddenly realize that it must be Ely S. Parker.[1] A chief of the Tonawanda Senecas who played a central role in their fight to reclaim their reservation in the wake of the supplemental Treaty of Buffalo Creek of 1842, Parker served as secretary and aide to Grant from Parker's enlistment in the army in 1863 through Grant's election as president. The men originally met in 1860 while Parker was serving as a civil engineer in Galena, Illinois.[2] The published screenplay confirms the historical identity of this figure on the screen, including Parker in the official cast of characters (Kushner, xvi).[3] In the scenes in which Grant appears, though, it never designates Parker by name, instead including him as one of the general's other unremarked "aides" (91), "officers" (140), or "staff" (157). Furthermore, at no point in the movie does he speak.

The film's screenwriter, Tony Kushner, clearly felt it necessary to represent Parker's existence for the sake of accuracy, but even as the movie captures his presence, it vacates that fact of any substantive significance, with Parker functioning more or less as a historical prop. I could not help reading the film's simultaneous awareness of his presence and failure to address it as a kind of allegory for the ways Native sovereignties, histories, and struggles with the U.S. settler-state cannot meaningfully enter into an historiographic imagination organized around the Civil War, especially one in which emancipation serves as the pivot point for narrating national time. Onto what other histories does Parker's presence open? If we were to approach *Lincoln* as something like a distillation of how the Civil War continues to be envisioned in the U.S., how might Parker's unnamed and silent appearance suggest the ways that such accounts of the U.S. past foreclose an engagement with Indigenous polities and geographies as well as the ongoing history of state assaults on them? In this way, Parker's passing and unremarked entry into the film's imagination can be read as a trace, pointing toward temporalities of indigeneity and settler colonialism that remain unintelligible within the narrative of the Civil War as epochal/redemptive break.[4]

Clearly a product of contemporary perspectives and sensibilities, *Lincoln* suggests the role the Civil War plays in current forms of national self-representation, particularly as they seek to cast the United States as a multicultural nation committed to modes of antiracist inclusion.[5] Within this vision of history, emancipation serves as a crucial marker of a national commitment to equality, but one that requires a break in the usual operation of the nation in order for the promise of liberty to be actualized. In *Lincoln*, the Civil War appears as a transformative caesura in the time/space of the nation, a state of exception in which the legal and political order of the country is suspended in the process of realizing national ideals. Giorgio Agamben suggests that "the state of exception appears as the legal form of what cannot have legal form," and he asks, "If the state of exception's characteristic property is a (total or partial) suspension of the juridical order, how can such a suspension still be contained within it?" (1, 23). A national norm of universal equality that has no precise legal status and that directly contravenes the institutionalized structure of chattel slavery ostensibly serves as the basis for a suspension of law in the war and the implementation of a new law that puts into legal form that which was always supposed to be, but never actually was, the legal order of the nation. This story, reiterated in *Lincoln*, presents increasing freedom as the truth of the nation's history and moral life (regardless of actually existing institutional structures at any particular moment), invoking the Civil War as the ever-present possibility of a break with the past but one through which the underlying democratic tendencies of the nation can be realized—a dynamic I describe as *the emancipation sublime*.

Lincoln predicates the resolution of the legacy of slavery on the ratification of the Thirteenth Amendment, which putatively remediates antiblack racism and institutionalized white supremacy,[6] and narrating the Civil War in this way circulates it as something of an allegory of national promise, as well as of the potentially ambiguous relation of the actual legal order to such putative ideals at any given time. However, when national history is cast as pivoting around the Civil War (itself presented as the rupture through which emancipation can be realized), what happens to the modes of exception through which Native peoples and lands are made "domestic"? What room is there for thinking about the ways that the union—and the need to resort to exceptional violence in its defense—does not so much make possible antiracist freedom as subject Indigenous nations to settler governance? As Jodi Byrd argues, "The generally accepted theorizations of racialization in the United States have, in the pursuit of equal rights and enfranchisements, tended to be sited along the axis of inclusion/exclusion," figuring oppression as able to be "redressed by further inclusion into the nation-state" in ways that present "the foundation for U.S. participatory democracy" as something other than "the colonization of indigenous peoples and lands" (xxiii, xx). In this vein, Ely S. Parker's mute, unnamed, and unnoted presence in the film can serve as an occasion for articulating an engagement with histories of settlement and Native survival as they transect the Civil War, specifically Parker's role in Indian affairs both before and after war (as protesting Seneca leader in the 1840s and 1850s and as Commissioner of Indian Affairs and implementer of Grant's "Peace Policy" twenty years later) and the Dakota War of 1862 (which ended with the mass hanging of thirty-eight Dakota men just weeks after the announcement of the Emancipation Proclamation). *Lincoln* illustrates the implications of contemporary citations of the Civil War: the ways it is used to divide up national time and the stakes of doing so in envisioning U.S. history as the antiracist realization of freedom. Conversely, attending to the histories of Native peoples and Indian policy effaced in enacting the emancipation sublime opens the potential for telling a different story of how the Civil War era fits into the national past. An alternative vision of the nation, and of the Civil War, emerges from highlighting Native histories. Focusing on Parker's career and the Dakota War emphasizes the roles played by discourses of temporality in U.S. Indian policy as well as varied Native experiences of temporality generated by the imposition of settler administrative procedures and legal geographies. Furthermore, attending to the ways the violence of settler colonialism need not primarily be understood as acting through exceptional events of spectacular violence (like the Civil War) opens the potential for narrating national history as an accumulation of mundane, state-sanctioned, and ongoing processes of exceptionalization by which Native sovereignty and self-determination are cast as forms of legal and temporal aberrance (as anomalous deviations from the liberatory baseline of national union), rather than as politically meaningful expressions of Indigenous peoplehood.[7]

What sustains the narrative of exception, historical overcoming, and legalization of national ideals that circulate around the contemporary figuration of the Civil War is the presumptive permanence and coherence of the nation—the union—itself. In *Arranging Grief*, Dana Luciano uses the term "chronobiopolitics" to indicate the ways temporal narratives can work to naturalize specific formations of gender, sexuality, and affect, and Jean O'Brien has theorized how the nineteenth-century erasure of the continuing presence of Native peoples in New England relies on "temporalities of race," in which the supposed "fact" that "Indians can never be modern" derives from the projection of a future of inevitable "mixture and degeneracy for Indians" as against a "narrative of progress" for nonnatives (O'Brien, 105, 107).[8] These bodily narratives, however, depend on what might be termed *temporalities of space*, holding constant particular jurisdictional mappings against which to project processes of change or becoming over time. Positing the givenness of national territoriality as a consistent background for the performance of Civil War memory/periodization enacts what might be termed a *chronogeopolitics*. The legal order of the union for which the war is fought, and which it simultaneously suspends in the cataclysmic violence it unleashes, itself rests upon the taken-for-grantedness of the settler-state's claims to exert jurisdiction over Indigenous polities and homelands. The Civil War functions as a key figure in a dominant narrative of national history (as in *Lincoln*), but its exceptional status relies on an unstated exceptionalization of Native peoples, a process less particular to the contemporary moment than a sustained feature of U.S. policy from the Revolution onward. As Aileen Moreton-Robinson suggests, "Slaves were brought to America as the property of white people to work the land that was appropriated from Native American tribes. . . . Thus, the question of how anyone came to be white or black in the United States of America is inextricably tied to the dispossession" of Indigenous peoples (84). If one foregrounds Indigenous self-determination, U.S. history appears as an endemic and irresolvable legitimacy crisis, in which the prior claims of Native peoples to the "domestic" space of the nation makes the assertion of U.S. jurisdiction utterly incoherent except as a colonial imposition. However, the U.S. government at all levels persistently has cast Native peoples as exceptions to the normal operation of law and politics, up through the present moment, and doing so allows the structural challenge they pose to national identity, authority, and morality to be bracketed.

In *Lincoln*, Ely S. Parker appears as an anomaly, a brief and narratively empty reminder of the presence of Native peoples in the period. That truncated gesture, though, can open onto another set of historical relations and identifications which can be placed alongside the war but are not organized through it: a critical performance of what Elizabeth Freeman has described as "temporal drag." She suggests that temporal drag might entail "mining the present for signs of undetonated energy from past revolutions" (xvi), or from those figures/events/relations that failed to produce a revolution as such. In this vein, the silent figure of Parker that appears in *Lincoln* in the present becomes the occasion for reading into the film what it cannot engage—the rhythms and ruptures of exception performed by Indian policy over the course of U.S. history (including the ways such policy mobilizes figures of time as part of legitimizing the extension of U.S. jurisdiction over Native peoples and lands). This form of temporal drag takes the Dakota War and Ely S. Parker's career as an alternative prism through which to consider the relation between law and violence in the construction and maintenance of settler jurisdiction, as well as the limits of the Civil War as a periodizing frame for understanding the dynamics and stakes of settler-Indigenous conflict. These examples illustrate the colonial processes through which the U.S. incorporated Native peoples into the union both before and after the Civil War, suggesting how such dynamics are effaced in a narrative structured around the eruptive/redemptive enactment of emancipation and indicating the possibilities for a genealogy of the chronogeopolitics of settlement in the United States opened by moving away from this story of Civil War exceptionalism.

The Civil War as the Exceptional Horizon for Emancipation

In the Foreword to the published screenplay for *Lincoln*, Doris Kearns Goodwin suggests, "In an age when we are cynical about politicians and frustrated by our political system, Tony Kushner's screenplay is a vivid testimony to the ultimate strength of our democratic form of government—the revolutionary idea, designed by our founding fathers and secured by the Civil War, that ordinary people can govern themselves without kings or queens, dictators or tsars" (ix). From this perspective, thinking about the Civil War allows Americans in the present to reinvest emotionally in the nation because that conflict helps realize "the revolutionary idea" ostensibly embodied in the existence of the U.S. government—namely, rule by the people. The bloodshed of the war makes possible the persistence of that "democratic form," serving a crucial role in the perpetuation of the ideal represented by the nation's existence. The vast violence of the war does not mark the failure of the juridical/political order but its reinvigoration: a sustaining rather than a suspension, or perhaps sustaining through suspension. Within this frame, emancipation as a specific set of political actions and their particular effects—in terms of the executive order by the Lincoln administration during the war or the ratification of the Thirteenth Amendment—takes part in the story of the Civil War as a triumph of democracy. Or, flipped over, such a story can be told about the Civil War because of the presence of emancipation, which itself serves as a sign of the nation's tendency to become ever more democratic. From a slightly different angle, the linkage of the Civil War with emancipation as its internal truth allows the work of preserving the union, and thus the union itself, to appear as a necessary precondition for the achievement of *democracy*. The structure of the U.S. state appears as the political "form" through which that "revolutionary idea" immanently will be materialized, even in the absence of a clear indication of such in the operation of the "political system" in any given moment. In this contemporary vision of the nation and its past, the Civil War *secures* the union as the precondition for emancipation, as the a priori vehicle that makes democracy possible. From this perspective, the war represents not a rupture but an exception, one through which the norm of democracy can be cast as (increasingly) animating the juridical structure of the U.S. state. *Lincoln* enacts this story of emancipation both as the fulfillment of national law (and of the national promise of democracy/equality) and as achievable only through the Civil War in its suspension of national law. That double narrative maneuver— emancipation redeems the immanent idea of the union and that redemption of the state requires the suspension of the law—can be characterized as the *emancipation sublime*.[9]

The film casts the war as most certainly about the struggle over slavery, and in doing so, it presents the conflict as itself a return to first principles. At the beginning of the movie, after encountering two black soldiers at the battlefield of Jenkins' Ferry in Arkansas who question Lincoln's commitment to integration and African American civil rights, Lincoln comes upon two white soldiers who quote to him from the Gettysburg Address, the one repeating, "our fathers brought forth on this continent a new nation, conceived in liberty," followed by the other saying, "Now we are engaged in a great civil war, testing whether that nation or any nation so conceived and so dedicated can long endure" (8). These parallel encounters, the one coming right after the other, raise the question of the extent to which the "liberty" in which the nation was "conceived," and for which a "great civil war" is being fought, applies across the color line. The movie answers this question somewhat decisively when Lincoln, talking to workers in the White House telegraph room, observes in commenting on Euclid's theorems that "it is a self-evident truth that things which are equal to the same thing are equal to each other. We begin with equality" (99). The promise of "equality," which appears as the substance of the "liberty" that the "new nation" of the U.S. was created to achieve, not only extends to African Americans, but the film depicts the effort to secure racial equality through the abolition of slavery as the normative aim of the war itself. At one point, Lincoln asks Elizabeth Keckley, Mary Todd Lincoln's African American dressmaker, what might follow "once slavery's day is done," and she responds, "I never heard anyone ask what freedom will bring. Freedom's first. . . . My son died, fighting for the Union, wearing the Union blue. For freedom he died. I'm his mother. That's what I am to the nation, Mr. Lincoln. What else must I be?" (115). In this scene, the film offers a syllogistic series as a moral certainty: to die in the war on the Union side is to die fighting for the national union; to fight for the national union entails a battle for an end to the institution of chattel slavery; and the elimination of that institution through a process of emancipation means the achievement of "freedom." While the latter has no clear referent other than the cessation of lawful enslavement, it functions as a self-evident aim that can provide significance for the deaths incurred in the war.

The term "freedom," treated as more or less synonymous with "equality," appears as if it were semiotically self-sufficient, as naming a "truth" that might be reflected *in* law but that transcends the definitional parameters *of* law. The question of what specific legal capacities, entitlements, and responsibilities might attach to "freedom" seems irrelevant to understanding its contours or promise.[10] Similarly, in a meeting with his cabinet, Lincoln asserts, "I can't accomplish a goddamned thing of any human *meaning or worth* until we cure ourselves of slavery and end this pestilential war. . . . *This amendment is that cure!* . . . Blood's been spilt to afford us this moment!" (127). The Thirteenth Amendment both instantiates something new (realizing the "cure") and merely reflects an existing ("first") principle of "liberty"—what "our fathers brought forth" in the Revolution. Ending slavery, then, gives the war, in all its carnage, "meaning" and "worth," such that emancipation provides the (somewhat catachrestic) guiding principle that stretches across the rupture that is the conflict itself. In a meeting at Fort Monroe in Virginia, the Vice-President of the Confederacy, Alexander Stephens, confronts Lincoln, saying, "How've you held your Union together? Through *democracy*? How many hundreds of thousands have died during your administration? Your Union, sir, is bonded in cannonfire and death," and Lincoln responds, "Say all we done is show the world that democracy isn't chaos, that there is a great invisible strength in a people's union? Say we've shown that a people can endure awful sacrifice and yet cohere? Mightn't that save at least the *idea* of democracy, to aspire to? Eventually, to become worthy of?" (154). This exchange highlights the gap between the union as ordered around a particular set of legal structures and the union as an attempt to realize the "*idea* of democracy," as well as underlining the ways the potential disjunction between the one and the other generates extraordinary violence in the effort to make them "cohere." In this way, the film partakes in the contemporary ideological formation that Chandan Reddy has described as "freedom through violence," "in which socially and institutionally produced forms of emancipation remain regulatively and constitutively tied to the nation-state form" (39), and as he later notes, "The irony, of course, is that the social history of the excluded community is now dependent for its conditions of representational existence on the popular affirmation of the norm from which it was excluded" (203). As part of a speech addressing the legality of the Emancipation Proclamation in a conversation with his cabinet, making an argument for the necessity of the Thirteenth Amendment, Lincoln observes, "I decided that the Constitution gives me war powers, but no one knows just exactly what those powers are. Some say they don't exist. I don't know. I decided I needed them to exist to uphold my oath to protect the Constitution" (35–36).[11] Here the film represents the Constitution less as a juridical framework than an idea of union, one legitimized through its ostensible connection to democracy/liberty/freedom/equality despite that idea's noncorrespondence to the actual "powers" granted and distributed in the Constitution as a legal document.

That nonequivalence, and the attendant invocation of *necessity* to justify the deferral of the law in the interest of preserving the political order of the union, is the state of exception. As Agamben suggests, "the theory of necessity is none other than a theory of the exception (*dispensatio*) by virtue of which a particular case is released from the obligation to observe the law" (25), and he adds that necessity "appears as an ambiguous and uncertain zone in which de facto proceedings, which are in themselves extra- or antijuridical, pass over into law, and juridical norms blur with mere fact— that is, a threshold where fact and law seem to become undecidable" (29). The need to preserve the union appears as a "fact" that at times requires the suspension of law—the invention of "powers" that may have no basis in the juridical structure of the nation as defined by the Constitution. The "case" of Confederate secession demands that the president "decide" he has authority that does not rest in the Constitution in order "to protect the Constitution," which in this case means maintaining the union as a coherent geopolitical entity. The "fact" of the union operates as a precondition for the exercise of "law," leading to an "undecidable" slide in which alegal actions become quasi-legal in preserving the idea(l) of the union as the animating, extralegal context for the law's possibility. From this perspective, the supposed necessity of preserving the union appears as such due to a declaration of that necessity, rather than as an a priori imperative inherent in the situation itself.[12] The need to be "released from the obligation to observe the law" in order to defend the union retroactively posits the union as an extralegal foundation that exists somehow outside of the juridical order of the state sanctioned by the Constitution. Such a dynamic opens the potential for a legally unregulated and unregulable "zone" of executive discretion, in which preserving the idea of the union from threats to it can license the assumption of all manner of authority (a point which will take on greater significance when we turn to Ely S. Parker and the Dakota War).

However, the film manages that juridical crisis by fusing it to emancipation. To the extent that ending slavery can be imagined as the aim of the war and as the realization of the liberty for which the nation was founded, this goal helps legitimize the defense of the union, as well as the "powers" invoked/invented in doing so. *Lincoln* casts the union as (inherently) bearing the ideal of racial equality. Moreover, the Thirteenth Amendment functions as the "cure," formally enshrining in the Constitution the idea of democracy/ equality for which the war ostensibly is fought and thereby creating a way out of the state of exception (even as it also licenses the exception as an extralegal vehicle for achieving justice). The necessity of holding the union together gains normative meaning and justification by its association with the movement for black freedom. As Roderick Ferguson suggests with respect to post–Civil Rights era discourses of racial equality, "the state manages diversity through political emancipation," engaging in a "promotion of diversity without ensuring equal opportunity" in ways that allow the state (and inclusion within it) to be cast as a vehicle for securing freedom/liberty without the prospect of a more far-reaching "antiracist redistribution" of material resources (170). Reciprocally, the bloodshed of the war and the potential violation of the law in its conduct look like temporary oddities when seen in light of (a narrative of) the immanent relation between law and democracy/ equality that characterizes the nation's governance. In this way, the film enacts a genealogy in which the Civil War operates as a signal moment in the becoming of American freedom, in which cohering the state's jurisdiction functions as a moral, antiracist necessity. Through this prism, the expansion of governmental authority and the eruption of state-licensed violence work in the service of an antiracist extension of the potential for democracy that dwells within the *idea* of the nation—if not, perhaps, its actual laws and juridical structure.

That very logic, though, can be understood as reinvesting in a settler colonial imaginary. It identifies the union as the political/normative "fact" that must be defended against all threats to it, including Native peoples whose claims to territoriality, sovereignty, and self-determination potentially challenge the legitimacy of the United States and its jurisdiction. Moreover, it licenses state-organized violence, in excess of any constitutional/legal framework, as the means of securing that union while positioning national law as the ultimate vehicle for remedying racial inequity. From such a perspective, the incorporation of Native peoples into the state/union constitutes a promise of liberty rather than an act of imperial subjection.[13] In this way, the film's contemporary vision of national history not only reinvests in the necessity of state violence in order to achieve (racial) justice, it recapitulates older narratives about the moral and political imperative of maintaining the union, stories of benevolent inclusion and national progress that functioned as a means of validating the imposition of U.S. jurisdiction on Native peoples—enacting a chronogeopolitics of settlement.

Inexplicable Violence

What place is there for thinking the violence of settlement within a narrative ordered around the Civil War as a bloody yet transcendent trajectory toward emancipation? Within this genealogy, not only do Indigenous histories and sovereignties seem almost entirely irrelevant, but understanding national temporality as pivoting around the Civil War, most centrally due to the importance of the struggle over slavery, displaces the importance of Indian affairs and Indigenous peoplehood in conceptualizing the meaning of the union.[14] If Indigenous peoples appear as something other than full polities, as anomalous populations inhabiting "domestic" space and thus subject to national authority, forms of aggression by them can be cast as a kind of eruption within the unfolding time of settler expansion. They form an exception to the laws of the union, and as such, the imposition of U.S. jurisdiction over them and their lands functions less as a colonial imposition than as the fulfillment of a (civilizational) process of U.S. national becoming. Within this frame, armed Native actions in response to these expropriations and the conditions of destitution created by Indian policy can be narrated as aberrations by U.S. officials, cast as discontinuous with circumstances before and afterwards such that the outbreak of violence appears as (Indian) oddity rather than symptomatic of broader, longstanding, and ongoing patterns of settler invasion. Such a counterinsurgent story of the exceptional atrocities of barbarous Indians functions as the dominant narrative in the wake of the Dakota War of 1862.[15]

After ceding millions of acres to the United States through treaties in 1837, 1851, and 1858, Dakota peoples in 1862 were confined to a seventy-mile strip along the southern bank of the Missouri River.[16] The Mdewakantons and Wahpekutes in 1837 ceded "all their land, east of the Mississippi river, and all their islands in the said river" (493). In 1851, they, along with the Sissetons and Wahpetons, relinquished "all their lands and all their right, title and claim to any lands whatever" in what would become the state of Minnesota (588, 591). While the treaties of 1851 originally had provided for reserved lands on both sides of the Minnesota River, that provision was struck out by the Senate, replaced with a supplemental article giving the president authority to designate lands elsewhere (590, 593), but the president allowed all four peoples to remain on the lands that had been reserved in the provision that was removed from the treaty. In 1854, Congress passed an act authorizing the president to confirm Dakota rights in perpetuity to that territory, but he never formally did so. The treaties of 1858 affirmed Dakota claims to the land south of the Minnesota River that had been promised in the provision omitted by the Senate in 1851, and they offered compensation for the territory north of the river should the Senate determine the Dakotas held a right to that land (781–82, 785–86).[17] In light of this vast constriction in access to hunting resources and other possibilities for securing subsistence, Dakota peoples had become increasingly dependent on treaty-guaranteed annuities in order to purchase needed goods from traders, who preyed on Dakota vulnerability while charging heavily inflated debts against federal funds.

In 1862, the annuity had not arrived by late spring, when it had been expected, and Dakotas at both agencies were starving.[18] The urgency of the situation was illustrated by the armed Native demand for access to the foodstores of the Upper Agency (at Yellow Medicine) beginning on August 4, which lasted until four days later when the recently appointed agent, Thomas J. Galbraith, finally capitulated. The event that immediately precipitated the war directly points to this broader context of destitution. Beginning as an attempt on August 17 by a small group of Mdewakanton warriors to steal eggs from Robinson Jones (a local settler with whom they had traded previously), the raid quickly escalated into the murder of Jones and his family. After retreating to consult the leaders of their village, Rice Creek, they and the rest of their band quickly decided to seek shelter with Little Crow, an important leader who had been a signatory to the treaties of 1851 and 1858.[19] The warriors from Rice Creek pressured him and his band to join them in hostilities, and on the morning of August 18, he took part in an assault on the Lower Agency (at Redwood) in which twenty Americans were killed and ten captured. Over the next week or so, Dakota forces attacked Fort Ridgely and various settlements in the area, particularly New Ulm. Upon hearing of the conflict on August 19, the governor of Minnesota, Alexander Ramsey, appointed the former governor and longtime Indian trader Henry H. Sibley as a colonel to lead state militia units.[20] When Sibley arrived on September 26 in the vicinity of Yellow Medicine at the camp occupied by the "peace party," which had established its own site separate from Little Crow and others who desired to continue the war,[21] he took into U.S. custody over 1,200 Dakotas, augmented by almost eight hundred more who came in over the next several weeks—including many who had left to travel westward with Little Crow but later decided to return or were captured in U.S. military raids to the west. By October 17, Sibley had almost 400 prisoners, and the dependents of those men numbered around 1,600.

On September 28, Sibley ordered the creation of a five-member military commission to try anyone who had participated in the attacks and had committed violence against settlers. After the conflict already had begun, General John Pope was reassigned from his previous station in northern Virginia to take command of the situation in Minnesota, largely as a punishment for his failures during the Second Battle of Bull Run in late August, and by early

October, Pope was in communication with his superior officers and the War Department about the trials occurring under Sibley. Although Pope had instructed Sibley to execute those found guilty and to send the remainder of the prisoners and their dependents to Fort Snelling, that order was countermanded by a message Pope received in mid-October indicating that President Lincoln wished to evaluate the findings of the military commission. The trials continued until November 2, and by the end of the process, 392 Dakota men had been tried, 323 convicted, and 303 sentenced to death. Those convicted were sent to Mankato, while all the other Dakotas held in custody were sent to Fort Snelling. Based on an assessment of the trial transcripts and the evidence presented in each case, Lincoln commuted the sentences of the vast majority of those convicted, and on December 26, thirty-eight Dakotas were hanged at one time as the penalty for their participation in the war. In the spring of 1863, those who had been convicted were sent to Camp McClellan in Davenport, Iowa, their dependents were removed from Fort Snelling to the Crow Creek reservation, and Congress passed a statute to remove remaining Dakota peoples from Minnesota. The remaining 177 Dakota prisoners who had survived their internment for over three and a half years were pardoned by President Andrew Johnson in March 1866.

In perhaps the clearest and most extensive official description of the war, the agent's report filed on January 27, 1863, Thomas Galbraith utterly refuses to conceptualize the events of the previous fall as a war. He describes Dakota actions as "the recent and, although smothered, yet existing rebellion, or murderous raid," as "atrocities and savage outrages of the Indians," and as an "outbreak."[22] Characterizing the conflict in these ways denies it the kind of political significance or intelligibility that would accompany its designation as a military clash between contending sovereigns. Instead, the language here suggests something like an act of treason, an attempt at theft accompanied by bloodshed, wholesale unmotivated slaughter, and a natural disaster on the order of an epidemic. Galbraith observes, "In the beginning it was the intention of [Little] Crow to make regular 'war' after the manner of white men, but his 'braves' having tasted of blood and plunder became wild and unmanageable and again yielded to the popular current, and 'Crow's war' degenerated into a savage, barbarous, and inhuman massacre" (32). The intent to engage in "war," performing violence in a proper political mode like "white men," quickly *degenerates* into a "wild and unmanageable" orgy of carnage driven by an insatiable "taste" for "blood." This depiction presents efforts to interpret such struggle in the ways one would if it were conducted by civilized nations as ridiculous, thereby forestalling an engagement with the questions of sovereignty at play in Dakota grievances and choices. Galbraith declares, "Whenever Indians on a large or small scale commit crimes, they should be promptly punished" (40).[23] Indian violence cannot constitute an act of "war," and therefore an expression of Indigenous sovereignty, because, instead, it needs to be explained and adjudicated as "crime."[24]

What law, though, comes to serve as the background against which to interpret Native uses of force as *criminality*? As discussed earlier, the Civil War might be interpreted/remembered as a state of exception in which the insistence on the political norm (of the nation's coherence, of democratic equality, of the supposedly necessary relation between the two) animates suspension of the formal legal system in order to (re)materialize that ideal. The Dakota War, however, is validated less as a suspension of law, in the interest of securing further freedom, than as the exercise of law on its proper subjects who are behaving in improper ways. This narrative of Native intransigence suggests a different kind of exception than that at play in Agamben's analysis. He argues, "The state of exception is not a special kind of law (like the law of war); rather, insofar as it is a suspension of the juridical order itself, it defines law's threshold or limit concept" (4), and he indicates that the "transformation of a provisional and exceptional measure into a technique of government threatens radically to alter . . . the structure and meaning of the traditional distinction between constitutional forms" (2). Law emerges for Agamben as the privileged way of naming a normative structure that serves as a bulwark against the prospectively unlimited use of force by the state represented by the exception, itself invoked as a temporary measure in the name of "security" (14). Rather than requiring the creation of a new zone of authority, at odds with the regular "technique of government," the punishment and removal of Dakota people(s) appear as actions by and under the law, as extensions of the normal operation of settler jurisdiction to subjects whose defiance is itself exceptional.

Dakota exceptionality inheres less in the need to enact a new policy to discipline them, one at odds with the regular regime of law, than in the fact of their *Indianness*. In seeking to answer the question, "What was the cause of the outbreak?" Galbraith insists that first "it will be necessary to strip the Indian of the filigree coloring of romance, which has been thrown around him by sentimental poets and lovesick novelists, and present him as he is, a matter of fact being."[25] Freeing this "fact" from "romance" entails recognizing that "the Sioux" "regard most of the vices as virtues. Theft, arson, rape, and murder are among them regarded as the means to distinction." Furthermore, "ignorance, indolence, filth, lust, vice, bigotry, superstition, and crime, make up the '*ancient customs*' of the Sioux Indians, and they adhere to the code with a tenacity and stoicism indefinable" (23–24). The "fact" at play here, in Agamben's terms, has less to do with a situation "in which the emergency becomes the rule" than with a population that needs to be subjected to the legal order but whose very nature proves resistant to such inclusion (22).[26] Jodi Byrd argues, "the United States has used executive, legislative, and juridical means to make 'Indian' those peoples and nations who stand in the way of U.S. military and economic desires" (xx), later suggesting that "all who can be made 'Indian' in the transit of empire, can be killed without being murdered" (227). In this vein, official accounts surrounding the Dakota War can be thought of as turning Indigenous *peoples* into *populations* by suspending the question of sovereignty, a process "of making racial what is international" (125). Describing Native "customs" as "crime" (including the legal charges of "theft, arson, rape, and murder") presents Native peoplehood as an accretion of collective forms of "vice," and doing so forecloses the possibility of recognizing the existence of an autonomous Dakota legal and political order (a "code") that would be at odds with the assertion of U.S. authority over them and their lands.[27] In this way, this discourse converts the possible understanding of Dakotas as outside the normal legal order due to their indigeneity into an attribution of anomaly to them as Indians that makes them subject to prosecution, such as in the trials that led to the mass execution of thirty-eight Dakota men (to which I will return shortly).

Even as officials tend to frame Dakota actions as criminal rather than military, and thus as lacking political content, their accounts register the ways that engagement with Native people(s) cannot be understood entirely as a matter within the ordinary operation of state law and the criminal justice system.[28] While denying the ultimate consequence of anything other than Indians' savage inclinations in causing the "outbreak," Galbraith does address prior treaties as an "inciting" element:

> From the best information which I have been able to obtain, it seems that at the time of the treaties of Mendota and Traverse des Sioux, in the year 1851, in order to induce the Indians to sign the treaties, very liberal, if not extravagant, promises were made to them—promises for the occasion, without regard to consequences. . . . This, I must say, however, that the alleged non-compliance with "promises" made "at the treaty" was the text and conclusion of nearly every Indian orator's speech which I have had the fortune to hear, (and I have heard not a few). (27)

Dakota people can engage in treaty-making as a diplomatic activity, in which formal "promises" are made by the U.S. government in exchange for territory over which the Dakota exercise authority. The fact of the treaty system and the uneven history of recognizing Dakota sovereignty pushes against narrating Native participation in the conflict as simply lawbreaking. The need to insist that Dakota actions do not constitute warfare as such indicates an awareness that, given the place of diplomacy in the prior cession of lands and the role of Native frustration with the nonfulfillment of those agreements in animating the turn to violence, Dakota uses of force might be interpreted as formal military engagement. During the conflict, Pope observes in his commands to Sibley, "It is idle and wicked, in view of the atrocious murders these Indians have committed, in the face of treaties and without provocation, to make treaties or talk about keeping faith with them": "They are to be treated as maniacs or wild beasts, and by no means as a people with whom treaties or compromises can be made."[29] The turn to violence by "these Indians" seems to license the suspension of treaties, both prior ones and the prospect of treaty-making as a vehicle of securing peace, and in committing "atrocious murders," the Dakota morph from "a people" into an aggregation without any cognizable political status— "maniacs or wild beasts."

However, the supposed violations for which Dakota combatants are tried by the military commission remain unclear. When commuting the death sentences of the hundreds of Dakota marked for execution by Sibley's commission, Lincoln cites a distinction between "participation in *massacres*" and "participation in *battles*," implying that the latter could not be tried since they were a regular part of combat.[30] In listing the people to be executed, though, that same message indicates that taking part in "battles" serves as one of the charges against seven of them and as the principal charge against two of them.[31] The president tries to frame actions as punishable due to their having violated the laws of war, rather than casting all uses of force by the Dakota as inherently punishable,[32] but that distinction collapses in the effort to provide a semi-legal means of disciplining Dakota insurgency, instituting a regime of "domestic" governance predicated on disavowing Native peoples' claims since they substantively challenge the coherence of settler sovereignty. Sibley's message to General Pope announcing the creation of a military commission notes that those appointed to it will see "if there are guilty parties among them" that "can be arrested and properly dealt with," two days later indicating, "If found guilty they will be immediately executed."[33] Of what precisely are they "guilty"? In the middle of his campaign, Sibley asserts with respect to Dakota actions, "This system of plunder must be suppressed and the criminals punished," and he observes in a letter three days later, "I will do all in my power to chastise the miserable savages who have devastated the frontier." Furthermore, Sibley characterizes those who took part in the conflict as "bad Indians," and both Sibley and Pope consistently refer to the entirety of the conflict as "the late outrages."[34] These comments do not distinguish between "battle" and "massacre," casting all use of arms by the Dakota as a violation of some unstated norm. In this vein, the *criminal* character of their "plunder" seems to lie in its disruption of settler inhabitance: to *devastate the frontier* makes one a *bad Indian* since doing so claims land that prospectively and rightfully belongs to nonnatives, which is the "outrage."

Scholars have addressed the legality of the trials themselves, tracing the categorical and procedural errors that undermine their legitimacy,[35] but the trials' failure to distinguish between regular criminal law and martial law indicates less an error that could have been rectified by applying the proper legal scheme ("war" rather than "crime") than the continuity between peace and war in the extension of settler authority and inhabitance. Official accounts project the potential for an unsullied future predicated on the immutability of settler occupancy, offering a spatiotemporal narrative in which Native peoples can be nothing but a drag on settler promise. In this way, they craft a genealogy of settlement that serves as the backdrop against which to assess the actions for which the Dakota prisoners are tried. At one point during the war, Sibley insists, "There is no use to disguise the fact that unless we can now, and very effectually, crush this rising, the state is ruined, and some of its fairest portions will revert for years into the possession of these miserable wretches," and Pope notes, "I have proposed to the government to disarm and remove entirely from the state all the annuity Indians, and all other Indians now within its boundaries, and to place them where they can no longer impede the progress of settlements nor endanger the settlers."[36] Armed conflict becomes the occasion for removing Dakota peoples from Minnesota, and while that dislocation might be narrated as a response to recent "outrages," it points toward "the progress of settlements" and the access of nonnatives to the "fairest portions" of the state as the horizon for policymaking.[37] Galbraith observes in his report that, in response to Dakota actions against the "peaceful and industrious frontier people," "If the sufferers are promptly compensated, the Indians removed, and the frontier secured against the reasonable probability of future raid [sic] of the kind, then the *effects* of the outbreak will soon comparatively disappear, and the frontier will, in a short time, resume its wonted prosperity" (33). The trial of combatants, then, operates as a part of a broader process of dispossession that makes land available to "peaceful and industrious" people who will bring "prosperity" to the "frontier." That connection appears perhaps most blatantly in a letter to Governor Ramsey from Morton S. Wilkinson, one of Minnesota's U.S. Senators, in which he asserts, "I have done all in my power to induce our President to have the law executed in regard to your condemned Indians," noting at the end of the correspondence, "If the people will be patient we will be able, I think, to dispose of those condemned, and will also succeed in removing the Sioux and Winnebago Indians from the state."[38] To fully *execute the law* entails not only punishing those Dakota pronounced "guilty" for their actions during the war but "removing" all Native peoples from Minnesota, even those who played no role in the conflict.

In other words, separate from reference to particular statutes, "the law" as a way of designating a normative order gains meaning here by signifying a juridical, economic, property, and temporal structure in which Natives cannot participate as peoples, in which their collective possession of territory constitutes an illegitimate, aberrant *impediment*—something like a blockage in the unfolding of settler time. If for Agamben the exception is "situated in an absolute non-place with respect to the law" (51), the rendering exceptional of Indigenous presence (as criminal, destructive, irrational, extrapolitical) creates the contours of (nonnative) place and history, making possible the construction of a proper sphere of application for the law (of the settler-state). Moreover, when considered in the context of policy prior to the war, this push for removal functions as a projection forward in time of the established pattern of increasing exertion of control over Dakota lands.[39]

The treaties in the decade before the conflict render ambiguous/anomalous the legal status of Native lands and peoples in ways that facilitate settler expropriation.[40] The Treaties of 1851, in the second article, indicate that Dakota peoples "do hereby cede and relinquish all their lands and all their right, title, and claims to any lands whatever" in Iowa and Minnesota (591),[41] and in doing so, they divest themselves of all territorial claims, such that they cease to possess any specific land rights based on their indigeneity in what would become the state of Minnesota. In the next article, stricken out by the Senate, the treaties specify the land that "the United States do hereby set apart for the future occupancy and home of the Dakota Indians, parties to this treaty, to be held by them as Indian lands are held" (593), suggesting not only a gift from the federal government (an impression intensified by the substitution for this article of a clause giving the president power to choose "such tracts of country" as he shall deem proper [593]) but an "occupancy" of a special, undefined nature. Given the previous surrender by the Dakota peoples of "all their right" in specific territories, this qualification—"as Indian lands are held"—implies a diminished, contingent inhabitance, one in which they do not exert a determinate political authority over that space. That impression seems confirmed by the provisions in Article 7: "Rules and regulations to protect the rights of persons and property among the Indian parties to this Treaty, and adapted to their condition and wants, may be prescribed and enforced in such manner as the President or the Congress of the United States, from time to time, shall direct" (592). More than gesturing toward the management of Indian–white relations, as in the regulation of nonnative presence on Native lands in the various federal Trade and Intercourse Acts, this clause seems designed to allow for U.S. superintendence of intrareservation dynamics among Native persons, and it envisions that the peculiar "condition and wants" of Indians license such intervention. In his annual report in 1851, in the wake of having helped negotiate the treaties,

Governor Ramsey places them in the context of the fact that "the relation of the government of the United States to the red races comprised within its limits is without a parallel in the history of other nations," and he says of Article 7 that it "introduces an entirely new relation between these Indians and the federal government. It disposes at once of the fanciful pretensions and artificial rules of construction to which the assumed *sovereignty* of Indian tribes has so often given rise."[42] Not only does the treaty ostensibly help bring a sense of order to the Dakotas, who "live almost without law,"[43] but it arises from an effort to resolve the apparent aberrance of Indian relations with the government, which themselves produce a "pretension" to sovereignty on the part of Native peoples.

The Treaties of 1858 extend such interference in Dakota affairs. They provide for the allotment of Dakota lands and the patenting of such allotments by the president "as members of said bands become capable of managing their business and affairs" (781), and it enables the Secretary of the Interior to use annuity funds as he "shall deem best calculated to promote their interests, welfare, and advance in civilization" (784), giving the Secretary complete power over Dakota monies so as to promote their *advancement*. In addition, the Treaties of 1858 make allotted and patented land "exempt from levy, taxation, sale or forfeiture, until otherwise provided for by the legislature of the State in which they are situated with the assent of Congress" (781), and they call on Dakotas to deliver up for trial anyone "belonging to said bands who may become offenders against the treaties, laws, or regulation of the United States, or the laws of the State of Minnesota" (783). By 1858, to occupy territory "as Indian lands are held" seems to mean being subject to the jurisdiction of Minnesota, casting the laws of the state as the prism through which to understand and assess Native presence and actions. Not only do the treaties project a horizon of diminished Dakota inhabitance but a process of becoming whereby they progressively are purged of their anomalous Indianness as they are integrated into the regular scheme of settler law. In his postwar report, Galbraith observes of the "immediate causes of the outbreak" that the previous agent had instituted "a new and radical system" put into place by "the treaties of 1858":

> The theory, in substance, was to break up the community system which obtained among the Sioux; weaken and destroy their tribal relations; individualize them by giving each a separate home, and having them subsist by industry—the sweat of their brows; till the soil; to make labor honorable and idleness dishonorable; or, as it was expressed in short, "*make white men of them*," and have them adopt the habits and customs of white men. (25)

From this perspective, to become lawful means to cease to exist as a people—to "destroy . . . tribal relations" in the interest of inculcating "the habits and customs" of bourgeois subjects.[44] This chronogeopolitics posits a progressive understanding of time whereby Native modes of inhabitance cease to disrupt the exercise of settler sovereignty. In this vein, the "outrage" of the war lies less in the specific actions of combatants than the refusal to accede to the staging of Dakota peoples as a spatiotemporal problem in need of resolution. The abrogation of former treaties with Dakota peoples and their statutory expulsion from Minnesota by Congressional fiat in February and March 1863 (Meyer, 140), then, can be understood less as an immediate response to the recent conflict than an expansion of existing aims justified as the spatial amplification of an inevitable settler futurity.

To represent the Dakota War of 1862 as a rupture, an anomalous event at odds with what precedes it, takes part in a process of rendering Native peoples exceptional, casting them as out-of-sync with the baseline temporality of settler law and jurisdiction. When viewed as an isolated event, the conflict can be treated as having no cause other than that of ingrained Indian propensities toward lawlessness, presenting Native warriors' employment of violence as an inherent tendency toward criminality that explains their violation of a social order organized around the terms of settler governance. As discussed earlier, Agamben defines the state of exception as one in which "law is suspended and obliterated in fact" (29), but in officials' accounts of the Dakota War, the exception operates in ways that cast the extension of the law as the means of resolving the aberrant "fact" of continuing Native presence as distinct peoples. Within this frame, the mobilization of violence as a vehicle of Dakota opposition to their increasing dispossession appears as an incongruous break in the unfolding of a history shaped by the enhancement and expansion of settler occupancy—a history of the increasing extension and perfection of the national union. To the extent that accounts of national history shaped around the Civil War emphasize a break in the national union which must be mended in the interest of democracy, they leave no room for addressing the imposition of the temporal narrative of national progress on Native peoples and for critiquing the geopolitical mapping of U.S. coherence such a narrative helps normalize.[45] The insistence on the necessity of the union, on the moral imperative of maintaining the jurisdictional integrity of the United States, is what produces Dakota peoples as an exception, and taking emancipation as a horizon for the unfolding of national history does not address that imperial process of imposition and interpellation.

Parker in Peacetime

Ely S. Parker's silent cameo in *Lincoln* does not directly point toward the Dakota War, or other important moments of state violence against Native peoples during the period (such as the Sand Creek Massacre or the Navajo Long Walk),[46] nor does it substantively gesture toward Parker's own role in Indian affairs prior to and after the Civil War. That very emptiness suggests how Indigenous histories and sovereignties become exceptional—anomalous, aberrant, atypical—within a historiographic narrative centered on the Civil War. His presence, though, also operates as a trace of possibilities that arise when the war no longer serves as the prism through which to narrate the U.S. past, opening the potential for performing an Indigenous-centered form of temporal drag. Officials' interpretations of Dakota actions as something other than true "war," as more like "crime" in their violation of an accepted standard of law, normalizes settlement as the background for perceiving national space and time. Conversely, the defense of Tonawanda lands (in which Parker was a key participant) and his service as Commissioner of Indian Affairs during the Grant administration highlight the ways Indigenous polities and landedness persistently trouble U.S. legal geographies. Tracking the political struggles generated by the effort to manage Native presence creates a sense of continuity that straddles the Civil War, indicating the significance of settler impositions and interpellations in the absence of armed conflict and drawing attention to the recurrent modes of translation through which Indigenous geopolitics gets cast as a disruption in the otherwise even, temporal flow of settler becoming.

Parker came to his role as representative for the Tonawanda Senecas in the early 1840s (first as the principal interpreter in 1844 and eventually as a Seneca sachem of the Iroquois League in 1851) in the wake of the supplemental Treaty of Buffalo Creek in 1842.[47] The initial treaty in 1838 had ceded four Seneca reservations (Buffalo Creek, Cattaraugus, Allegany, and Tonawanda) in exchange for lands in the Kansas territory, but after extensive Seneca protest about the validity of the process through which that treaty was negotiated, a new agreement was reached four years later, brokered by the Society of Friends with virtually no Seneca input.[48] That treaty agreed to cede Buffalo Creek and Tonawanda in order to be able to retain Cattaraugus and Allegany. However, the Tonawandas refused to assent to this trade and continued to insist on the illegitimacy of both treaties, especially given the absence of Tonawanda consent. After over fifteen years of struggle, the Tonawandas finally in 1857 were able to secure a reduced version of their reservation by agreeing to buy the land from the official property holders, selling the territory in Kansas they putatively possessed through the treaty of 1842 in order to do so.[49] Their central antagonist in this conflict was the Ogden Land Company, which as of 1811 held preemption rights to Seneca lands.[50] This chain of prospective title reached back to an agreement in 1786 between New York and Massachusetts that resolved a boundary dispute by declaring a particular stretch of territory to be under the jurisdiction of the former while giving the latter the right to retain the funds generated by selling it to private purchasers. It passed through a series of hands prior to 1811, providing much of the impetus for the Treaty of Big Tree in 1797 in which the Senecas ceded all of their lands in the state with the exception of eleven reservations (including the four that would be at stake in the Treaties of Buffalo Creek). Once it acquired the preemption right, the Ogden Land Company began its decades-long campaign to gain access to the rest of Seneca territory (as well as that of other Haudenosaunee peoples in what had become central and western New York).[51] The claims of the Ogden Company to territory they did not actually own, the federal government's acceptance of this supremely fantastic form of legal fiction, the collusion of numerous U.S. officials in facilitating the realization of this phantom title-in-potential (including many on the payroll of the Ogden Company), and the suffering caused by the resulting displacement of Seneca people and flouting of Seneca sovereignty together constitute a slow-motion invasion over more than half a century.

That dynamic does not take the form of an explosive occurrence: there is no moment of "war," "insurgency," or "emergency." Rather, this insistent pressure, imposition, and dispossession by settler corporations backed (sometimes implicitly, sometimes explicitly) by the U.S. government over the course of generations can be characterized as, in Elizabeth Povinelli's terms, a "quasi-event." She defines that concept as circumstances in which "nothing rises to the level of an event let alone a crisis" (4)—"legal forms of bad faith" or "not being killed by the state in any way that would be recognizable as state killing" (118). One might describe such relations as a temporality of attrition, a relentless assault on Indigenous occupancy and placemaking conducted largely through nonmilitary, bureaucratic means, justified on the basis of an official narrative of continuing advancement—a chronogeopolitics of progress. Treaties serve as the mechanism for such lawful dispossession, the form suggesting a diplomatic relation but in practice functioning as, in Agamben's terms, "law's threshold or limit" in order to sanctify relations of force as consensual.[52] Referring to the ways Native leaders who did not sign their names would indicate their assent on treaty documents, Scott Richard Lyons observes, "The x-mark is a contaminated and coerced sign of consent made under conditions that are not of one's making. It signifies power and a lack of power, agency and a lack of agency. It is a decision one makes when something has already been decided for you, but it is still a decision," and he argues that "there is always the prospect of slippage, indeterminacy, unforeseen consequences, or unintended results: it is always possible, that is, that an x-mark could result in something good" (3), later noting, "an x-mark is a commitment to living in new and perhaps unfamiliar ways" (169). While not seeking to portray the treaty process as completely unilateral or as a fall from a sense of prelapsarian Indigenous wholeness, I want to emphasize the ways that the coercive influence of state imperatives does not cease with the signing of a single treaty and that later possibilities for Native agency remain affected by the momentum of earlier and ongoing impositions of settler law and administrative mappings. As Dale Turner suggests in his discussion of policy in Canada, "there are intellectual landscapes that have been forced on Aboriginal peoples. . . . These intellectual traditions, stained by colonialism, have created discourses on property, ethics, political sovereignty, and justice that have subjugated, distorted, and marginalized Aboriginal ways of thinking" (Turner, 88). As part of this list, one might add discourses on *futurity*: institutionalized temporal narratives that treat settler legal and political norms as given and in which Native peoplehood, therefore, appears as an aberration whose endurance indicates less sovereignty than oddity. Moreover, having to negotiate and live within such spatiotemporal frames generates accreting effects over time, potentially producing forms of rage, despair, and/or exhaustion which can be seen in both the Dakota War and Ely S. Parker's later career in Indian affairs. Such policy and affective tempos of settler colonial occupation do not fit the model of rupture and redemption that characterizes the story of the Civil War as a(n emancipatory) pivot point in U.S. national history.

Official accounts of the 1838 treaty present supposed Seneca acquiescence as a temporal rubicon that once crossed cannot be retreated from, and they further situate the effects of that assent within another story of the necessary progress of Seneca people toward "civilization." After having worked out a deal with the Ogden Company and the federal government for the Senecas to retain the Cattaraugus and Allegany reservations, the Society of Friends met with Seneca representatives in April 1842 to explain the situation as they saw it. Describing the compromise that had been reached, without Seneca input, Quaker representatives indicate, "The well-known policy of the government to remove all the aboriginal race beyond the Mississippi forbids the idea that the treaty would be suffered to remain a lifeless form," adding that "the expulsion of the Senecas at the point of the bayonet is a circumstance which could not be contemplated without horror."[53] While taking some form of removal (and the larger aim of displacing Native peoples as such) as a necessary frame for considering possibilities for the future, the Quakers also disavow violence as a vehicle for enacting that policy imaginary. What remains unclear, though, is how this self-evident unfolding of nonnative occupation will occur without force given clear Seneca opposition. In response to this implicit question, the Quakers make the potential for continued Seneca inhabitance on any part of their lands contingent on their ceasing to be aberrant with respect to settler spacetime. In that same council in 1842, the Quakers observe, "We have seen that from the day when the *white men* first set their feet on your land *they* have been *increasing*, and the *red men* have been *decreasing*," and they add, "we believe it is not too late to reform. If you will take our advice now," which entails adopting Euramerican heterodomesticity, private property, and commercial agriculture, "then will your nation grow and increase, and become strong," whereas the alternative is "extinction."[54]

In this vein, treaties signal the exceptional character of Indigenous peoples within the scheme of U.S. law and policy, indicating less the survival of an alternative sovereignty than a noncoercive process by which Native peoples will merge into a future defined with respect to settler jurisdiction and patterns of land use. In the council at Buffalo Creek in May 1842 with federal treaty commissioners, the state representative from New York observes, "You are under the protection of the laws of this State, and to a degree you are liable to their exactions and restrictions, like our own citizens. Ours is a government of laws, and not of force. It is impossible to protect our own citizens against improvident contracts of their own making."[55] The Treaty of 1838 functions as a "contract" to which the Senecas, ostensibly including the Tonawandas, have agreed, and by that fact, they have submitted to the "laws" promulgated by the "government." After 1842, when Tonawandas insist that the treaty is invalid with respect to their reservation given the absence of their consent to it, various governors tell them that state officials have no authority to act. In 1844, New York Governor William C. Bouck insists, "I had no power as Governor of the state of New York, legally to interfere in your difficulties with the Ogden Company. The treaty under which they claim your land was with the President & Senate of the United States. It is not within my province to inquire into the legality of this treaty," and two years later, Governor Silas Wright observes, "I have examined the subject carefully and do not find that I have any power to interpose on your behalf and prevent the execution of the Treaties. They were made with the authorities of the United States, and are as binding upon us as they are upon you," adding, "If I were to exert the authority of this state by force to prevent the execution of these Treaties, I should be guilty of insurrection under the laws of the United States."[56] The status of the treaty system as a federal matter supposedly binds the hands of state officials, even though the state previously had engaged in numerous treaties with Haudenosaunee peoples absent any federal oversight,[57] and the specialness of federal-Native relations means that treaties must de facto be considered lawful and binding, as to do otherwise would constitute "insurrection." Similarly, in the same letter, Wright warns the Tonawandas "to do nothing in violation of the law, or to the interruption of the public peace," noting, "If the Treaties have conveyed away your rights in the reservation, you cannot get them back by acts of violence." Given their (posited) prior assent, Tonawanda resistance to their dispossession now constitutes a "violation of the law" and can be constellated with "acts of violence" as a mode of aggression against the sociopolitical order instituted through treaties. The quasi-events of transgenerational invasion disappear behind the narrative of Native acquiescence, via treaties, to the legalities and mappings of the settler-state: a process of geopolitical becoming which apparently has nothing to do with the exertion of "force" (such as would be the case in the deployment of the military).

However, Tonawanda accounts in the period between 1842 and 1857 (largely translated, delivered, and/or authored by Ely S. Parker) refuse that story of amicable and nonantagonistic development and the attendant citation of treaties as signs of the absence of violence. In a memorial from numerous Tonawanda chiefs and warriors to the president and Senate, they observe that they have been "informed that the legal tribunals cannot look behind or below the outward face of treaties which have been ratified, and inquire into the *manner or means* whereby they were obtained. The courts of law, therefore, cannot reach the evil or do us justice," and they respond by noting, "The United States government, which authorized a commissioner to make these treaties, can authorize another commissioner to unmake them, and we on our part, as a nation, will most gladly assent."[58] "Law" does not equal "justice," and to the extent that treaties stand beyond the jurisdiction of "legal tribunals" in which questions might be raised about their validity, they function as an "outward" sign of legitimacy for a fundamentally corrupt process of *obtaining* Native territory. Moreover, the Tonawandas inquire why federal authority with respect to treaties somehow recedes in the wake of their ratification, especially when one of the putative signatories challenges the authenticity of the agreement. In an 1848 letter to the Commissioner of Indian Affairs, Parker asserts, "The Tonawanda Senecas will not surrender to the Ogden Land Company the Tonawanda reservation, because they are no parties to the Treaties under which the Ogden Company claim their lands, and by which they propose to remove them."[59] What prevents such treaties from being *unmade*? The apparent answer is the presumption that Indigenous lands eventually will and must be given over to nonnative forms of inhabitance and jurisdiction, such that moves in that direction cannot be undone.

As against that temporality of "civilized" progress, Tonawandas assert a different genealogy, one organized not only around their indigeneity but also the broader context of their decades-long struggle to retain their homeland. In an 1845 memorial to Governor Wright, Tonawanda leaders insist, "The justness of our cause we think to be approved by the Great Spirit, who has given the lands we occupy to our forefathers, who gave it to us in trust for our children, and we do not wish to violate that trust which is so sacred to us."[60] Enduring Seneca occupation of this territory suggests a kind of claim, one "approved by the Great Spirit," which cannot be reduced to the terms of U.S. law, indicating a "sacred" connection passed down from "forefathers." That intergenerational belonging offers a very different sense of time than that at play in Quaker articulations of Seneca prospects or in the treaty system. In addition, the memorial draws attention away from the scene of consent that appears in the events immediately surrounding any given treaty and toward the broader pattern of settler intrusion over time that shapes the circumstances of that negotiation. After reminding Governor Wright of the Treaty of Canandaigua (1794), in which Haudenosaunee peoples were promised the possession of their existing lands in perpetuity, the chiefs observe:

> citizens of the United States hav[ing] the name of the Ogden Company have for many years past, in direct violation of this provision of a Treaty, harassed us in the quiet possession of our lands and homes. They have sold our lands at public auction against our consent and the consent of the people we represent; and we did publicly protest against the sale of our lands time after time, but seemingly with no effect, for the purchasers have now come and settled upon our lands under the title of the Ogden Company, and we do not wish to remove them by force, because we should then violate the treaties of peace we have made.

The prior and ongoing violations of the Treaty of Canandaigua by "citizens of the United States" do not signify for U.S. officials as a prism through which to interpret the Treaty of Buffalo Creek and its aftermath. That history of *harassment*, however, provides the framework for Tonawanda interpretations of the events of the late 1830s and 1840s. Not only did they not consent to those later "treaties," but the possibility of meaningful consent is vitiated by the persistent patterns of settler action, seemingly unregulated and at times actively supported by the government, in disturbing Tonawandas' "quiet possession" and thereby breaching the prior treaty. Further, Senecas have not responded to such acts of aggression (ultimately countenanced by the United States under the cover of legal "title") through recourse to violence, due to their commitment to upholding the terms of extant "treaties of peace."[62] The Tonawandas situate the treaty system as it actually functions within a historicity of dispossession in which the law operates as a retrospective projection to validate forms of appropriation enacted by U.S. subjects. In this way, Seneca opposition to removal in the 1840s and 1850s refuses the supposed fact of Indian anachronism (with which the law must struggle), instead presenting the fact and continuing history of persistent settler lawlessness as the principal challenge to the potential for just U.S.–Native relations predicated on treaties as vehicles of diplomatic good faith.

As a central figure in the Tonawanda struggle to retain their lands, Ely S. Parker took part in shaping their response and played a crucial role in the process of negotiating the repurchase of their reservation. His brief appearance in *Lincoln*, however, offers no hint of the existence of this conflict. In the film, and in the broader discourse of national periodization to which it contributes, the union functions as a normative frame for conceptualizing the rupture of the war as a challenge to the democratic promise of the nation, as well as an opportunity to redeem it through emancipation. In the Tonawandas' struggle, though, the presumption of the union operates as a means of projecting the coherence of national jurisdiction over Native lands, such that the continuing pressure on Native peoples to cede them appears less as a form of imperial force than the (inevitable) fulfillment of national progress.

Parker's official communications on Indian affairs after the Civil War reflect the prewar experience of the Senecas, noting the ways the treaty system helps validate a state-sanctioned process of nonnative annexation but also accepting the temporal narrative of settler development and expansion as the frame through which to approach U.S.–Native relations. In his 1867 recommendations for rethinking Indian policy, requested by the Secretary of War, Parker emphasizes how the treaty process has served as a license to white aggression. He observes of the system's ostensible aims, "The plan of removal was adopted as the policy of the government, and, by treaty stipulations, affirmed by Congress; lands were set apart for tribes removing into the western wilds, and the faith of a great nation pledged that the homes selected by the Indians should be and remain their homes forever, unmolested by the hand of the grasping and avaricious white man."[61] From this perspective, Native peoples accepted new lands in exchange for the ones they currently occupied, with the proviso that those to which they would be removed would be held by them "forever," and such a promise by the federal government was meant permanently to hold at bay "grasping and avaricious" U.S. citizens. However, the repeated use of treaties as the vehicle for accomplishing transfers of this kind ended up sanctioning nonnative incursions: "as the hardy pioneer and adventurous miner advanced into the inhospitable regions occupied by the Indians, in search of the precious metals, they found no rights possessed by the Indians that they were bound to respect. The faith of treaties solemnly entered into were totally disregarded, and Indian territory wantonly violated."[63] Even as nonstate actors would assert claims to treaty-guaranteed territory, the government either would look away or negotiate another treaty to cover this most recent wave of dispossession, such that "the Indians" effectively have "no rights" that settlers are "bound to respect." Drawn from the infamous *Dred Scott* case in 1857, which denied African Americans national citizenship,[64] this phrasing intimates the ways that the recursive dynamics of nonnative invasion faced by Native peoples exceed the terms of emancipation and reconstruction through which *Dred Scott* legally was superseded. Parker adds that "if any tribe remonstrated against the violation of their natural and treaty rights, members of the tribe were inhumanly shot down and the whole treated as mere dogs. Retaliation generally followed, and bloody Indian wars have been the consequence."[65] The eruption of armed conflict, such as in the Dakota War, needs to be understood as part of a cycle of settler intrusion backed by violence that leads to Native response but in which only the latter becomes visible as a disruption of the extant legal order, as an exception that needs to be handled as an emergency/crisis/"outrage." While such white actions often violate treaty terms, Parker implies that they are driven by a broader temporality of treaty-making that projects future cessions as the means of retroactively legitimizing these putatively illegal forms of trespass by citizens.

By the time he becomes Commissioner of Indian Affairs in 1869, Parker's perspective on the treaty system has become even bleaker.[66] In his annual report for that year he states, "Arrangements now, as heretofore, will doubtless be required with tribes desiring to be settled upon reservations for the relinquishment of their rights to the lands claimed by them and for assistance in sustaining themselves in a new position, but I am of the opinion that *they should not be of a treaty nature*."[67] If treaties have functioned as a means of validating the transfer of territory from Native control and making it part of the regular jurisdictional hierarchies of the United States, often as a retrospective measure in the wake of existing settler encroachments, Parker argues that legal fiction should be suspended due to the falseness of its premises. He asserts, "A treaty involves the idea of a compact between two or more sovereign powers, each possessing sufficient authority and force to compel a compliance with the obligations incurred. The Indian tribes of the United States are not sovereign nations," and "great injury has been done by the government in deluding this people into the belief of their being independent sovereignties, while they were at the same time recognized only as dependents and wards."[68] In light of the fact that Indian tribes are deemed "dependents and wards" in federal law,[69] narrating them as "sovereign nations" simply for the purposes of concluding treaties that ease the exchange of land can only be a vicious pretense, one especially pernicious given that it trades on the inability of Native peoples to enforce the terms of these agreements against the United States and, thus, to prevent continuing breaches of them prior to the next round of treaties/cessions. Parker adds, though, "In regard to treaties now in force, justice and humanity require that they be promptly and faithfully executed, so that the Indians may not have cause of complaint, or reason to violate their obligations by acts of violence and robbery."[70] Fulfillment of treaty obligations appears as something of a cynical means of deferring Indigenous "complaint," so as to prevent the outbreak of kinds of activity deemed criminal by U.S. officials (such as in the Dakota War).

The sort of peace secured by treaties, or whatever "arrangements" might replace them,[71] gains meaning within a vision of futurity defined by the inexorable movement of nonnatives onto Indigenous lands. In his recommendations in 1867, Parker suggests that in explaining to Native peoples why they should concentrate themselves on much smaller landbases and take up "agricultural and pastoral pursuits," as well as "the habits and modes of civilized communities," that "they could probably be made to comprehend that the waves of population and civilization are upon every side of them; that it is too strong for them to resist; and that, unless they fall in with the current of destiny as it rolls and surges around them, they must succumb and be annihilated by its overwhelming force."[72] The chronogeopolitics of settlement—"waves" of development—here provides the background against which to assess the (im)possibilities for the continuance of Native polities. In his 1867 recommendations, he observes, "Originally their greatest desire was to be left undisturbed by the overflowing white population that was quietly but surely pressing to overwhelm them, and they have been powerless to divert or stem the current of events," further noting that "naturally many of them at times have sought by violence the redress of what they conceived to be great and heinous wrongs against their natural rights."[73] In contrast to the characterization of violent response as savagery or crime, as in officials' accounts of the Dakota War discussed earlier, Parker insists that such actions are attempts to "redress" white "wrongs." Even if understood as a "heinous" violation of "natural" law, though, the expansion of white occupancy, and attendant extension of U.S. modes of governance, possesses an *overwhelming* momentum that fundamentally (re)shapes the relation between the present and the future: "the current of events." If Agamben presents the state of exception as one in which "law is suspended and obliterated in fact" (29), here the facticity of continued Native presence and existence as polities appears as a drag on the operation of U.S. law, casting acknowledgment of Indigenous "rights" as a limited diversion/suspension of the overpowering flow of settler governance.

While presenting Native peoplehood as something of a vestigial anomaly, and at times arguing for the necessity for Indians to move away from communalism,[74] Parker also highlights the importance of acknowledging existing forms of Indigenous territoriality, even if such recognition can function in somewhat carceral ways. Discussing the general terms of federal Indian policy, he observes in his 1869 report that Indians "should be secured their legal rights; located, when practicable, upon reservations; assisted in agricultural pursuits and the arts of civilized life; and that Indians who should fail or refuse to come in and locate in permanent abodes provided for them, would be subject wholly to the control and supervision of the military authorities, to be treated as friendly or hostile as circumstances might justify."[75] Still reserving the military as the insurance that Native movement, grievance, and/ or warfare will not disrupt nonnative geographies of property, transit, and commerce, Parker concedes that Indigenous peoples have specific "legal rights," largely derived from extant treaties, and that they should not be deprived of tribally specific landbases, even while they are being trained out of such collective attachments via education in "agricultural pursuits" and the individualized/privatized cartographies of "civilized life." If the experience of the Senecas—and the Tonawandas in particular—illustrates for Parker the potential violence of the treaty system, including the ability of the U.S. government to utilize such apparent consent as a means of legally validating an ongoing process of expropriation and displacement, Seneca struggles also indicate the persistent commitment of Native peoples to retaining separate governance over homelands that remain apart from the regular jurisdiction of the settler-state.[76] Parker often stages his own engagement with this fact as a confrontation in the present with a residual formation that, for better or worse, cannot be sustained in the face of nonnative advancement (whether cast as invasion or progress) and the increasing integration of the national union as such. Yet his insistence, albeit uneven, on the need to honor extant treaties and to provide a legal status for collective Indigenous occupancy through reservations suggests that, whatever may occur in the future, Native peoples as landholding, self-governing entities exist now and must be reckoned with as such.

Inasmuch as the Civil War is taken as paradigmatic, as the prism through which to understand the U.S. past, the conceptual and normative coordinates through which its centrality gets mapped obscure both the dynamics of settler colonialism and the temporal narratives of exception employed to normalize such occupation/dispossession. To the extent that the violence of the Civil War and its challenge to national jurisdiction can be recast as a process of democratic becoming via the war's linkage to emancipation as its immanent horizon, the periodization of national history around the war imbues the union, and the force exerted in preventing its fracture, with the sense of realizing freedom and racial justice. In such a periodizing narrative, the union functions, in Agamben's terms, as the fact behind/beyond the law that works "to maintain the law in its very suspension" (59), as the extralegal necessity that both subtends and suspends the juridical order. Within that story, enacted by the film *Lincoln*, there is no place for engaging with Indian policy and Indigenous sovereignties as anything but a curiosity, an oddity that does not fit. Like Ely S. Parker in the film, they may appear as a marker of accuracy—these things happened—while remaining silent and marginal with respect to the central drama of national (re)formation. However, Parker's appearance suggests the potential for a different kind of history—for enacting a form of temporal drag that runs against the grain of the national plot in which the Civil War serves as the transcendent/redemptive exception. Parker's presence in the film suggests the conceptual and historiographic possibilities opened by foregrounding his role in Indian policy and settler–Indigenous relations during the Civil War itself. Attending to official accounts of the Dakota War (and their efforts to distinguish that "outbreak" from the events, negotiations, and conflicts of the prior decades) and to Parker's antebellum and postbellum participation in Indian affairs reveals how U.S. legal and administrative discourses have sought to manage indigeneity by coding it as (temporal) anomaly, but doing so also suggests the ways one might offer an alternative narrative to one centered on the Civil War as the sublime crisis of the union through which emancipation is realized.

Instead, one could trace the history of how the state generates geopolitical cohesion for itself in any given moment by projecting a futurity predicated on expansive settler inhabitance. Native peoples and sovereignties appear as a temporal aberration within a geography defined by the normalization of settler law. In this way, the projection of the inevitability of the union—the geopolitical cohesion of the United States—works through a cross-referencing and mutually defining set of spatial and temporal strategies that could be characterized as settler spacetime. From this perspective, the history of settlement in the nineteenth century appears less as a series of eruptive episodes of armed conflict than a more slow-motion temporality of expropriation. It becomes a series of *quasi-events*, largely enacted via the treaty system, through which Native nations are subjected to the union. Addressing performances of mourning in the nineteenth century, Dana Luciano suggests that they can "rearrange the dominant chronobiopolitical dispositions of the historical moments in which they were produced," engendering "a self-conscious distance from the 'official' materials of history" (21). Focusing on the silence of Ely S. Parker brings to the fore the histories of Indigenous struggle, survival, and self-determination toward which his presence gestures. Doing so allows for an attention to the *chronogeopolitical* dynamics of settler colonialism, in terms of the operation of policy discourses in the nineteenth century as well as the (later) elision of Indigenous peoples in the process of periodizing the U.S. past and performing national genealogies in the present. Casting the Civil War as the turning point in U.S. history perpetuates a metanarrative of Indian irrelevance, one made even more pernicious by being yoked to a story of the war as the achievement of liberty/freedom/democracy: the performance of the emancipation sublime. Parker's fleeting, mute presence provides an opening to a different kind of political vision, one in which Indigenous histories, polities, sovereignties, and futures cease to be exceptional.

MARK RIFKIN is professor of English and women's and gender studies at University of North Carolina at Greensboro. He is the author of *The Erotics of Sovereignty* (Minnesota, 2012) and *Settler Common Sense* (Minnesota, 2014).

Notes

1. While incited by my thoughts after viewing *Lincoln*, this essay also was greatly inspired by C. Joseph Genetin-Pilawa's reimagining of Parker's career in *Crooked Paths to Allotment*.

2. See Armstrong, 71–121.

3. For quotations from the film, I will refer to the published screenplay by Tony Kushner.

4. As Michelle Raheja argues, Indian images in popular media can reinforce existing settler narratives, but "these cinematic and televisual experiences also enable Indigenous [and I would add nonnative] spectators to engage critically with the artifacts of imagined cultural knowledge produced by the films and their long political, narrative, and historical context" (2010, xi).

5. Thanks to one of the anonymous readers of the manuscript for highlighting this point. On the work of multicultural forms of racial inclusion and the ways they continue to animate modes of erasure and destitution, see Chow; Ferguson; Lee; Melamed; and Reddy. On the ways the Civil War serves as a normative frame for narrating U.S. history, see Blight 2011; Hogan; Kelman; Schwartz. For recent scholarship that performs this framing, see Finkelman; Guelzo; Holzer; Neely; Schwartz; Witt.

6. On the failures and inaccuracies of such a narrative with respect to African American freedom, see Blight 2001; Dayan; Hartman; McCurry; Stanley.

7. For varied ways of mobilizing Agamben's analysis for thinking about U.S. federal Indian policy, see Byrd, 185–220; Rifkin 2009a; Shaw. Thanks to Jason Cooke and Beth Piatote for suggesting to me the productiveness of thinking more intently about the relations between discourses of Indianness and settler temporality.

8. While O'Brien focuses on popular accounts (specifically town histories) and their emplotment of Indian disappearance, I'm interested in the work of the historiographic paradigm of the Civil War in displacing discussion of Indian affairs entirely through its normative emphasis on (the crisis of) the union. Reciprocally, I attend to the ways official discourses of (temporal) exception

throughout U.S. history disavow Native sovereignties through a similar emphasis on the self-evidence of the jurisdictional imaginary of the state. On the recurrent popular trope of Indian presence as oddity, see Deloria.

9. For alternative accounts that emphasize the ways the ideal of equality articulated in the Revolution and in its wake gains meaning within the context of extant racialized systems of value, see Kazanjian; Silva; Sweet.

10. On this specific legal aporia for African Americans and its legacy after the war, see Crenshaw; Harris; Hartman; Wagner.

11. On the constitutional controversies created by Lincoln's assertions of various kinds of executive authority, see Neely.

12. Giorgio Agamben notes that one cannot presume "the very nature of necessity, which writers continue more or less unconsciously to think of as an objective situation": "This naïve conception—which presupposes a pure factuality that the conception itself has called into question—is easily critiqued by those jurists who show that, far from occurring as an objective given, necessity clearly entails a subjective judgment, and that obviously the only circumstances that are necessary and objective are those that are declared to be so" (28).

13. On this dynamic more broadly, see Byrd; Jackson; Moreton-Robinson; Rifkin 2009a ; Rifkin 2009b; Wolfe.

14. Moreover, the Civil War can be understood as about what modes of settler inhabitance and production would dominate in the occupation of Indigenous lands. While noting the increasing importance of questions about differentiating "slave" and "free" territory in the decades leading up to the war, scholars do not necessarily address how that crisis depends on holding constant nonnative rights to lands incorporated into U.S. "domestic" space. See Guelzo, 54–93. On this dynamic, see Kelman, 1–43. Such a reinterpretation of the Civil War would align with work in the last twenty years that has reframed the American Revolution as a conflict among nonnatives over the possibilities of settlement. See Calloway; Jones; White; Yirush.

15. I use "Dakota" rather than "Sioux," since the former conforms more to the self-designation of the peoples in question (Mdewakantons, Wahpekutes, Sissetons, and Wahpetons) and the latter has a wider frame of reference. Sometimes the term "Dakota" is used to refer to all seven peoples commonly grouped together as "Sioux," but I am drawing on the term's common use to refer to the four eastern peoples of those seven (not including the Yankton, Yanktonai, and Lakota or Teton). On counterinsurgent historiography, see Guha, 37–44.

16. For the text of the treaties, see Kappler, 493–94, 588–93, 781–89. I will cite page numbers parenthetically. For discussion of the process through which these treaties were negotiated and the history surrounding them, see Anderson 1997, 130-260; Gilman, 62–134; Hyman, 39–92; Meyer, 72–108.

17. In 1860, the Senate finally resolved that the Dakotas did have such a right, and they set compensation at thirty cents an acre, funds which largely were claimed by traders to pay back debts supposedly owed to them (Anderson 1997, 231).

18. On Dakota history leading up to the war, the conflict itself, and its immediate aftermath, see Anderson 1986, 89–179; Anderson and Woolworth; Berg;

Board of Commissioners, 162–326; Chomsky; Gilman, 162–209; Herbert; Hyman, 93–142; Martínez; Meyer, 109–54; Nichols, 61–128; Wilson.

19. Little Crow had been removed as speaker for the Mdewakanton quite recently due to his being perceived as not committed enough to the project of "civilization" privileged by the Indian agent. See Anderson 1986, 119–21.

20. Reinforcements of about twelve hundred men led by Sibley arrived at Fort Ridgely on August 27, and relatively soon thereafter, this increase in U.S. forces in the vicinity of the fort brought an end to active conflict in the south. During this time, Dakotas had been gathering in Little Crow's village, which came to serve as their base of operations through August 25, at which point they decided to move northward to try to join with Sissetons and Wahpetons at the Upper Agency. Leaving on August 26 in a train five miles long, they arrived at Yellow Medicine two days later, leading to an extended debate over the next two weeks about participation in the war and the formation of the "peace party" (which began gathering and protecting white and mixed-blood prisoners captured during the course of the war). On September 21, news reached Little Crow's camp that Sibley's forces were just south of the Upper Agency, and after a failed attack on them at dawn the next morning, Little Crow counseled those who wanted to continue the war to head toward the plains.

21. Since there was no centralized authority for all the bands of a given people, they did not function like a state that declares war as a unit, so leaders and members of different peoples took various positions. However, the alignments tended to follow a split between those peoples connected to the Lower Agency (Mdewakanton and Wahpekute) and those connected to the Upper Agency (Sisseton and Wahpeton).

22. See Message of the President of the United States in Answer to A resolution of the Senate of the 5th instant in relation to the Indian barbarities in Minnesota. 37th Cong., 3rd sess. S. exec. Doc. 7. 68, 9, 10, 23, 25, 31, 33. Further citations will be parenthetical.

23. Similarly, in a memorial to the president in late 1862 on the subject of what to do with the Dakotas who already had been tried, the Minnesota congressional delegation notes, "These Indians are called by some prisoners of war. There was no war about it. It was wholesale robbery, *rape, murder*. These Indians were not at war with their murdered victims," adding, "the people of Minnesota . . . have *not* violated the *law*" (Ibid., 4).

24. In his dispatches to various officials and military personnel during the Dakota War, Sibley repeatedly refers to Native combatants as "guilty." See Board of Commissioners, 165–282.

25. For similar statements by Alexander Ramsey, who in his role as territorial governor of Minnesota also served as superintendent of Indian affairs in the area, see Annual Report of Office of Indian Affairs (1850), 76–77; Annual Report of Office of Indian Affairs (1851), 411. Galbraith attributes Dakota actions to ingrained propensities toward lawless savagery despite noting a range of sources of Dakota resentment and desperation prior to the war, including starvation due to the delay of the annuities, longstanding concerns about the amount of Dakota funds given over by the government to nonnative traders,

the nonfulfillment of treaty promises, and discontent with the agent's efforts to turn them into Euramerican farmers.

26. Galbraith further asserts, "Whilst I must confine myself to the Sioux, I cannot keep out the fact that what is generally true of the Sioux is also generally true of all our other Indian tribes" (36).

27. For discussion of a similar discursive and policy nexus through which Native actions in the period are understood as crime, see Rand, 58–92.

28. Governor Ramsey does describe recent events as an "Indian war" in a letter to Lincoln on September 6, 1862, but then describes it as "being equally cruel and barbarous with those waged by that race which have preceded it in the history of our country." In a letter to the War Department that same day, Ramsey describes it as a "national war" in order to insist on the need for "the general government" to intervene, and in a letter to General Pope on September 19, Colonel Sibley also describes it as a "war" while then immediately shifting the frame of reference by characterizing the Dakotas as "the most warlike and powerful of the tribes on this continent." See Board of Commissioners, 224–25, 234. These moments cite the name of war but qualify it by its association with Indianness, suggesting the term serves less as an indication of the political stakes of the conflict than the savagery of the scope and modes of Indian violence. Moreover, Dakota Indian agent and northern superintendency reports from the 1850s routinely use the term "war" to discuss conflicts among Native peoples, particularly the Dakota and Ojibwe, suggesting something other than, in Galbraith's terms, *regular war*. For examples, see Annual Report of the Office of Indian Affairs (1850), 107; Annual Report of the Office of Indian Affairs (1851), 280; Annual Report of Office of Indian Affairs (1854), 273; Annual Report of Office of Indian Affairs (1856), 604; Annual Report of Commissioner of Indian Affairs (1859), 449; Annual Report of Commissioner of Indian Affairs (1860), 285.

29. Board of Commissioners, 257.

30. Message of the President, S. Ex. Doc. 7, 2. For a critique of efforts to exonerate Lincoln or ameliorate his role in the executions, see Martínez.

31. Message of the President, S. Ex. Doc. 7, 7–8. Battles are included in the charges against prisoners No. 5, No. 12, No. 19, No. 24, No. 35, No. 67, No. 70, and they are the principal charge against No. 19 and No. 35.

32. On the emergence of new understandings of the laws of war during the Civil War, see Witt. However, he does not consider the role of settler–Indigenous conflict as itself potentially formative in the construction of the laws of war from the eighteenth century onward.

33. Board of Commissioners, 256.

34. Ibid., 233, 236, 262, 270, 272, 279.

35. See Chomsky; Herbert; Martínez; Witt, 330–35.

36. Board of Commissioners, 198, 288.

37. For similar sentiments in relation to Dakota lands, see Annual Report of Office of Indian Affairs (1850), 77; Annual Report of Office of Indian Affairs (1851), 416–20; Annual Report of Office of Indian Affairs (1852), 419.

38. Board of Commissioners, 291.

39. Colette A. Hyman has characterized this time in Dakota history, during the war and in the years immediately in its wake, as specifically genocidal (93–94). Without minimizing the violence done to Dakota people(s) in this period, I want to highlight the continuities of political imagination in government discourses between times of "peace" and "war" in order to emphasize that U.S. settler colonialism does not rely primarily on military intervention to displace Native peoples and secure state jurisdiction. On this point, see also Rockwell. On the circumstances of deprivation for prisoners and noncombatants in the wake of the war, see Canku and Simon; Hyman, 93–142. On contemporary nonnative responses to Dakota characterizations of nonnative policy and actions during and after the war, particularly the forced marches and imprisonment of noncombatants, see Nunpa.

40. For discussion of a similar dynamic in treaty-making with respect to the Kiowa in the same period, see Rand, 33–57. Dakota bands, though, did not necessarily conform to the geographies of federal policy. For discussion at the time of Dakota refusal to occupy the lands designated for them within extant law and Indian policy, see Annual Report of Office of Indian Affairs (1855), 378–79; Annual Report of Office of Indian Affairs (1856), 604–6; Annual Report of Commissioner of Indian Affairs (1858), 387; Annual Report of Commissioner of Indian Affairs (1859), 455; Annual Report of Commissioner of Indian Affairs (1860), 283–85.

41. The treaties of 1851 are almost identical in their provisions for the Mdewakanton and Wahpekute and for the Sisseton and Wahpeton, as are the treaties of 1858.

42. Annual Report of Office of Indian Affairs (1851), 411, 417. In 1850, Ramsey refers to "the suppositious independence of the Indian" as "but another of the anomalies . . . of which the general subject of the relative rights and duties of a civilized and barbarous people is so fruitful" (Annual Report of Office of Indian Affairs [1850], 80).

43. Annual Report of Office of Indian Affairs (1850), 80. For similar sentiments in relevant agency and superintendency reports prior to the war, see Annual Report of Office of Indian Affairs (1850), 107; Annual Report of Commissioner of Indian Affairs (1858), 388; Annual Report of Commissioner of Indian Affairs (1861), 703–4.

44. For similar statements in relevant agent and superintendent reports prior to the Dakota War, see Annual Report of Office of Indian Affairs (1850), 107; Annual Report of Office of Indian Affairs (1851), 281–83, 413–14; Annual Report of Office of Indian Affairs (1852), 350; Annual Report of Commissioner of Indian Affairs (1858), 387; Annual Report of Commissioner of Indian Affairs (1859), 419–21; Annual Report of Commissioner of Indian Affairs (1861), 699–700.

45. Some at the time did seek to interpret the Dakota War as brought on by Confederate agitators. See Berg 99–100; Board of Commissioners, 260, 274; Gilman, 177; Nichols, 78–79.

46. See Denetdale; Kelman; Nichols, 161–201.

47. On Parker's participation in the Tonawandas' struggle to regain their

reservation, see Armstrong, 20–70; Genetin-Pilawa, 29–50; Hauptman 2011, 75–113; Parker 1919, 71–93. On the structure of the Iroquois League and its sachemships, see Fenton; Parker.

48. On the treaties of 1838 and 1842, see Conable; Genetin-Pilawa, 29–50; Gonzales, 182–220; Hauptman 1999, 175–212; Society of Friends; Valone.

49. On the Tonawandas' struggle to regain their reservation after 1842, see Conable, 283–324; Genetin-Pilawa, 29–50; Hauptman 2011.

50. On the history of this preemption claim and the role of the Ogden company in Seneca politics in the first half of the nineteenth-century, see Conable; Densmore; Ganter; Hauptman 1999; Wilkinson.

51. Haudenosaunee is the name used by the peoples themselves for what conventionally is known as the Iroquois League or Six Nations. This confederacy includes the Mohawks, Oneidas, Onondagas, Cayugas, Senecas, and Tuscaroras.

52. For an overview of the history of treaty-making under the U.S. from the perspective of U.S. officials, see Prucha. For an account of the history of treaty-making more focused on the meaning of such agreements to Native peoples, especially prior to the early nineteenth century, see Williams.

53. Report of the Committee on Indian Affairs, 61.

54. Ibid., 65–66.

55. Ibid., 87.

56. Letter from the Governor of New York, June 17, 1844, Ely S. Parker Papers (American Philosophical Society); Letter From the Governor of New York Stating That He Has No Power to Prevent the Execution of the Treaties, April 18, 1846, Ely S. Parker Papers (American Philosophical Society).

57. See Graymont; Hauptman 1999; Tiro.

58. Report of the Committee on Indian Affairs, 115.

59. Difficulties between the Tonawanda Senecas and the Ogden Land Company, Jan. 21, 1848, Ely S. Parker Papers (American Philosophical Society).

60. Tonawanda Chiefs to Governor Silas Wright, Appeal for Justice Till Difficulties are Settled, Feb. 22, 1845, Ely S. Parker Papers (American Philosophical Society).

61. The Tonawandas, though, also were able to make use of the government's official disavowal of coercion as the means of acquiring Native lands. In the case of *Fellows v. Blacksmith* (60 U.S. 366, 1857), the U.S. Supreme Court finds that the Ogden Company has no legal right to resort to violence as a means of gaining access to the land it supposedly acquired in the Treaty of Buffalo Creek, instead indicating that the federal government has exclusive authority to manage the process of Seneca removal as it sees fit.

62. Letter from the Secretary of War, Addressed to Mr. Schenck, chairman of the Committee on Military Affairs, transmitting a report by Colonel Parker on Indian affairs, 39th Cong., 2nd sess., H. mis. docs. 37, 4. In his reading of Parker's postwar career, Genetin-Pilawa emphasizes this dimension of Parker's thinking (61–72, 84–90). On Parker's term as Commissioner of Indian Affairs, see Armstrong, 137–65; Parker 1919, 150–61.

63. Letter from the Secretary of War, 2.

64. *Dred Scott v. Sanford*, 60 U.S. 393 (1857), 407.

65. Letter from the Secretary of War, 2.

66. Parker's statements as Commissioner of Indian Affairs, though, should not be taken as necessarily typifying his perspective on Native landedness in his later years. In a letter to a friend in 1887, he observes, "The tenacity with which the remnants of this people have adhered to their tribal organizations and religious traditions is all that has saved them thus far from inevitable extinguishment; when they abandon their birthright for a mess of Christian pottage they will then cease to be a distinctive people" (Parker 1919, 176), and his speech on the twenty-fifth anniversary of the Gettysburg Address features discussion of the Delaware chief Tammany and the violence of the history of white expropriations (Parker 1919, 181–88). See also Raheja 2006.

67. Annual Report of Commissioner of Indian Affairs (1869), 448.

68. Ibid.

69. This formulation dates back to the majority decision in the U.S. Supreme Court case of *Cherokee Nation v. Georgia* (30 U.S. 1, 1831), which invented the category "domestic dependent nation" as a way of characterizing the legal status of Native peoples while also describing their relation to the U.S. government as like that of a "ward" to his "guardian." For citations by agents and superintendents of such wardship with respect to the Dakota, see Annual Report of Office of Indian Affairs (1851), 281, 416; Annual Report of Commissioner of Indian Affairs (1858), 387; Annual Report of Commissioner of Indian Affairs (1859), 418–19, 421; Annual Report of Commissioner of Indian Affairs (1861), 698.

70. Annual Report of Commissioner of Indian Affairs (1869), 448. C. Joseph Genetin-Pilawa also addresses Parker's complicated attitude toward treaty-making in the wake of the Civil War in "Ely S. Parker and the Paradox of Reconstruction Politics in Indian Country" (unpublished essay in the author's possession).

71. In his annual report in 1870, Parker notes, "although I do not recommend that treaties be made with the Apaches and the several bands of Utes . . . , yet I would present for the consideration of Congress the importance of these bands being properly cared for. . . . As soon as practicable they should be placed upon a reservation, and furnished with whatever may be required to enable them to become self-sustaining" (Annual Report of Commissioner of Indian Affairs [1870], 469). He suggests some alternative to treaty-making that could create a "reservation" but does not specify the mechanism or legal theory for doing so. Treaty-making formally was ended by Congress in 1871. On this decision and the temporal narratives mobilized to legitimize it, see Bruyneel, 65–96.

72. Letter from the Secretary of War, 5.

73. Letter from the Secretary of War, 6.

74. In addressing the consequences of this settler tsunami, Parker's rhetoric at times seems almost boosterish of the civilization program, resembling the kinds of remarks made by Galbraith and Sibley discussed earlier. At one point, he claims, "the clouds of ignorance and superstition in which many of this people were so long enveloped have disappeared, and the light of Christian civilization seems to have dawned upon their moral darkness, and opened up a brighter future" (Annual Report of Commissioner of Indian Affairs [1869], 445),

and he endorses "the policy of giving to every Indian a home that he can call his own" by which "the Indians would be more rapidly advanced in civilization than they would if the policy of allowing them to hold their land in common were continued," also indicating the need for Indians to "progress toward that healthy Christian civilization in which are embraced the elements of material wealth and intellectual and moral development" (Annual Report of Commissioner of Indian Affairs [1870], 473–74).

75. Annual Report of Commissioner of Indian Affairs (1869), 447.

76. On the continuing struggle over Seneca lands in the late nineteenth century, including during the Civil War, see Hauptman 1993.

Bibliography

Agamben, Giorgio. (2003) 2005. *State of Exception*. Trans. Kevin Attell. Chicago: University of Chicago Press.

Anderson, Gary Clayton. (1984) 1997. *Kinsmen of Another Kind: Dakota–White Relations in the Upper Mississippi Valley, 1650–1852*. St. Paul: Minnesota Historical Society Press.

———. 1986. *Little Crow: Spokesman for the Sioux*. St. Paul: Minnesota Historical Society Press.

Anderson, Gary Clayton, and Alan R. Woolworth, eds. 1988. *Through Dakota Eyes: Narrative Accounts of the Minnesota Indian War of 1862*. St. Paul: Minnesota Historical Society Press.

Annual Report of Commissioner of Indian Affairs (1858). 35th Cong, 2nd sess. S. exec. doc. 1/9.

Annual Report of Commissioner of Indian Affairs (1859). 36th Cong., 1st sess. S. exec. doc. 2/5.

Annual Report of Commissioner of Indian Affairs (1860). 36th Cong., 2nd sess. S. exec. doc. 1/4.

Annual Report of Commissioner of Indian Affairs (1861). 37th Cong., 2nd sess. S. exec. doc. 1/5.

Annual Report of Commissioner of Indian Affairs (1869). 41st Cong., 2nd sess. H. exec. doc. 1/11.

Annual Report of Commissioner of Indian Affairs (1870). 41st Cong., 3rd sess. H. exec. doc. 1/11.

Annual Report of Office of Indian Affairs (1850). 31st Cong., 2nd sess. S. exec. doc. 1/3.

Annual Report of Office of Indian Affairs (1851). 32nd Cong., 1st sess. S. exec. doc. 1/12.

Annual Report of Office of Indian Affairs (1852). 32nd Cong., 2nd sess. S. exec. doc. 1/5.

Annual Report of Office of Indian Affairs (1854). 33rd Cong., 2nd sess. S. exec. doc. 1/7.

Annual Report of Office of Indian Affairs (1855). 34th Cong., 1st sess. S. exec. doc. 1/7.

Annual Report of Office of Indian Affairs (1856). 34th Cong., 3rd. sess. S. exec. doc. 5/6.

Armstrong, William H. 1989. *Warrior in Two Camps: Ely S. Parker, Union General and Seneca Chief.* Syracuse, N.Y.: Syracuse University Press.

Berg, Scott W. 2012. *38 Nooses: Lincoln, Little Crow, and the Beginning of the Frontier's End.* New York: Pantheon Books.

Blight, David W. 2011. *American Oracle: The Civil War in the Civil Rights Era.* Cambridge, Mass.: Harvard University Press.

———. 2001. *Race and Reunion: The Civil War in American History.* Cambridge: Harvard University Press.

Board of Commissioners, eds. 1893. *Minnesota in the Civil and Indian Wars, 1861–1865,* vol. 2: *Official Reports and Correspondence.* St. Paul, Minn.: The Pioneer Press Company.

Bruyneel, Kevin. 1997. *The Third Space of Sovereignty: The Postcolonial Politics of U.S.–Indigenous Relations.* Minneapolis: University of Minnesota Press.

Byrd, Jodi. 2011. *The Transit of Empire: Indigenous Critiques of Colonialism.* Minneapolis: University of Minnesota Press.

Calloway, Colin G. 2006. *The Scratch of a Pen: 1763 and the Transformation of North America.* New York: Oxford University Press.

Canku, Clifford, and Michael Simon, eds. 2013. *The Dakota Prisoner of War Letters: Dakota Kaŝkapi Okicize Wowapi.* St. Paul: Minnesota Historical Society Press.

Chomsky, Carol. 1990. "The United States–Dakota War Trials: A Study in Military Injustice." *Stanford Law Review* 43:13-96.

Chow, Rey. 2002. *The Protestant Ethnic and the Spirit of Capitalism.* New York: Columbia University Press.

Conable, Mary H. 1994. "A Steady Enemy: The Ogden Land Company and the Seneca Indians." PhD. Diss. University of Rochester.

Crenshaw, Kimberlé. 1995. "Race, Reform, and Retrenchment: Transformation and Legitimation in Anti-discrimination Law." In *Critical Race Theory: The Key Writings That Formed the Movement,* ed. Kimberlé Crenshaw, Neil Gotanda, Gary Peller, and Kendall Thomas, 103–22. New York: The New Press.

Dayan, Colin. 2011. *The Law Is a White Dog: How Legal Rituals Make and Unmake Persons.* Princeton, N.J.: Princeton University Press.

Deloria, Philip J. 2004. *Indians in Unexpected Places.* Lawrence: University of Kansas Press.

Denetdale, Jennifer Nez. 2007. *Reclaiming Diné History: The Legacies of Navajo Chief Manuelito and Juanita.* Tucson: University of Arizona Press.

Densmore, Christopher. 1999. *Red Jacket: Iroquois Diplomat and Orator.* Syracuse, N.Y.: Syracuse University Press.

Fenton, William N. 1998. *The Great Law of the Longhouse: A Political History of the Iroquois Confederacy.* Norman: University of Oklahoma Press.

Ferguson, Roderick. 2012. *The Reorder of Things: The University and Its Pedagogies of Minority Difference.* Minneapolis: University of Minnesota Press.

Finkelman, Paul. 2009. "Lincoln and the Preconditions for Emancipation: *The Moral Grandeur of a Bill of Lading.*" In *Lincoln's Proclamation: Emancipation*

Reconsidered, ed. William A. Blair and Karen Fisher Younger, 13–44. Chapel Hill: University of North Carolina Press.

Freeman, Elizabeth. 2010. *Time Binds: Queer Temporalities, Queer Histories.* Durham, N.C.: Duke University Press.

Ganter, Granville, ed. 2006. *The Collected Speeches of Sagoyewatha, or Red Jacket.* Syracuse: Syracuse University Press.

Genetin-Pilawa, C. Joseph. 2012. *Crooked Paths to Allotment: The Fight over Federal Indian Policy after the Civil War.* Chapel Hill: University of North Carolina Press.

Gilman, Rhoda R. 2004. *Henry Hastings Sibley: Divided Heart.* St. Paul: Minnesota Historical Society Press.

Gonzales, Christian Michael. 2010. "Cultural Colonizers: Persistence and Empire in the Indian Antiremoval Movement, 1815–1859." PhD. Diss. University of California, San Diego.

Graymont, Barbara. 1976. "New York State Indian Policy after the Revolution." *New York History* 57, no. 4: 438–74.

Guelzo, Allen C. 2012. *Fateful Lightening: A New History of the Civil War and Reconstruction.* New York: Oxford University Press.

Guha, Ranajit. 1988. "On Some Aspects of the Historiography of Colonial India." In *Selected Subaltern Studies,* ed. Ranajit Guha and Gayatri Chakravorty Spivak, 37–44. New York: Oxford University Press.

Harris, Cheryl I. 1993. "Whiteness as Property." *Harvard Law Review* 106, no. 8: 1707–91.

Hartman, Saidiya. 1997. *Scenes of Subjection: Terror, Slavery, and Self-Making in Nineteenth-Century America.* New York: Oxford University Press.

Hauptman, Laurence M. 1999. *Conspiracy of Interests: Iroquois Dispossession and the Rise of New York State.* Syracuse, N.Y.: Syracuse University Press.

———. 1993. *The Iroquois in the Civil War: From Battlefield to Reservation.* Syracuse, N.Y.: Syracuse University Press.

———. 2011. *The Tonawanda Senecas' Heroic Battle against Removal.* Albany: State University of New York Press. Herbert, Maeve. 2009. "Explaining the Sioux Military Commission of 1862." *Columbia Human Rights Law Review* 40:743–98.

Hogan, Jackie. 2011. *Lincoln, Inc.: Selling the Sixteenth President in Contemporary America.* New York: Rowman & Littlefield.

Holzer, Harold. 2012. *Emancipating Lincoln: The Proclamation in Text, Context, and Memory.* Cambridge, Mass.: Harvard University Press.

Hyman, Colette A. 2012. *Dakota Women's Work: Creativity, Culture, and Exile.* St. Paul: Minnesota Historical Society Press.

Jackson, Shona. 2012. *Creole Indigeneity: Between Myth and Nation in the Caribbean.* Minneapolis: University of Minnesota Press.

Jones, Dorothy V. 1982. *License for Empire: Colonialism by Treaty in Early America.* Chicago: University of Chicago Press.

Kappler, Charles J. 1929. *Indian Affairs: Laws and Treaties*, Vol. 2. Washington, D.C.: Government Printing Office.

Kazanjian, David. 2003. *The Colonizing Trick: National Culture and Imperial Citizenship in Early America.* Minneapolis: University of Minnesota Press.

Kelman, Ari. 2013. *A Misplaced Massacre: Struggling over the Memory of Sand Creek.* Cambridge, Mass.: Harvard University Press.

Kushner, Tony. 2012. *Lincoln: The Screenplay.* New York: Theatre Communications Group.

Lee, James Kyung-Jin. 2004. *Urban Triage: Race and the Fictions of Multiculturalism.* Minneapolis: University of Minnesota Press.

Luciano, Dana. 2007. *Arranging Grief: Sacred Time and the Body in Nineteenth-Century America.* New York: New York University Press.

Lyons, Scott Richard. 2010. *X-marks: Native Signatures of Assent.* Minneapolis: University of Minnesota Press.

Martínez, David. 2013. "Remembering the Thirty-Eight: Abraham Lincoln, the Dakota, and the U.S. War on Barbarism." *Wicazo Sa Review* 28, no. 2: 5–29.

McCurry, Stephanie. 2009. "War, Gender, and Emancipation in the Civil War South." In *Lincoln's Proclamation: Emancipation Reconsidered,* ed. William A. Blair and Karen Fisher Younger, 120–50. Chapel Hill: University of North Carolina Press.

Melamed, Jodi. 2011. *Represent and Destroy: Rationalizing Violence in the New Racial Capitalism.* Minneapolis: University of Minnesota Press.

Meyer, Roy W. 1993. *History of the Santee Sioux: United States Indian Policy on Trial.* Rev. Ed. Lincoln: University of Nebraska Press.

Moreton-Robinson, Aileen. 2008. "Writing off Treaties: White Possession in the United States Critical Whiteness Studies Literature." In *Transnational Whiteness Matters,* ed. Aileen Moreton-Robinson, Maryrose Casey, and Fiona Nicoll, 81–96. New York: Rowman & Littlefield.

Neely, Mark E., Jr. 2011. *Lincoln and the Triumph of the Nation: Constitutional Conflict in the American Civil War.* Chapel Hill: University of North Carolina Press.

Nichols, David A. (1978) 2012. *Lincoln and the Indians: Civil War Policy and Politics.* St. Paul: Minnesota Historical Society Press.

Nunpa, Chris Mato. 2004. "Dakota Commemorative March: Thoughts and Reactions." *American Indian Quarterly* 28, no. 1-2: 216–37.

O'Brien, Jean M. 2010. *Firsting and Lasting: Writing Indians Out of Existence in New England.* Minneapolis: University of Minnesota Press.

Parker, Arthur Caswell. (1926) 1967. *The History of the Seneca Indians.* Long Island, N.Y.: Ira J. Friedman, Inc.

———. 1919. *The Life of General Ely S. Parker: Last Grand Sachem of the Iroquois and General Grant's Military Secretary.* Buffalo, N.Y.: Baker, Jones, Hausauer, Inc.

Povinelli, Elizabeth. 2011. *Economies of Abandonment: Social Belonging and Endurance in Late Liberalism.* Durham, N.C.: Duke University Press.

Prucha, Francis Paul. 1994. *American Indian Treaties: The History of a Political Anomaly.* Berkeley: University of California Press.

Raheja, Michelle H. 2006. "'I leave It with the People of the United States to Say': Autobiographical Disruption in the Personal Narratives of Black Hawk and Ely S. Parker." *American Indian Culture and Research Journal* 30, no. 1: 87–108.

———. 2010. *Reservation Reelism: Redfacing, Visual Sovereignty, and Representations of Native Americans in Film.* Lincoln: University of Nebraska Press.

Rand, Jacki Thompson. 2008. *Kiowa Humanity and the Invasion of the State.* Lincoln: University of Nebraska Press.

Reddy, Chandan. 2011. *Freedom with Violence: Race, Sexuality, and the U.S. State.* Durham, N.C.: Duke University Press.

Report of the Committee on Indian Affairs, to whom were referred sundry petitions and memorials from Citizens of New York, and others, praying that the Tonawanda band of the Seneca tribe of Indians may be exempted from the operation of the treaty of the 20th May, 1842. 29th Cong., 2nd sess. S. doc. 156.

Rifkin, Mark. 2009a. "Indigenizing Agamben: Rethinking Sovereignty in Light of the 'Peculiar' Status of Native Peoples." *Cultural Critique* 73 (Fall): 88–124.

———. 2009b. *Manifesting America: The Imperial Construction of U.S. National Space.* New York: Oxford University Press.

Rockwell, Stephen J. 2010. *Indian Affairs and the Administrative State in the Nineteenth Century.* New York: Cambridge University Press.

Schwartz, Barry. 2008. *Abraham Lincoln in the Post-heroic Era: History and Memory in Late-Twentieth-Century America.* Chicago: University of Chicago Press.

Shaw, Karen. 2004. "Creating/Negotiating Interstices: Indigenous Sovereignties." In *Sovereign Lives: Power in Global Politics,* ed. Jenny Edkins, Véronique Pin-Fat, and Michael J. Shapiro, 165–87. New York: Routledge.

Silva, Denise Ferreira da. 2007. *Toward a Global Idea of Race.* Minneapolis: University of Minnesota Press.

Society of Friends. 1840. *The Case of the Seneca Indians in the State of New York: Illustrated by Facts.* Philadelphia: Merrihew and Thompson.

Sweet, John Hope. 2006. *Bodies Politic: Negotiating Race in the American North, 1730–1830.* Philadelphia: University of Pennsylvania Press.

Stanley, Amy Dru. 1998. *From Bondage to Contract: Wage Labor, Marriage, and the Market in the Age of Slave Emancipation.* New York: Cambridge University Press.

Tiro, Karim M. 2011. *The People of the Standing Stone: The Oneida Nation from the Revolution through the Era of Removal.* Amherst: University of Massachusetts Press.

Turner, Dale. 2006. *This Is Not a Peace Pipe: Towards a Critical Indigenous Philosophy.* Toronto: University of Toronto Press.

Valone, Stephen J. 2001. "William Seward, Whig Politics, and the Compromised Indian Removal Policy in New York State, 1838–1843." *New York History* 82, no. 2: 107–34.

Wagner, Bryan. 2009. *Disturbing the Peace: Black Culture and the Police Power after Slavery.* Cambridge, Mass.: Harvard University Press.

White, Ed. 2005. *The Backcountry and the City: Colonization and Conflict in Early America*. Minneapolis: University of Minnesota Press.

Wilkinson, Norman B. 1979. "Robert Morris and the Treaty of Big Tree." In *The Rape of Indian Lands,* ed. Paul Wallace Gates, 257–78. New York: Arno Press.

Williams, Robert A. 1997. *Linking Arms Together: American Indian Treaty Visions of Law and Peace, 1600–1800*. New York: Oxford University Press.

Wilson, Angela Cavender. 2004. "Decolonizing the 1862 Death Marches." *American Indian Quarterly* 28, no. 1-2: 185–215.

Witt, John Fabian. 2012. *Lincoln's Code: The Laws of War in American History.* New York: Free Press.

Wolfe, Patrick. 2000. "Settler Colonialism and the Elimination of the Native." *Journal of Genocide Research* 8, no. 4. 387–409.

Yirush, Craig. 2011. *Settlers, Liberty, and Empire: The Roots of Early American Political Theory, 1675–1775*. New York: Cambridge University Press.

LAUREN GREWE

"To Bid His People Rise":
Political Renewal and Spiritual Contests
at Red Jacket's Reburial

PRESERVED IN A TEXTUAL STANDOFF over the meaning of a local historical event are three unlikely interlocutors: Mohawk poet and performer E. Pauline Johnson, Seneca sachem and Civil War veteran Ely Parker, and American poet Walt Whitman. Brought together in the Buffalo Historical Society's publication *Obsequies of Red Jacket at Buffalo,* these authors propose competing spiritual and political visions of how to memorialize the Seneca leader and orator Red Jacket's reburial ceremony at the Forest Lawn Cemetery in Buffalo, New York on October 9, 1884. On that day, the Buffalo Historical Society reinterred Red Jacket and five other leaders from the Six Nations (also known as the Haudenosaunee or Iroquois), eventually constructing a monument to Red Jacket that features prominently in the cemetery to this day.[1] An important literary figure himself, Red Jacket is at the center of a constellation of literary moments involving a surprising range of American Indian, First Nations, and European American authors. Woven into the *Obsequies,* in addition to Red Jacket himself, are Mary Jemison, Walt Whitman, George Copway, E. Pauline Johnson, and, distantly, John Greenleaf Whittier.

My close reading of the Buffalo Historical Society's slim volume *Obsequies of Red Jacket at Buffalo* will reveal the competing visions, both spiritual and political, surrounding Red Jacket's reburial in October of 1884. Although the creators of *Obsequies* denied that the Six Nations had a continuing political presence at the reburial, the Historical Society's minutes and the participation of representatives from the Six Nations suggest a different story. Native speakers and participants used the event for their own purposes, whether to debate about Christianity, to assert Native land rights, or to forge and renew important social ties and intertribal alliances.

Amid the political work unfolding at Red Jacket's reburial, three voices stand out for their competing visions of the spiritual significance of the event: those of the poet Walt Whitman, the Seneca sachem and Civil War veteran Ely S. Parker, and the Mohawk poet and performer E. Pauline Johnson. After engaging briefly with Buffalo's religious history, Red Jacket's life, and Native dispossession and reorganization in the Buffalo area, I will turn to these three authors' different interpretations of the reburial as published in the Buffalo Historical Society's pamphlet. Whitman's poem about the reburial, "Red Jacket, (From Aloft.)," applauds the spiritual impulse behind the reinterment but questions the need for material monuments. His U.S. nationalist vision of Red Jacket's reburial concerns the proper memorialization of national heroes, even as he contemplates his own memorialization. In his speech as recorded in *Obsequies,* Parker subtly undermines the spiritual premise of the event, asserting that Red Jacket was not a Christian but, in his words, a pagan. Therefore, he argues, the Christian reburial was a farce, and thus the Buffalo Historical Society was unable to incorporate Red Jacket within its nationalist vision of Buffalo's importance. Johnson, however, counters Parker's argument with her poem "The Re-interment of Red Jacket." She offers a different model of Native Christianity while using the elegy to establish her own poetic authority. More important, in "The Re-interment of Red Jacket," Johnson for the first time acknowledged her own Indian ancestry, counteracting Whitman's spectral Indian with her own living presence at the reburial.

While Johnson attended the reburial ceremony as part of a delegation of Six Nations citizens from both the United States and Canada, Whitman likely heard about the event from the publicity it gained in newspapers and periodicals across the United States. The day after the reburial, on October 10, 1884, the *Philadelphia Press* published the poem "Red Jacket (From Aloft.)."[2] On first glance, Whitman's poem commemorates Red Jacket's reburial as part of the vanishing Indian myth so often found in nineteenth-century European American representations of Indians. In Whitman's poem, Red Jacket witnesses the event from above as a specter, appearing not as a human voice but as "a towering human form." Figured as "some old tree, or rock or cliff," the "Product of Nature's sun, stars, earth direct," Red Jacket lacks the ability to act in the poem, in spite of being "arm'd with the rifle." The poem makes no direct mention of the living Indians who took a central part in the event— among them Johnson and some of Red Jacket's descendants, including Parker. Instead Whitman erases Native agency entirely, representing the reburial as the product of European American "fashion, learning, wealth" rather than as a collaboration between Indians and European Americans. Despite its nuanced critique of the commercialism of monuments, "Red Jacket, (From Aloft.)" seems easily legible within the common analytical framework of the spectral Indian narrative.[3]

If we step back, however, from Whitman's ghostly portrayal of Red Jacket, what might "Red Jacket, (From Aloft.)" signify next to Johnson's poem, "The Re-interment of Red Jacket"? Whitman offered a poem that, while spiritual and nationalist, conforms to neither the designs of the Buffalo Historical Society nor the Christian perspectives of Johnson. As both a participant in the event and a member of the Mohawk Nation, Johnson opens up less hegemonic ways of interpreting the event, allowing us to regard it as the locus of a spiritual contest involving multiple European American and Indian groups. Moreover, as Johnson's first public claim of Indianness, "The Re-interment of Red Jacket" constitutes a key moment in Johnson's emergence as an author.[4] In contrast, by the time "Red Jacket (From Aloft.)" was published in the *Philadelphia Press* (and later in the 1888 edition of *November Boughs* and the 1891–92 edition of *Leaves of Grass),* Whitman was an established poet contemplating how to ensure his own monumentalization. By reading Johnson's poem in juxtaposition with Whitman's, we move beyond nationalist frames to address the heterogeneity of claims, spiritual, literary, and historical, that materialized in response to Red Jacket's reinterment at Buffalo.

My discussion of Johnson and Whitman's memorializations of Red Jacket in this way responds to the recent call of scholars to contemplate the relationship between the literary and the historical with the goal of writing Native history differently. "The line between what is literary and what is historical, particularly in Native American writing," Lisa Brooks notes, "may be as problematic as the divide between imagery, orality, and the written word." Similarly, Matt Cohen argues, "History must be written using different evidence and different methods when indigenous North Americans are part of the story." The story of Red Jacket's reburial is both literary and historical, and as a "publication event," an "embodied act of information exchange," it involved not only the print publication of Johnson and Whitman's poems but also the presence of Six Nations people and the proclaiming of speeches at the reburial itself.[5] In exploring the religious and spiritual aspects of Red Jacket's reburial and the poems and speeches written for its occasion, I also respond to scholarly reconsiderations of Christianity's place within Native American communities. Native American converts "tapp[ed] Christianity to oppose the forces of destruction, to defend Native American communities, and to strengthen Native American sovereignty, in spite of the odds," as Joel W. Martin argues in the introduction to *Native Americans, Christianity, and the Reshaping of the American Religious Landscape,*[6] Contrary to the claims of the secularization thesis, religion remained integral to ideas about politics and aesthetics for the authors discussed in this essay. Religion does not coincide neatly with tribal affiliation, race, or nationality in this story. This essay uses the Buffalo Historical Society's small pamphlet *Obsequies of Red Jacket at Buffalo* as a lens for analyzing this publication event, which is best understood as a series of performances of competing spiritual visions of what Red Jacket's reburial meant for Buffalo, for the Six Nations people, and for the United States, with competing political ambitions tied to each vision.

The utterances surrounding Red Jacket's reburial exemplify the often neglected religious or spiritual elements at play in such historical ceremonies and their literary components. The impulse toward memorialization of Indians during the nineteenth century was rooted not only in the political contest over land and sovereignty but also in a complex spiritual contest over bodies and their potential meanings—an aspect of monumentalization undertheorized even in criticism today, even as it increasingly returns religious matters to analytical centrality. Attending to heterogeneity—of religion, tribal affiliation, or class—at Red Jacket's reburial allows us to understand the varying stakes of the conflict. After all, the claims of tribal outsiders such as Whitman and Johnson cannot be subsumed into the concerns of the Seneca nor of the Buffalo Historical Society.

The story of Red Jacket's reburial is a complicated one. The civic ceremony of Red Jacket's reinterment by the Buffalo Historical Society elides

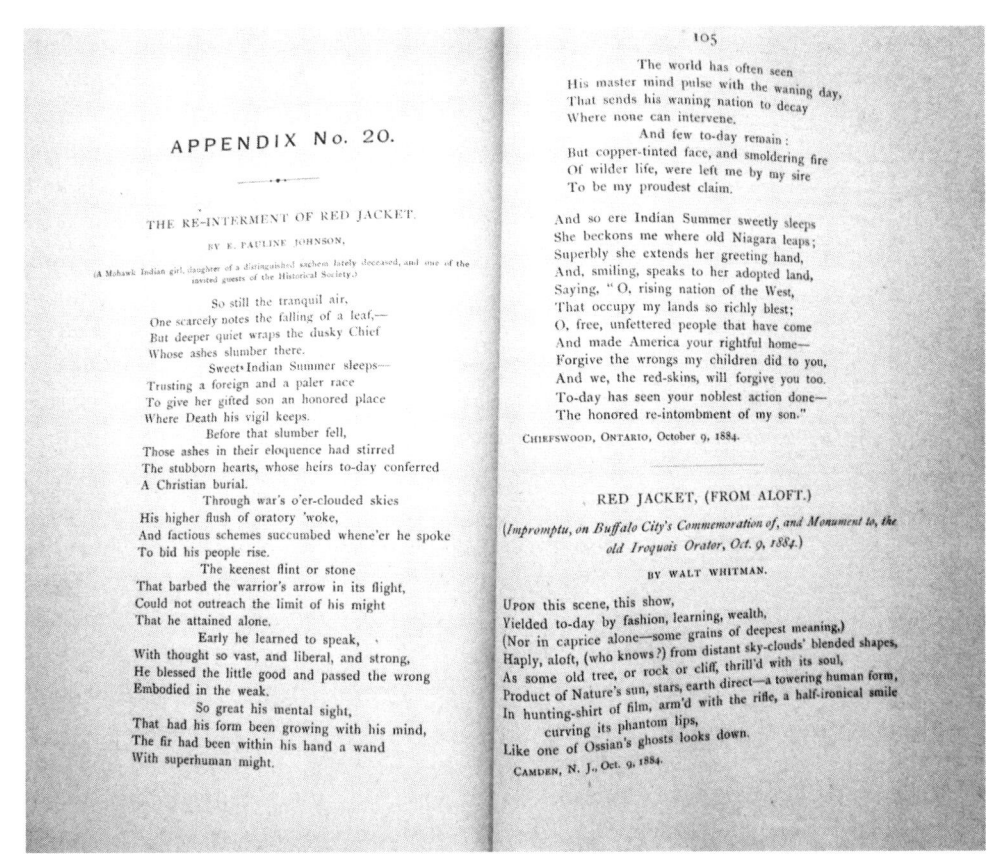

FIGURE 1. Side-by-side, surprisingly, in Appendix 20 of the Buffalo Historical Society's publication *Obsequies of Red Jacket at Buffalo*, E. Pauline Johnson and Walt Whitman memorialize the occasion of the Seneca leader and orator Red Jacket's reburial. Photograph by the author.

this complicated history by using the reburial to assert Buffalo's place within the national history of the United States. Even as the ceremony promotes Buffalo's national history, it slights Buffalo's local histories of immigration and European dispossession of Indians by figuring Six Nations Indians as belonging to the past rather than the present. At the Buffalo Historical Society's ceremony, however, were Natives who challenged such a tale. Following this narrative that Natives helped to create will take us from Buffalo's religious landscape and Six Nations political formations to the memorializations by Whitman, Parker, and Johnson. Varying affiliations with different strands of Christianity, American and Canadian governments, and tribal communities complicate Six Nations identity at the reburial. Addressing the event as a spiritual contest allows us to appreciate these tensions and how they shaped Red Jacket's reburial.

As the "nexus of an important 'political hub,'" Buffalo Creek had long been a stop on what Robert Warrior describes as the "intellectual trade routes" of the American Northeast. Important to Six Nations political structures, Buffalo Creek "effectively maintained the values of the longhouse, the traditional council fire of the old confederacy." In Christine DeLucia's terms, Buffalo might be called a "memoryscape," composed of a "constellation of spots on the land that have accrued stories over time, transforming them from blank or neutral spaces into emotionally infused, politically potent places." As such, Buffalo Creek was important not only to the Seneca but also to the Six Nations. "Buffalo Creek is the story of a people recalling, re-establishing, and maintaining their relationship to the reservation," writes Alyssa Mt. Pleasant, "in ways that define it as a Haudenosaunee place." As the seat of the council fire of the confederacy, Buffalo Creek helped maintain the Gayaneshagowa, the "Great Law of Peace" that united the Mohawk, Oneida, Onondaga, Cayuga, and Seneca nations.[7]

In addition to being an important place for the Six Nations, Buffalo had a long history of religious heterogeneity and revival. Called the "Burned-Over District," Western New York in the early nineteenth century was "a volatile, erratic, unsettled religious landscape," filled with interdenominational conflict, evangelical revivals, utopias, and other social experiments. The religious landscape of Buffalo in the 1880s and 1890s was far from homogenous. A city map from 1901 shows that Buffalo contained Baptist, Congregationalist, Episcopalian, Presbyterian, Lutheran, Methodist, Unitarian, and Roman Catholic churches as well as several synagogues.[8] For the Seneca, this heterogeneous religious landscape meant juggling relations to and with Christian denominations throughout the nineteenth century, a situation Senecas could turn to their own benefit by "play[ing] one denomination off against another" and selectively adopting practices of religious groups, defying missionaries' attempts to convert the Seneca fully. Red Jacket himself often invoked this religious heterogeneity to condemn European American attempts to convert the Seneca, drawing particular attention to sectarian conflict among Christians.[9]

Best known for his skill in council, not in war, Red Jacket participated in political affairs from 1775 to his death in 1830. Never a great warrior, Red Jacket opposed involvement in the Revolutionary War, although he ultimately lost the argument when the Seneca sided with the British. The 1790s were the period of Red Jacket's greatest influence, and the Treaty of Canandaigua in 1794 was his greatest contribution to the Six Nations politically. This treaty "sets out the basis for the relationship between the United States and the Indians in New York State" and was "in large measure the result of the negotiations between Timothy Pickering and Red Jacket from 1790 to 1794." During the 1820s and following the so-called Christian—Pagan split, Red Jacket supported the faction of the Seneca in favor of continuing Seneca religious belief, and his policy after 1810 was resistance to attempts to purchase reservation land by European Americans and to the attempt to move the Seneca west. Red Jacket was known as "the defender of the Seneca traditions and lands against the attacks of land speculators and missionaries." By the time of his reburial, however, Red Jacket was better known for his eloquent reply to Reverend Cram in 1805 about religion and colonialism than he was for his work on Six Nations treaties.[10]

The Seneca religious revival led by Handsome Lake at the end of the eighteenth century provided another response to religious heterogeneity in western New York. A socially conservative movement, particularly concerning gender and sexuality, the religious teachings of Handsome Lake "reflected the prolonged intercultural conversation between Seneca religious traditions and various representatives of Christianity, which had begun in the seventeenth century and would continue into the nineteenth century and beyond." Handsome Lake's religion emphasized sobriety, the practice of agriculture by men, the abandonment of witchcraft and a shift to emphasizing husband—wife rather than mother—daughter relations in an attempt to stabilize the nuclear family. As Matthew Dennis argues, Handsome Lake's death and resurrection closely resemble those of leaders of other religious revivals at the time. In addition to emphasizing a form of millennialism, Handsome Lake's visions included George Washington as well as Jesus Christ, endowing his teachings with both political and moral significance.[11]

The Buffalo Historical Society's reburial of Red Jacket also took place in the wake of a history of Native land dispossession in the Buffalo area. Following the Revolutionary War, Seneca land rights in New York State became more precarious. Seneca land eventually fell under the right of preemption, wherein private companies and people could gain exclusive right to purchase

Native land by obtaining the consent of the federal government to execute these land sales. Under these conditions, several land companies converged on the Seneca, among them the Ogden Land Company, which made a series of shady land purchases from the Seneca in the 1820s and 1830s, culminating in the disastrous 1838 Treaty of Buffalo Creek.[12] Under this treaty, the Seneca lost all their remaining New York lands except the one-mile square Oil Spring Reservation. While the supplemental treaty of 1842 returned the Allegany and Cattaraugus Reservations to the Seneca, the Buffalo Creek Reservation remained under the control of the Ogden Land Company. Moreover, from this point forward, New York state officials increasingly tried to extend their jurisdiction over the Seneca as Buffalo's growth "depended on its extinguishment of Indian land titles to this immense reservation that bordered the city on the east and south."[13]

Although the speeches of European American civic leaders largely consigned Senecas to the past, a closer examination of Red Jacket's reburial reveals that Indians participating in the event also took advantage of the occasion, using the event in ways that exceed the official vanishing-Indians narrative of the Buffalo Historical Society. Despite European American attempts to confine history and memory to written records, Andrew Newman contests, "Memories are shared through media, including spoken and written language, images, relics, and monuments." Reading these alternative memories requires paying attention to what Grey Gundaker terms "vernacular practices," ways that take place outside of conventional literacies. At moments such as Red Jacket's reburial, a kind of cultural "interference" takes place, the "ambiguating effect that results when disjunctive networks overlay, interface, and shift, with changing points of view." Red Jacket's reburial witnessed this kind of cultural overlap, as Indians and European Americans brought different and unstable religious and cultural frameworks to the event.[14]

Despite the Buffalo Historical Society's insistence upon the lack of political organization among the Six Nations Indians present at the reburial, political organization did in fact take place behind the scenes in the historical society's own rooms. In *Obsequies of Red Jacket,* we can see brief glimpses of a Six Nations council from the afternoon preceding Red Jacket's reburial, October 8, 1884. During this time, the text notes, "the visiting Indians assembled . . . and listened to addresses by Mr. William C. Bryant, himself a Seneca by adoption, and Gen. Ely S. Parker, of New York, one of the fifty sachems of the allied Six Nations." "The latter's speech," the document continues, "was especially interesting and affecting to the Indians present, and was interpreted in their dialect by his brother, Chief Nicholas H. Parker. A council was then organized to make final preparations for the burial ceremonies." Over thirty years earlier, the Senecas had elected Ely Parker as a grand sachem of the Six Nations at the age of twenty-three and given him the name Do-ne-ho-ga-wa or "Open Door," a name that historically conferred with it the title of Keeper of the Western Door of the Six Nations.[15]

In contrast to images of Native decline, the Buffalo Historical Society's commemoration of Red Jacket seems to have brought estranged Six Nations tribes back into communication with each other, thus renewing, not destroying, Six Nations alliances. Elsewhere, the Buffalo Historical Society calls this "council of the sachems, chiefs and warriors of the Six Nations" the "first general council of the united Iroquois . . . since the conclusion of the Revolutionary War, and the consequent disruption of the League." *Obsequies* stipulates, however, that "when this gathering and council was first proposed the Canadian Iroquois refused to unite with their estranged brothers who lived in the State of New York." Nevertheless, in the rooms of the Historical Society, "A few moments' conference . . . and a few bursts of Indian eloquence, melted all their hearts into a feeling of common sympathy, and the council proceeded with kindly and fraternal feeling."[16]

While official narratives at Red Jacket's reburial focused on the Confederacy's end, Indians at the event engaged in information exchange and organization that, in the long run, may have been as important as the Confederacy in maintaining the political viability of the Six Nations tribes. Gathered together for Red Jacket's reburial, tribes based both in Canada and the United States could share information about sovereignty struggles and financial compensation; relatives could meet and tell stories; economic deals could be formed; trust and communication could be renewed. Through these public memorializations—officially, narratives of death—the political formations of Six Nations tribes transformed and contributed to the cultural, social, and economic survival of Indian tribes in this area.

While Whitman's poem, "Red Jacket, (From Aloft.)" contests this vision of Six Nations survival, the poem nevertheless commemorates Red Jacket's reburial by applauding the spiritual impulse behind the event and questioning the need for material monuments. The poem was one of a series that Whitman published between 1879 and 1887 in the *Philadelphia Press* on famous people and public events. Under the poem's title, a note specifies that the poem was composed "Impromptu on Buffalo City's commemoration of and monument to the old Iroquois orator, October 9, 1884." Whitman likely read about the reburial in the September 27, 1884 issue of *The Critic,* which contains an article on the upcoming event entitled, "Honoring a Dead Indian." This article provides an important context for interpreting Whitman's poem, as it emphasizes the material aspects of the monument to be erected in Red Jacket's honor, noting:

> This monument, which is to stand in a lot containing 1500 square feet of ground, will be built of granite, in the form of a hexagon, one side for each of the Six Nations—Mohawks, Oneidas, Tuscaroras, Onondagas, Cayugas, and Senecas. A bronze statue of Red Jacket, heroic in size, will surmount it, making the total height about forty feet.

Although Red Jacket's reburial occurred in October 1884, the monument itself was not built until some years later, its dedication occurring in June 1892. The proposed design of the Red Jacket monument appearing in *The Critic* resonates with Whitman's portrayal of Red Jacket floating spectrally above the scene of the reburial. As "a towering human form," Red Jacket anticipates his own towering monument, his "ghostliness" forming a stark contrast with the solidity of the proposed bronze and granite monument.[17]

Whitman's gentle mocking of the proceedings further situates this event as a contest about proper memorialization of national heroes. As the unseen witness to this event, Red Jacket smiles "a half-ironical smile" as he looks down "Upon this scene, this show, / Yielded to-day by fashion, learning, wealth." In the poem, Whitman portrays Red Jacket as both physically and spiritually distant from the spectacle occurring below. On the one hand, by representing Red Jacket as a ghost, Whitman performs what Renée Bergland identifies as the literary removal of Indians from American lands by placing them "instead, within the American imagination." This position in the imagination is also, however, that of the aloof, spiritual artist, as Red Jacket watches the pomp of the reburial with silent derision. Nevertheless, Whitman allows that the reburial is not "in caprice alone" but contains "some grains of deepest meaning." Whitman lauds, in other words, the spiritual impulse behind the event—the impulse Red Jacket himself seems to embody, as the poem's allusion to Ossian's ghosts will demonstrate—even as the reburial itself devolves into a gaudy, overly material western spectacle.[18]

Whitman's placement of "Red Jacket (From Aloft.)" in the 1888 *November Boughs* collection and the *Sands at Seventy* section of the 1891–92 edition of *Leaves of Grass* further reinforces the poem's relation to questions of proper memorialization, particularly in the wake of the U.S.'s monument-building craze from the 1850s to 1880s. In both cases, a poem entitled "Death of General Grant" precedes "Red Jacket (From Aloft.)," while "Washington's Monument, February, 1885" follows it. The poems are not chronologically ordered: "Death of General Grant" first appeared in *Harper's Weekly* on May 16, 1885, while "Washington's Monument" appeared in the *Philadelphia Press* on February 22, 1885. This organization suggests that Whitman deliberately arranged these poems, previously published in periodicals, into a poetic "cluster" about monuments first in the 1888 edition of *November Boughs* and then in the 1891–92 edition of *Leaves of Grass*. In "Death of General Grant," Whitman mourns the loss of Ulysses S. Grant as the disappearance of yet another of "the lofty actors, / From that great play on history's stage eterne." "Red Jacket, (From Aloft.)" builds on this trite image of history as a stage with its emphasis on the theatricality of Red Jacket's reburial. "Washington's Monument," meanwhile, takes the misgivings of "Red Jacket" even further, insisting that material monuments do Washington's memory injustice, since "Wherever Freedom, pois'd by Toleration, sway'd by Law, / Stands or is rising thy true monument." Although not portrayed as a specter, Washington nevertheless possesses distinctly ethereal qualities in this poem; he is free to roam "Wherever sails a ship, or house is built on land, or day or night, / Through teeming cities' streets, indoors or out, factories or farms, / Now, or to come, or past." As in the case of Red Jacket and his statue, Whitman criticizes Washington's monument's inability to represent his spirit: "Ah, not this marble, dead and cold: / Far from its base and shaft expanding—the round zones circling, comprehending, / Thou, Washington, art all the world's, the continent's entire—not yours alone, America." The spirit of Washington—less

FIGURE 2. Red Jacket's monument and related graves, including that of Ely S. Parker, are sited at Forest Lawn Cemetery in Buffalo, New York. Photograph by the author.

literalized than that of Red Jacket but no less "comprehending"—surpasses the limits of its expensive but inert monument to wander the earth.[19]

As these three poems reveal, for Whitman the spiritual elements of memorialization take precedence over the building of "dead and cold" monuments. It is at this spiritual knowledge that Red Jacket's ghost hints when "a half-ironical smile / curv[es] his phantom lips" as, "Like one of Ossian's ghosts [he] looks down."[20] Although the revelation that James Macpherson invented the Scottish bard Ossian emerged after his death at the end of the eighteenth century, American writers like Whitman interested in romanticism and nationalism continued to read and be influenced by his poetry.[21] In a group of manuscripts from Duke likely dating from the 1850s, Whitman writes about Ossian, "very likely a myth altogether," drawing a pointing hand for emphasis.[22] Yet Whitman associates Ossian with a kind of primal paganism, effusing in 1888, "Ossian is of the Biblical order—is best to one who would come freshly upon it—to one who knew nothing of the Hebrew Bible."[23] By calling Red Jacket "one of Ossian's ghosts," Whitman aligns him with this conception of pre-Judaic, mythical knowledge, Red Jacket's "half-ironical smile" perhaps suggesting that the Christian burial occurring below is ineffectual since Red Jacket himself belongs to an "older" form of spiritualism.

Like Red Jacket watching the materialistic scene below him, Ossian's ghosts also appear as the Gaelic "natives" who emerge to "fortel [sic] futurity" in cases of death or misfortune.[24] The ghost Crugal's appearance in the second book of *Fingal*, moreover, bears a more than passing resemblance to Whitman's Red Jacket. "His face is like the beam of the setting moon," the description reads, "His robes are of the cloud of the hill. His eyes are like two decaying flames. . . . The stars dim-twinkled through his form. His voice was like the sound of a distant stream."[25] Red Jacket thus becomes the ghost to Whitman's Ossian, warning the American people of the impending dangers of the materialism evident in his own memorialization. By providing the American version of Ossian's ghosts, Whitman, as Bergland might put it, trades his own "ancestral specters" for "American specters."[26] Perhaps more important for Whitman, however, in *Leaves of Grass,* he replaces the European Ossian with a new "American" mythmaker: himself.

Despite Whitman's ghostly portrayal, in the case of Red Jacket's memorialization, Natives (as well as spiritual outsiders like Whitman) were a part of the event and its publication. In his speech, the only full Native speech recorded in the Buffalo Historical Society's pamphlet, Seneca sachem and Civil War veteran Ely Parker subtly employs Christianity to critical rhetorical effect, linking the desecration of Red Jacket's grave to Native dispossession and perhaps undermining the spiritual and sentimental premise of the event itself. A Tonawanda Seneca, Parker was a member of the Wolf clan, and he was related to Red Jacket through his mother, who was also a direct descendent of Handsome Lake. Ely's father, William Parker, served under Red Jacket during the War of 1812, and Red Jacket frequently visited the Parkers until his death when Ely was two years old. "Red Jacket's skill as a speaker and his cowardice on the battlefield," writes William Armstrong, "were part of the family's common memories." From an early age, Ely Parker was a renowned speaker. In 1842, after attending a Baptist mission school near the reservation and

FIGURE 3. In this view, Red Jacket's statue, added after the reburial, towers over Forest Lawn Cemetery in Buffalo, New York. Photograph by the author.

living in Canada for a few years, Parker attended Yates Academy, where he perfected his English. As a member of the Euglossian Society, a literary group, he was famous for his speeches, and it was at Yates that he developed an interest in Christianity. Although Parker was never baptized or a church member, "he was eagerly trying on the white man's religion, as he had tried on his language and his culture, and it seemed to him that the fit was good."[27]

Parker was also attaining prominence among the Tonawanda Senecas. At fourteen he became an interpreter for the Tonawanda chiefs and would interrupt his studies many times to travel on their behalf to Washington, D.C., to meet with members of Congress and deliver petitions to the president. During this time, Ely began to study law, and he also became a member of the Masonic Lodge in 1847. As a Mason, Ely would often deliver speeches and exhibit the Red Jacket peace medal with which he was invested at the age of twenty-three, the same age at which he became a grand sachem of the Six Nations with the title Keeper of the Western Door. After the government denied him the right to take the bar on the grounds that he was not a citizen of the United States, Parker started a career first as an engineer, then, when the Civil War broke out, as a captain and then a military secretary on General Ulysses S. Grant's personal staff. At the conclusion of the war, Parker attained an appointment as an Indian commissioner who met with the Indians of the Southwest. Following Grant's election as president, Parker was appointed commissioner of Indian affairs from 1869 until his resignation following a bitter trial for misconduct two years later. Shifting his attention from the Masons to veterans' groups, Parker became a member of the Grand Army of the Republic, where he found a welcome place among other Civil War veterans. In 1881, he met the poet and Indianologist Harriet Maxwell Converse, whose friendship rekindled his interest in Indian matters. Instead of seeing Christianity as the solution to the "Indian Problem," Parker professed that education held the key to solving the Indians' problems.[28]

Parker had at first objected to the plan to rebury Red Jacket, but when the Seneca Nation approved the event, he agreed to attend the ceremonies. Parker even proposed his own design for Red Jacket's memorial, suggesting an aged tree trunk as fitting the aging Confederacy and corresponding to one of Red Jacket's speeches. Appearing at Red Jacket's reburial after a series of long addresses by European Americans on Six Nations history and wearing full military dress, Parker turns, in his conclusion, from land observations to questions about the legitimacy of Red Jacket's reburial itself. Parker notes:

> [O]ne of [Red Jacket's] last requests is said to have been that white men should not dig his grave and that white men should not bury him. But how forcibly now comes to us the verity and strength of the saying that "man proposes, but God disposes."

Parker then retells the story of Red Jacket's reburial, stating that because of the Senecas' forced removal shortly after his death, "Red Jacket's grave remained unprotected, and ere long was desecrated." Parker's use of the passive voice to describe the desecration of Red Jacket's grave is important because it leaves the identity of the desecrators unclear. This ambiguity opens up, among other potential meanings, the possibility that the desecrators include the members of the Buffalo Historical Society before him; after all, it was these people who kept Red Jacket's body in a bank vault for several years before his reinterment. It is through a biblical reference, however, that Parker connects this observation about the violation of Red Jacket's reburial to the question of Native dispossession. He concludes:

> While a silent spectator of the ceremonies to-day, the words of the blessed Saviour forcibly presented themselves to my mind, "the foxes have holes and the birds of the air have nests, but the Son of Man hath not where to lay His head." I applied this saying to the Indian race. They have been buffeted from pillar to post. They once owned much, but now have hardly anything they can call their own. While living they are not let alone—when dead they are not left unmolested.

Rather than interpreting this scriptural passage in the usual sense as a command to abandon all possessions and follow Jesus, Parker turns it to his own purposes. He uses the passage to show how European Americans robbed Indians of their homes, forcing them to move "from pillar to post." His final sentence, "While living they are not let alone—when dead they are not left unmolested," connects the living and the dead, and, by implication, ongoing acts of land theft, grave theft, and reburial. "Red Jacket's grave is desecrated," Maureen Konkle summarizes, "as the Seneca lands are stolen and desecrated." European American usurpation of the Seneca land in which Red Jacket was buried is of a piece with the subsequent disturbances of Red Jacket's grave, demonstrating how questions of burial, religion, and land rights become inextricably intertwined in this history.[29]

Parker's coup de grace, however, comes in his reminder that Red Jacket was not a Christian. "From the bottom of my heart," Parker states, "I believe that Red Jacket was a true Indian and a most thorough pagan." By linking the conception of a "true Indian" to "pagan[ism]," Parker seems to accept European American assertions that "true Indian[s]" are disappearing. He continues: "[Red Jacket] used all the powers of his eloquence in opposition to the introduction of civilization and Christianity among his people. In this, as in many other things, he signally failed." Many Senecas have embraced Christianity, testifying to the failure of Red Jacket's influence. Yet, like Whitman's sly portrayal, Red Jacket may in fact get the last laugh in Parker's version of events. Understanding "the white man and his ways and methods," Red

Jacket requested that "white men should not dig his grave and that white men should not bury him." Again, elite European Americans tried to assimilate Red Jacket into the commemorative and Christian landscape of the rural cemetery by reburying him at Forest Lawn. By stipulating that Red Jacket was pagan, however, Parker denies this fantasy, replacing it with his version of events. "Red Jacket has been honorably reburied with solemn and ancient rites," Parker insists, "and may his remains rest there in peace until time shall be no more." Although educated at a Baptist mission school, Parker explicitly rejects the Christian version of final judgment and resurrection in the case of Red Jacket, replacing it with the more evasive, "until time shall be no more." Moreover, by using the ethnographic language of "solemn and ancient rites," language Parker probably learned from friends like Lewis Henry Morgan and Harriet Maxwell Converse, Parker favors Six Nations rituals over Christian ones, perhaps comparing Red Jacket's reburial to a condolence ceremony, at which the Seneca not only buried their dead leaders but also chose new ones. According to Parker, in an observation suggestively similar to Whitman's, Red Jacket's paganism may have been his trump card, foiling, as it does, European American plans to make his body signify properly within a Christian cemetery and lending the reburial an element of the Six Nations condolence ceremony.[30]

Countering Parker's version of events, E. Pauline Johnson's poem "The Re-interment of Red Jacket" provides a different model of Native Christianity at Red Jacket's reburial.[31] Part of a Mohawk Christian elite running the Confederacy Council in Brant, Ontario, and known for "their command of English, their intermarriage, their education, their Christianity, and their material prosperity," Johnson's family was not always well received by other Six Nations tribes. Educated by Anglican missionaries, Johnson's Mohawk father, George, later became interpreter for the Anglican Church and solidified ties with that community when he married Englishwoman Emily Howells in 1853. George's family was opposed to the marriage since it meant that the children would inherit their father's Mohawk status by federal but not tribal law. After their marriage, the Johnsons moved into an impressive house called Chiefswood, where the Johnson children enjoyed a "middle class lifestyle" with aristocratic flair, complete with servants, literature, music, governesses, and private and collegiate schools. As Strong-Boag and Gerson argue, Johnson's familial and class background caused her to "rouse mixed feelings among the people she publicly celebrated as her own."[32]

When Johnson's father died of pneumonia in February 1884—a situation complicated by his failing health after several brutal, partisan assaults—Johnson's financial situation became more perilous.[33] After 1885, the Johnsons could not afford to live at Chiefswood and moved to nearby Brantford, where Johnson began to contribute to the family's survival by publishing her work in newspapers and periodicals.[34] It was during this period in Johnson's life, between her father's death and her family's removal to Brantford, that she attended Red Jacket's reburial and composed her elegy to Red Jacket. Prior to this poem, Johnson had placed just a few sentimental poems in the American periodical *Gems of Poetry*. As Johnson's first poem published outside of *Gems of Poetry,* her first Indian-themed poem, and the first poem in which Johnson acknowledged her Native ancestry, "The Re-interment of Red Jacket" played a vital role in Johnson's literary career.[35]

Moreover, since Johnson only began performing her literary works in costume in the early 1890s and "never wore Indian dress" growing up, Johnson likely began to formulate her own ideas of Indian performance in attendance at memorializations like Red Jacket's reburial and Brantford's Joseph Brant monument dedication in 1886.[36] Since Johnson published at her own financial risk, using her performances to pay the print publication costs of her first two poetry collections *The White Wampum* (1895) and *Canadian Born* (1903), these performances, or recitals, were important as a way to "profitably publish her writing."[37] Ever mindful of how she could use her social ties to further her literary career, Johnson also likely used Red Jacket's reburial as a way to meet influential people, both Native and European American. At Red Jacket's reburial, Johnson met the adopted Seneca poet and ethnologist Harriet Maxwell Converse. A close friend of Ely Parker's, Converse would later buy artifacts from Johnson during financial need and host the poet during her trips to New York City. Attending Red Jacket's reburial at Buffalo thus likely furthered Johnson's career on several levels.[38]

Johnson's elegy to Red Jacket appears both in Appendix 20 of *Obsequies* and as an "unidentified clipping" in the Chiefswood scrapbook. According to the editors of Johnson's collected poems, Johnson created the Chiefswood scrapbook from about 1888 to 1895, "past[ing] many clippings of her poems and a few other mementos into a commercially produced blank book." The scrapbook contains notes and corrections in Johnson's hand as well as "copious comments by Hector Charlesworth . . . a close friend in the early 1890s."[39] Several differences emerge between the Chiefswood scrapbook version of "The Re-interment of Red Jacket" and the Buffalo Historical Society version. Most significant among these is the break between the first nine quatrains (in alternating iambic trimeter and pentameter) and the last stanza in the *Obsequies* version. Moreover, in the *Obsequies* version, this stanza consists of twelve lines of iambic pentameter couplets rather than three quatrains, as found in the Chiefswood version. This last stanza of the *Obsequies* version resembles the kinds of codas often found in elegies for famous figures, suggesting that the *Obsequies* version was more attuned to the memorialization theme at the Buffalo Historical Society's reburial of Red Jacket. Since the clipping found in the Chiefswood scrapbook remains unidentified and little is yet known about Johnson's own editorial practices, it is difficult to justify privileging one text of the poem over another. Instead, it is important to acknowledge the differences and explore how these variants affected the joint production of "The Re-interment of Red Jacket" by Johnson and the Buffalo Historical Society.

A highly flexible poetic form, the elegy does not follow strict poetic conventions of meter and rhyme. According to an 1824 article in *London Magazine*, however, the English elegy most often consists of a "stanza of four lines in which the rhimes [sic] alternate," a description that fits both versions of "The Re-interment of Red Jacket."[40] Thematically, the elegy most often follows the pattern of "lamentation, praise and consolation."[41] The stanzas of Johnson's poem conform to this pattern, beginning with images of the cemetery setting, progressing to praise of Red Jacket's oratorical skills, and ending with Johnson's revelation of her Indian ancestry and appeal to European American sympathy. In contrast to Parker, Johnson portrays Red Jacket's memorial as "A Christian burial," implying that he was given an individually marked grave as well as perhaps a Christian ceremony.[42] Thus, in opposition to Parker, Johnson, from the beginning, argues that Red Jacket's reburial was Christian, regardless of Red Jacket's own religious beliefs.

Racialized ideas of poetic form in the nineteenth century likely contributed to Johnson's use of conventional forms and metrics in the elegy to establish her own poetic authority. In his 1880 *Elements of English Prosody: For Use in St. George's Schools*, John Ruskin matches poetic meters with their pace relative to the moving human body. Ruskin's privileging of English, Latin, and Greek languages becomes most clear as he writes:

> In this power, the Spondeus, or time of the perfect pace of a reasonable two-legged animal, has regulated the verse of the two most deliberate nations of the earth—the Greek and Roman; and, through their verse, has regulated the manner, the mien, and the musical ear of all educated persons, in all countries and times.

He continues, "our own rhythms are all derived from [Greek and Latin], in proper subjection to our own tempers and tongues."[43] Ruskin mixes popular contemporary racialist ideas about temperament and nationality with his evaluations of the merits of different poetic forms. By reading for poetic meter, Ruskin seems to suggest, one can read for purported racial characteristics. As the child of an interracial marriage, Johnson was no doubt aware of this kind of literary discrimination. Her highly metrical poetic form may have been in part a response to it.

Johnson does not just respond to such notions, however; she capitalizes on them. Her use of the elegiac form, with its Greek and Latin associations, exploits the tendency of Europeans to name the Iroquois the Romans and Greeks of the Americas.[44] Moreover, in "The Re-interment of Red Jacket," Johnson acknowledges her Indian ancestry, doing so within the elegiac framework as a kind of consolation for Red Jacket's death. After the line, "And few to-day remain," which ends in a colon in *Obsequies* and a semi-colon in the Chiefswood scrapbook, Johnson surprises the reader with a shift in voice and another revelation: "But copper-tinted face, and smoldering fire / Of wilder life, were left me by my sire / To be my proudest claim."[45] Prompted perhaps by the knowledge that the Buffalo Historical Society would include a description of her as "A Mohawk Indian girl" and no doubt influenced by the recent death of her father, Johnson discloses her Native heritage to her audience.[46] This disclosure, of course, would figure largely in her later oral performances, with Johnson dressing in a Minnehaha-inspired costume for part of her recitals and an evening gown for the other part, visually juxtaposing for her audiences the "Indian" and the "Englishwoman."[47] Johnson's performance of the metrically savvy Englishwoman who reveals her Indian heritage toward the end of "The Re-interment of Red Jacket" thus prefigures her more famous stage performances.

With the next stanza—the epitaph in *Obsequies* and the last three quatrains in the Chiefswood version—Johnson builds upon this change in voice, signified by her shift to first-person pronouns, to provide the required consolation for Red Jacket's death according to the elegy form. At this same moment, she also accelerates her poem by switching from embedded rhyme to couplets. This movement from loss to praise to consolation forms an essential aspect of elegies. "Elegies cannot just describe loss," as David Kennedy puts it, "they have to require it as a species of transformation and provide an early glimpse of an afterlife for their subject."[48] It is in this final motion, however, that the heretofore straightforward voicing of Johnson's poem becomes more ambiguous. Although in the previous stanza Johnson allied herself with the first-person voice and a claim of Indian heritage, she complicates that association with her next stanza by returning to the feminized figure of "Indian Summer," which she earlier portrays as not dead, but "sleep[ing],— / Trusting a foreign and a paler race / To give her gifted son an honored place / Where Death his vigil keeps." With this stanza, the first-person pronouns multiply:

> And so ere Indian Summer sweetly sleeps
> She beckons me where old Niagara leaps;
> Superbly she extends her greeting hand,
> And, smiling, speaks to her adopted land,
> Saying, "O, rising nation of the West,
> That occupy my lands so richly blest;

> O, free, unfettered people that have come
> And made America your rightful home—
> Forgive the wrongs my children did to you,
> And we, the red-skins, will forgive you too.
> To-day has seen your noblest action done—
> The honored re-intombment of my son."[49]

This coda becomes the most dramatic moment in the poem, with the first-person speaker and Indian Summer traveling to Niagara Falls where Indian Summer, in turn, speaks to the "rising nation of the West." At the liminal location of Niagara Falls, the question arises: to which "rising nation" does Indian Summer speak? By moving the setting of Red Jacket's elegy from the Forest Lawn Cemetery to Niagara Falls, Johnson transforms the dialogue surrounding Red Jacket's reburial from one of loss and mourning to one of citizenship and national belonging. Addressing Europeans, seemingly both Canadian and American, Indian Summer welcomes them with hospitality as she smiles and extends to them "her greeting hand."

Within Indian Summer's speech, however, variations exist between the two versions of the poem. The Chiefswood version uses "occupies my land" instead of "occupy my land," and "To make America your rightful home" instead of "And made America your rightful home."[50] Although small, these changes in tense significantly change the meaning of Indian Summer's address to Europeans, lending Europeans a permanence in the *Obsequies* version that they do not quite possess in the Chiefswood version. Whether these differences reflect the choices of Johnson or the Buffalo Historical Society is difficult to tell. Nevertheless, they suggest that Johnson was, at some point, experimenting with the tenses in this last section of her poem, demonstrating an awareness of how memorializations like her elegy to Red Jacket affect perceptions of time as well as space. Johnson's changes in tense in the Chiefswood version work against the tendency in European memorializations of Indians to place Natives in the past and deny them a collective future. Extending a welcoming hand to Europeans at a nationally ambiguous site, Indian Summer asserts both her indigeneity and futurity. It is Europeans—not recent immigrants or Indians—who are the newcomers in Johnson's version of Red Jacket's memorialization: Indian Summer welcomes them as if they had just landed on the shores of the Americas again.

The multiple and often conflicting viewpoints on the subject of Red Jacket's reburial reveal the stakes involved in any attempt of memorialization. Power at these events was by no means unilateral, as Indians brought their own material and spiritual frameworks to Red Jacket's reinterment, adding to the multiplicity of meanings already at play. Christianity proves important to both Indians and European Americans in interpreting Red Jacket's reburial at Forest Lawn Cemetery. A shared, material understanding of Christianity motivates many of the conflicting viewpoints operating simultaneously at the reburial.

Such heterogeneity surfaced at Red Jacket's reburial in numerous ways. From disagreements about Christianity's effects to how to respond to land theft and relocation, Natives at Red Jacket's reburial used the event as an opportunity to debate and reconsider these important issues. Paramount among these concerns was the question of how to transform (or not) long-standing intertribal conflicts in light of pressures from European colonization, pressures that, as Red Jacket's reburial shows, both estranged tribes and brought them back together.

Taking into account European colonization in a similar way, and bringing tribes back together, the protagonist Almost Browne of Gerald Vizenor's short story "Feral Lasers" creates "postshamanic laser holotropes" that hover first over the reservation, then over the interstate and the cities. These laser holograms include naked presidents from old peace medals, western explorers, bears, and a version of the Mount Rushmore National Memorial. Almost Browne gets kicked off the reservation for these laser holograms, then tried in federal court for his light shows in the city. By the end of the story, however, the judge has sided with Almost Browne in favor of his "light rights." The laser shows catch on, as "in old and troubled cities across the nation, people by the thousands bought lasers to revise histories, to hold their memories, and to create a new wilderness over the interstates."[51] As monuments, the laser holograms are performances of history, living records. They are also, however, critical records, or records that transform the living by transfiguring the dead. On one hand, this transfiguration is the kind of work that the Buffalo Historical Society performed in its reburial of Red Jacket in service of Buffalo's national history. On the other hand, the laser holograms exceed this singular vision of history as Browne shows multiple sides of the story and his technology is used by many different people. By enlivening the figures of history, his laser holograms revise both the approach to simulation that Red Jacket's graveyard monument represents and the monumentalization movement more broadly.

In the middle of *Obsequies,* following Ely Parker's speech, is another peace medal, a reproduction of Red Jacket's peace medal, presented to him by George Washington and at that time under the care of Parker himself. Dressed "in black and white wampum," Parker brought the medal to Red Jacket's reburial and displayed it at the end of his speech, as he had brought it to many Masonic meetings and even to the Civil War.[52] Upon Parker's death, the Buffalo History Museum (formerly the Buffalo and Erie County Historical Society) bought the peace medal. It is currently displayed in their permanent installation, the John R. Oishei Native American Gallery, which also includes a walk-in longhouse. The medal depicts George Washington and an Indian man, presumably representing Red Jacket himself, Washington supporting a long peace pipe and Red Jacket smoking the pipe. In the background a farmer plows a field with a pair of oxen; a small house sits in the distance. Washington's face is stern, and he is dressed in full Continental officer regalia as he extends the pipe to Red Jacket uncharacteristically clad in a skirt of leaves or feathers with feathers on his head, not in the red jacket in the British-officer style that was his namesake garb. The scene clearly depicts the forging of peace between the newly formed American government, represented by Washington, and the Six Nations. One detail sticks out as odd, however: although peace has just been agreed upon—the pipe is still smoking—Red Jacket already wears a peace medal in the picture.

This representation of an alliance between the new American government and the much older Indian governments effectively collapses time, skipping the moment of contact, asserting European American primacy and presenting peace to Indians as a foregone conclusion. Through this temporal trick, the European creators of the peace medal erase their own immigrant status as well as the time required to reach diplomatic agreements between nations. Monumentalizations of the American past perform a similar trick. Such monuments speak across time, impressing themselves on a Native landscape and making it tell a certain story. Most often, those stories are the ones preferred by elites, and they work to consolidate power. These monumentalizations deal with heterogeneity by creating a kind of veneer, an illusion of collapsing time and space together within a hegemonic narrative. Alive within these memorializations, however, a different image persists, one that preserves the messy debates over religion, land settlement, citizenship, and transforming Native governments that actual memorialization ceremonies create. Through the very means by which elite European Americans imagined themselves as quarantining politics emerges an explosion of conflicting viewpoints and the regeneration of Native communities. At Red Jacket's reburial, Senecas and Mohawks, historical societies and Six Nations tribes, and aging and budding poets performed acts of memorialization that used Red Jacket's reburial to voice their survival and advance their own careers, religions, and social interests.

LAUREN GREWE is a PhD student in the Department of English at the University of Texas at Austin.

Notes

I am deeply grateful to Matt Cohen for his insight, support, and guidance. My thanks to James H. Cox, Coleman Hutchison, and Michael Winship, who read drafts of this essay and provided thoughtful feedback. I also thank Wayne Lesser and Alyssa Mt. Pleasant for their help along the way. My gratitude goes as well to the Buffalo and Erie County Historical Society and especially to Cynthia Van Ness.

1. E. Pauline Johnson, "The Re-interment of Red Jacket," in *Obsequies of Red Jacket at Buffalo, October 9th, 1884* (Buffalo, N.Y.: Buffalo Historical Society, 1885), 104–5; Walt Whitman, "Red Jacket, (From Aloft.)," in *Obsequies of Red Jacket at Buffalo, October 9th, 1884* (Buffalo: Buffalo Historical Society, 1885), 105. According to the Buffalo Historical Society, the other Indians buried with Red Jacket were The Young King or Gui-en-gwàh-toh, Captain Pollard or Ga-on-do-wau-na, Little Billy or Jish-ge-ge, Destroy-Town or Go-non-da-gie, Tall Peter or Ha-no-ja-cya, Two Guns, Twenty Canoes, John Snow, White Chief, and five other "unknown braves." *Obsequies of Red Jacket at Buffalo, October 9th, 1884* (Buffalo, N.Y.: Buffalo Historical Society, 1885), 85.

2. For newspaper articles on Red Jacket's reburial, see: "Honoring a Dead Indian," *The Critic: A Literary Weekly, Critical and Eclectic (1884–1885)*, 149; "Red Jacket," *Bismark Daily Tribune* (Bismark, N.D.), April 15, 1887; "Red Jacket," *Salt Lake Weekly Tribune* (Salt Lake City, Utah), Sept. 25, 1884; "News by Telegraph," *San Francisco Bulletin*, Jan. 12, 1884; "Current Gossip," *Trenton State Gazette* (Trenton, N.J.), Feb. 4, 1884; "Red Jacket's Bones," *Wheeling Register* (Wheeling, W.V.), Mar. 21, 1884; "Personals," *Christian Advocate* (New York, N.Y.), Jan. 31, 1884. Numerous local articles on Red Jacket's reburial can also be found in *Buffalo Courier, The Buffalo Morning Express, Buffalo Evening News*, and *Evening Republic* newspapers. Walt Whitman, "Red Jacket, (From Aloft.)," *Walt Whitman Archive*, 2012, http://www.whitmanarchive.org/published/periodical/poems/per.00069.

3. Whitman, "Red Jacket, (From Aloft.)," *Obsequies of Red Jacket at Buffalo*, 105; I employ the term "collaboration" here in the sense that Eric Cheyfitz gives it as "running the gauntlet from cooperation to coercion." Eric Cheyfitz, "The (Post)Colonial Construction of Indian Country: U.S. American Indian Literatures and Federal Indian Law," in *The Columbia Guide to American Indian Literatures of the United States since 1945*, ed. Eric Cheyfitz (New York: Columbia University Press, 2006), 7.

4. Veronica Jane Strong-Boag and Carole Gerson identify "The Re-interment of Red Jacket" as Johnson's "first identifiably Indian poem." Veronica Jane Strong-Boag and Carole Gerson, *Paddling Her Own Canoe: The Times and Texts of E. Pauline Johnson (Tekahionwake)* (Toronto: University of Toronto Press, 2000), 147.

5. Lisa Brooks, *The Common Pot* (Minneapolis: University of Minnesota Press, 2008), xxiii; Matt Cohen, *The Networked Wilderness* (Minneapolis: University of Minnesota Press, 2010), 23, 7.

6. Joel W. Martin, introduction to *Native Americans, Christianity, and the Reshaping of the American Religious Landscape,* ed. Joel W. Martin and Mark A. Nicholas (Chapel Hill: University of North Carolina Press, 2010), 3.

7. Phillip H. Round, *Removable Type* (Chapel Hill: University of North Carolina Press, 2010), 84; Robert Warrior, *The People and the Word* (Minneapolis: University of Minnesota Press, 2005), 182; Christine DeLucia, "The Memory Frontier," *Journal of American History* (2012): 977; Alyssa Mt. Pleasant, "After the Whirlwind" (PhD diss., Cornell University, 2007), 10–11; 54.

8. Matthew Dennis, *Seneca Possessed: Indians, Witchcraft, and Power in the Early American Republic* (Philadelphia: University of Pennsylvania Press, 2010), 57; Charity Organization Society, *Map of Buffalo Church Districts, January 1st, 1901,* Map (Buffalo, N.Y.: Matthews-Northrup, 1901), from Buffalo and Erie County Historical Society, Buffalo, N.Y.

9. Dennis, *Seneca Possessed,* 58; 58–59.

10. Christopher Densmore, *Red Jacket: Iroquois Diplomat and Orator* (Syracuse: Syracuse University Press, 1999), xiv, 11–12, 125, xvi, 72; Alyssa Mt. Pleasant, "Debating Missionary Presence at Buffalo Creek: Haudenosaunee Perspectives on Land Cessions, Government Relations, and Christianity," in *Ethnographies and Exchanges,* ed. A. G. Roeber (University Park: Pennsylvania State University Press, 2008), 176, xviii.

11. Dennis, *Seneca Possessed,* 70; Anthony F. C. Wallace, *Revitalizations and Mazeways* (Lincoln: University of Nebraska Press, 2003), 57, 63; Dennis, *Seneca Possessed,* 62, 67.

12. Dennis, *Seneca Possessed,* 181, 193. According to lawyer Stuart Banner, preemptive rights accelerated the devastation of Native land rights in the nineteenth and twentieth centuries. He writes, "When Indian land could be bought and sold with the Indians still on it, the Indians' right to the land started to feel, to the buyers and sellers, less like simple fee ownership." Banner qtd. in Dennis, *Seneca Possessed,* 181.

13. Laurence M. Hauptman, *Conspiracy of Interests: Iroquois Dispossession and the Rise of New York State* (Syracuse: Syracuse University Press, 1999), 176, 191, 210–11, 102.

14. Andrew Newman, *On Records: Delaware Indians, Colonists, and the Media of History and Memory* (Lincoln: University of Nebraska Press, 2012), 10; Grey Gundaker, *Signs of Diaspora, Diaspora of Signs: Literacies, Creolization, and Vernacular Practice in African America* (New York: Oxford University Press, 1998), 4, 8, 6.

15. *Obsequies of Red Jacket at Buffalo,* 12. William H. Armstrong, *Warrior in Two Camps* (Syracuse: Syracuse University Press, 1978), 49.

16. *Obsequies of Red Jacket at Buffalo,* 12.

17. "Philadelphia Press," *Walt Whitman Archive,* 2012, http://www.whitmanarchive.org/published/periodical/periodical_titles/per.00171; Whitman, "Red Jacket, (From Aloft.)," *Obsequies of Red Jacket at Buffalo,* 105; "Honoring a Dead Indian." *The Critic,* 149; "Red Jacket Statue: Unveiling Ceremonies at Forest Lawn," Programme (Cemeteries Folder: Forest Lawn, Buffalo and Erie County Historical Society, Buffalo, N.Y., 1892); Whitman, "Red Jacket, (From Aloft.)," Ob-

sequies of Red Jacket at Buffalo, 105; Renée Bergland, *The National Uncanny: Indian Ghosts and American Subjects* (Hanover: University Press of New England, 2000), 1.

18. Whitman, "Red Jacket, (From Aloft.)," *Obsequies of Red Jacket at Buffalo,* 105; Bergland, *The National Uncanny,* 4; Whitman, "Red Jacket, (From Aloft.)," *Obsequies of Red Jacket at Buffalo,* 105.

19. *The Public Art of Civil War Commemoration: A Brief History with Documents,* ed. Thomas J. Brown (New York: Bedford, 2004), 5; Walt Whitman, *Leaves of Grass (1891–92), Walt Whitman Archive,* 2012, http://www.whitmanarchive.org/published/LG/1891/index.html; "Harper's Weekly Magazine," *Walt Whitman Archive,* 2012, http://www.whitmanarchive.org/published/periodical/periodical_titles/per.00162; "Philadelphia Press," *Walt Whitman Archive;* Walt Whitman, "Death of General Grant," *Walt Whitman Archive,* 2012, http://www.whitmanarchive.org/published/LG/1891/poems/331; Walt Whitman, "Washington's Monument," *Walt Whitman Archive,* 2012, http://www.whitmanarchive.org/published/LG/1891/poems/333.

20. Whitman, "Red Jacket, (From Aloft.)," *Obsequies of Red Jacket at Buffalo,* 105.

21. Andrew Ladd, "Macpherson, James ("Ossian") (1736–1796)," in *Walt Whitman: An Encyclopedia,* ed. J. R. LeMaster and Donald D. Kummings (New York: Garland Publishing, 1998), 415–16.

22. Walt Whitman, "—Even Now Jasmund," in *Walt Whitman: Notebooks and Unpublished Prose Manuscripts, Vol. IV: Notes,* ed. Edward F. Grier (New York: New York University Press, 1984), 1432–33.

23. Horace Traubel, *With Walt Whitman in Camden (July 16, 1888–October 31, 1888)* (New York: Mitchell Kennerley, 1915), 17–18.

24. Hugh Blair, "A Critical Dissertation on the Poems of Ossian the Son of Fingal," in *The Poems of Ossian,* trans. James Macpherson (Edinburgh: Thomas Nelson, 1842), 134.

25. James Macpherson, "Fingal," in *The Poems of Ossian,* trans. James Macpherson (Edinburgh: Thomas Nelson, 1842), 318–19.

26. Bergland, *The National Uncanny,* 19.

27. Armstrong, *Warrior in Two Camps,* 15–19.

28. Ibid., 19–165.

29. Ibid., 178–79. *Obsequies of Red Jacket at Buffalo,* 43, 44; Maureen Konkle, *Writing Indian Nations: Native Intellectuals and the Politics of Historiography, 1827–1863* (Chapel Hill: University of North Carolina Press, 2004), 286.

30. *Obsequies of Red Jacket at Buffalo,* 43, 44.

31. E. Pauline Johnson, "The Re-interment of Red Jacket," *Obsequies of Red Jacket at Buffalo,* 104–5.

32. Strong-Boag and Gerson, *Paddling Her Own Canoe,* 35–36, 47, 48, 47, 49, 51, 37.

33. Contributing to this financial instability was the fact that Howells' attempts to gain a widow's pension were denied by both the Indian superintendent and the Confederacy Council. Ibid., 48.

34. Ibid., 50. Paula Bernat Bennett, *Poets in the Public Sphere: The Emanci-*

patory Project of American Women's Poetry, 1800–1900 (Princeton: Princeton University Press, 2003), 103.

35. Strong-Boag and Gerson, *Paddling Her Own Canoe*, 100, 219–20, 147.

36. Ibid., 41, 42, 191; Mary Elizabeth Leighton, "Performing Pauline Johnson: Representations of 'the Indian Poetess' in the Periodical Press, 1892–95," *Essays on Canadian Writing* 65 (1998): 7; Strong-Boag and Gerson, *Paddling Her Own Canoe*, 51.

37. Sabine Milz, "'Publica(c)tion': E. Pauline Johnson's Publishing Venues and their Contemporary Significance," *Studies in Canadian Literature/Études en littérature* 29, no. 1 (2004): 130, 128.

38. William Dean Howells was Johnson's cousin, but he kept his distance from Emily Howells and her family. The Confederacy Council's practice of ceremonially adopting influential visiting British aristocrats and military and religious officials, however, gave Johnson a set of kinship ties that she would later draw upon to advance her career. Strong-Boag and Gerson, *Paddling Her Own Canoe*, 49, 39, 41, 54.

39. E. Pauline Johnson, "The Re-interment of Red Jacket," *Obsequies of Red Jacket at Buffalo*, 104; *E. Pauline Johnson, Tekahionwake: Collected Poems and Selected Prose*, ed. Carole Gerson and Veronica Strong-Boag (Buffalo: University of Toronto Press, 2002), 291, 289.

40. "On English Versification," *London Magazine*, July 1824, 29.

41. Max Cavitch, *American Elegy: The Poetry of Mourning from the Puritans to Whitman* (Minneapolis: University of Minnesota Press, 2007), 92.

42. Johnson, "The Re-interment of Red Jacket," *Obsequies of Red Jacket at Buffalo*, 104.

43. John Ruskin, *Elements of English Prosody: For Use in St. George's Schools* (Kent: George Allen, 1880), 4, 4–5, 6.

44. Strong-Boag and Gerson, *Paddling Her Own Canoe*, 32.

45. Johnson, "Re-interment of Red Jacket," *Obsequies of Red Jacket at Buffalo*, 105; Johnson, "The Re-interment of Red Jacket," *E. Pauline Johnson, Tekahionwake*, 11.

46. Johnson, "Re-interment of Red Jacket," *Obsequies of Red Jacket at Buffalo*, 104.

47. Bennett, *Poets in the Public Sphere*, 104; Milz, "'Publica(c)tion': E. Pauline Johnson's Publishing Venues": 129–30.

48. David Kennedy, *Elegy* (New York: Routledge, 2007), 20.

49. Johnson, "Re-interment of Red Jacket," *Obsequies of Red Jacket at Buffalo*, 104, 105.

50. Ibid.; Johnson, "The Re-interment of Red Jacket," *E. Pauline Johnson, Tekahionwake*, 12.

51. Gerald Vizenor, "Feral Lasers," in *Landfill Meditation* (Hanover: Wesleyan University Press, 1999), 13, 21.

52. *Obsequies of Red Jacket at Buffalo*, 44.

JANICE CINDY GAUDET

Rethinking Participatory Research with Indigenous Peoples

Introduction: Situating Research and Researcher in the Participatory Paradigm

CONCEIVING CREATIVE WAYS to engage in participatory research in spite of contradictory norms, knowledge, and values is often a challenge for both community members and academic researchers (Colorado 1988). A relatively new approach in academia, participatory research is both a theoretical and a methodological inquiry that emerged with the rise of critical Indigenous space and scholarship, encouraged among authors by internationally recognized Māori scholars Linda Tuhiwai Smith (1999; 2000) and Russel Bishop (1998; 2005). The emergence of participatory research within social and health sciences stems from the awareness that research initiatives are sustainable with the participation of the people themselves (McTaggart 1994; Minkler 2005; Smith 1999).

In the last few decades, researchers have been encouraged to reexamine epistemological foundations as part of the methodological shift from an objective model of science to a humanistic approach (Colorado 1988). Colorado reminds us that "the ground rules that should guide new practices are not immediately evident" (98). Despite the uncertainties of new practices, there is an increasing push to improve collaborative research partnerships with Indigenous communities; the literature suggests an urgency to taking ownership and responsibility of our human actions and choosing to do research differently. As a result, the differing views of ethics, science, and human action have brought to the forefront what Leroy Little Bear refers to as "jagged worldviews colliding" (Castellano 2004, 103). "Aboriginal world views assume that human action, to achieve social good, must be located in an ethical spiritual context as well as its physical and social situation" (103). This speaks to a more holistic approach and resituates the hierarchical way of doing research.

Some scholars argue for a participatory process that directly addresses the inevitable issues of power and control, thereby mutually recognizing the limitations of the methodology (Varcoe et al. 2011). In this essay, I seek to understand the ways in which participatory research either reinscribes or challenges dominant relations of power. This is a step toward what Māori education scholar Bishop describes as "participatory mode of consciousness" (quoted in Denzin, Lincoln, Smith 2008, 14). "The participatory mode of knowing privileges sharing, subjectivity, personal knowledge, and the specialized knowledge of oppressed groups. It uses concrete experience as a criterion for meaning and truth" (Denzin, Lincoln, Smith 2008, 14). From this empirical understanding of "participatory," I will integrate within the literature glimpses of the teachings that emerged from my incipient stages as an Indigenous researcher.

The literature emerging over the past few decades offers ethical thought, guidelines, and experiences geared toward research practices that cease to reinforce imbalanced power relations (Castellano 2004; Denzin, Lincoln, Smith 2008; Smith 1999). To highlight its practical application, Castellano explains ethics in a manner that allows for the sought-after humanistic approach to research: "Ethics, as the rules of right behaviour, are intimately related to who you are, the deep values you subscribe to and your understanding of place in the spiritual order of reality" (103). In reflecting on this claim, an ethical relationship with the self at the center of our research practices can help to move away from subjugation and toward engagement with others involved in the research. Such a way of conceiving ethics serves to remind the researcher that relationship comes from an understanding of where we place ourselves in the "spiritual order of our reality" (Castellano 2004, 103). With that, the mode of participatory engagement is defined by one's epistemological foundation and a theoretical framework that emerges from the meaning and thought behind what is true for the participants themselves (Denzin, Lincoln, Smith 2008). This way of positioning theory as congruent to methodology inspires a shift in researcher-and-researched power dynamics.

Castellano's terms of reference in relationship to ethical understanding helps me to learn and unlearn how I am meant to "do" and to "be" in research. Prior to the ambiguous idea of a relationship-building field trip to Moose Factory First Nations community, Maria Campbell, Métis elder, educator, and artist, strongly advised me to be grounded in who I am and from where I come. "Otherwise people will know you are snooping around in their business," she said. Well, she was right. A few days into the trip, a young woman from the community asked me, in the midst of rhetorical questioning, if I was an undercover cop. It was a revealing moment and I immediately understood the Elder's forewarning. The young women's keen perception welcomed an examination of my transparency and seriousness. The quiet voice from within nudged me to disclose my academic research insecurities. In addition, I further shared the teachings passed on by Maria before my departure. The young woman's tender words, "I'd like to be an undercover cop someday," put me at ease and further confirmed that the youth have much to teach me. This exchange was the beginning of what would continue to inform a human and ethical approach to participatory research. It further helped me contextualize what scholars mean by "participatory" within Indigenous methodological and theoretical research principles.

Given my interests in applying critical Indigenous theories and methodologies to my research study, I have examined mainstream literature in addition to literature by Indigenous scholars on participatory research and its subtypes, which include participatory action and community-based research. Literature on these methodologies offers varied insights into the ways in which dominant relations of power are challenged or reinscribed. I will weave throughout the paper some of the distinctions that are represented by Indigenous scholars. The focus on Indigenous epistemology offers a distinct perspective into the power differentials that play out in the current research initiatives that concern the health and well-being of Indigenous peoples (Louis 2007).

Power relations remain central to the participatory research theme as the political, economic, spiritual, and social landscapes of Indigenous communities continue to be fraught with proverbial undercover cops (Louis 2007; Simpson 2001). Decentering power and knowledge from academia to the periphery arguably supports a transformative and healing approach to research that moves beyond a western-based participatory framework often upheld with the repetition of superficial checks and balances (Chilisa 2011; Louis 2007). Implying that there is a singular methodology compartmentalizes the power upheld by research participants themselves. When working within an Indigenous context, participatory research is meant to uphold at its center the view of Indigenous peoples (Smith 1999). This presumption leads me to another exchange that revealed the struggle of weaving three threads of balance: academia, prayer, and truth.

During my first visit with the people of Moose Factory, the community was bustling with their annual cultural gathering called GOOP (Gathering Of Our People), which included feasts, dancing, artisans, traditional teachings, and entertainment. I felt quite at home in the space as a Métis woman and I seemingly blended in; nevertheless, Wapistan, a gentleman from the community, approached me and asked me what I was doing there. Excited that someone asked, I immediately blurted out my research interests and the possibility of working more closely with the community on a research project. He listened. Then he placed his hand on my shoulder, and advised me to approach everything I do with eyes of innocence, a beginner's mind, and an open heart.

With the utmost respect, he said, "You know nothing about these people, their history, their present, and their way of life." I listened and immediately felt relieved at the permission to drop the academic persona, and to remain present without any agenda to somehow evoke community interest in my research. I murmured words of gratitude as I placed my hands at the center of the heart. He has since become a mentor and sounding board in regard to the research journey with his community. The vulnerability of our exchanges demand that I become "absent of a need to be in control, by a desire to be connected to and to be part of a moral community where a primary goal is the compassionate understanding of another's moral position" (Denzin, Lincoln, Smith 2008, 11). A few days later, Wapistan invited me to a sweat lodge ceremony. I accepted the invitation and opened myself to receive guidance from within the lodge itself. During the third round of the ceremony, the lodge keeper said out loud, "Open your eyes." It was not only a message to literally open my eyes but figuratively to see beyond my limited vision. A quiet and familiar whisper emerged from the lodge, "Ask the community to help you in your research; you need their help, more than they need yours." Soon thereafter, I felt a tear roll down my cheek. My eyes were open. I felt sober. There were no other instructions, at least not on that day.

Attempting to work from within a participatory methodology requires a surrendering of what I as the "researcher" think the process should be like, what data is required, what theoretical lens to apply, and the need to look for something in particular. It is humbling and at times deeply uncomfortable. Yet I have had moments of feeling liberated in the abandonment of internalized academic and intellectual rigor. I am reminded of this moment with every transfer from the Air Canada flight to Thunder Air or Air Creebec or when I embark on the Polar Bear express train. The landscapes, the vastness, the generosity of the people remind me to see, sense, perceive, and hear from the mother's womb. Although this may seem like a radical approach in the world of research that demands results, hypotheses, proof, and timelines, it is becoming a way to remain grounded and in relationship with a force greater than my own. I am comforted by the Kaupapa Māori research model, which asks us to consider more deeply the principles of participatory and collaborative research that are epistemologically inspired and defined (Denzin, Lincoln, Smith 2008). As Wapistan urged, "relax."

Defining Participatory Research

Some basic definitions of the participatory subtypes can assist us to resituate ourselves within a research methodology. Community-based research is defined as an approach that focuses on community as opposed to individuals

(Horowitz, Robinson, and Seifer 2009). It is a collaborative research process that "engages multiple stakeholders, including the public and community providers, who affect and are affected by a problem of concern" (Horowitz, Robinson, and Seifer 2009, 2633). Ideally, the problem of concern emerges directly from the community itself (Denzin, Lincoln, and Smith 2008). The initiation of the research itself differs according to various factors. In some cases the community independently initiates the research and works in collaboration with a researcher or research community (Horowitz, Robinson, and Seifer 2009).

Participatory Action Research is another approach that includes well-thought-out planning strategies and stages to direct action and social change (McTaggart 1994). Parker (1993) refers to participatory action research as "a means of putting research capabilities in the hands of the deprived and disenfranchised peoples so that they transform their lives for themselves" (1). Chilisa (2012) presents two types of participatory action research, "one with an emphasis on participants as coresearchers and another with an emphasis on personal and social transformation" (225). At the outset, these diverse explanations embody a prevailing belief that participation is unequivocally beneficial for the community. For such reasons, Smith (2000) poses a series of critical questions to assist the researcher in challenging structures of oppression: "What research do we want to do? Whom is it for? What difference will it make? Who will carry it out? How do we want the research done? How will we know it is worthwhile? Who will own the research? Who will benefit?" (239). Denzin, Lincoln, and Smith (2008) further explain "that these eight questions serve to interpret critical theory through a moral lens, through key indigenous principles" (10). They serve to create a space beyond privilege and leading toward what Frye (1998) calls circle consciousness.

Among the different ways in which the various subtypes of participatory research, such as community-based research and participatory action research, are described, there is a general emphasis on its tenets. The literature includes principles of co-learning, experiential methods, shared knowledge practices, respectful relationships, and mutually beneficial results (Getty 2010; Minkler 2005; Smith 1999). Reflecting on the implications, we are cautioned about assigning meaning without a careful examination of epistemological understanding (Getty 2010). "Accordingly, these may require reflection to identify historically bound belief and power systems that explicate domination or marginalization" (Getty 2010, 11). It is increasingly evident from the literature that the epistemological tensions emerge through participatory efforts (Chilisa 2011; Getty 2010). In seeking to examine this emerging theme, I refer back to the epistemological participatory approach found in the Kaupapa Māori Research model in New Zealand. Their model of a theoretical and humanistic approach to research destabilizes dominant power relations (Battiste 2000; Castellano 1993; Chilisa 2011; Smith 1999).

I feel fortunate as a scholar to have on hand an array of literature and guidance that seeks to break down the hierarchical barriers within participatory research (Colorado 1988; Getty 2010; Smith 1999). These leanings have led to integrating ethical rigor concerning ownership, community control, and decision-making processes into research practices, facilitating equitable partnerships between community members and academic researchers (Getty 2010; Minkler 2005). The emphasis on community participation in research has resulted in another analysis of study, analyzing the epistemic differentials inherent in a mode of inquiry. This awareness is increasingly being applied in research. It has led to critical thinking as to whether Western models continue to prevail in a knowledge-making that can unknowingly masquerade under the participatory umbrella.

Situating Distinctions in Knowledge

Much of the literature addresses the complexities and varying factors that influence participatory legitimacy and its effectiveness in overcoming and reinforming relations of power (Castellano 1993; Varcoe et al. 2011). Discourse on dominant relations of power within the context of participatory research can be obscured when examining the acquisition of knowledge and its source, legitimacy, and production (Smith 1999). While seeking to discuss the power differential within the institution—community collaborative paradigm, scholars have not arrived at an absolute position defining and opposing principles on this issue. It is important to note that critical thinking is not meant to further polarize epistemological differences and knowledge systems. On the contrary, the participatory research process is shaped by the quality of the relationships, the dynamics and competing interests between the various parties, the various levels of authority (within the community, the researched population, and the researcher and/or the funding body), and the sociopolitical and cultural environment (Castellano 1993; Minkler 2005; St. Denis 1992; Varcoe et al. 2011). St. Denis (1992) forewarns that "it is unrealistic to expect homogeneity in any community or group" (64). There is no single Indigenous epistemology, as each person and/or community expresses knowledge uniquely based on stories, personal experiences, and ways of knowing and being (Deloria 1991, 1999). Beck, Walters, and Francisco (1977) explain that there is no homogenous template and no mathematical formula to explain what is logical at the depth of one's humanity.

Literature on Indigenous epistemology concludes that no cookie-cutter system of actually coming to knowledge exists (Battiste and Youngblood

Henderson 2000; Deloria 1999; Ermine 1995; Turner 2006). Yet there are laws, practices, protocols, and standards that distinguish what Colorado describes as "Native Science" (1988) and what Deloria (1999) refers to as the "Science of wholeness." Although group ethics are situated in a local context, ways of coming to knowledge are diverse, personal, and intimate, and incapable of being reduced to one another (Battiste and Henderson 2000; Ermine 1995; Kovach 2005).

The phrase "coming to knowledge" as expressed by Colorado (1988) signifies the reciprocal approach in which Indigenous people relate to knowledge. Battiste and Henderson (2000) expand on the value of reciprocity and relationship to ensure that methodologies "flow from Aboriginal values, such as community accountability, giving back, and benefitting the community, and that the researcher is a helper committed to doing no harm" (48). Notably, expecting intellectual conformity and linearity in participatory research re-inscribes dominant relations of power. As such, it becomes difficult to connect deeply with the heart of the people and our own humanity (Holmes 2000; Kovach 2005). Subscribing knowingly or unknowingly to an imposing approach to research (such as predetermined questions, process, and results, as I shared earlier), leads to re-enacting epistemological conflict and risks dismissing Indigenous knowledge (Battiste 2000; Castellano 1993, 2000; Simpson 2001; Varcoe et al. 2011). It further compromises the collective capacity to creatively explore and experience new mutual forms of dialogue and power.

Knowledge and Purpose

St. Denis (1992) addresses the relevance of examining notions of equality at the forefront of community-based research because "for so long First Nations communities have been led to believe and forced to accept that members of the colonial society can and should act on their behalf" (65). Notions of equality consumed in sameness and conformity, as Ermine (1995) suggests, constrict the self-actualization of the research goal itself and further re-enforce a Eurocentric roadmap to research. Barnhardt and Kawagley (1999) demonstrate how knowledge for Indigenous peoples has been informed through a process of observing and living within their relationship to others, including place, land, nature, and cosmology. Louis (2007) explains that "from an Indigenous perspective, research, the search for knowledge is considered to be a spiritual journey" (134).

Beck, Walters, and Francisco (1977) explain that knowledge developed through oral traditions is embodied in the flesh of Native American people and thus counters dominating discourses that falsely portray Indigenous peoples' way of life as uncivilized. More recent literature continues to reference ways in which the western mindset and western science differ from Indigenous thought and philosophy (Barnhardt and Kawagley 2005; Getty 2010). Within this dichotomy, the western mindset or worldview is predisposed to produce knowledge for the purposes of progress and at times simply to further our own academic endeavours. The Indigenous worldview produces practical knowledge for specific cultural effects and for preserving a respective society's social order (Battiste and Youngblood Henderson 2000; Kovach 2005). To begin, it is important to be aware of the differences as a means of fostering maturity in our research practices.

Castellano (2004) explains that the focus on cultural renewal speaks to "restoring order to daily living in conformity with ancient and enduring values that affirm life" (100). Holmes (2000) speaks of the purpose of knowledge to "incite humans to act in such ways as to ensure the protection and reproduction of all creations in the universe" (37). Deloria (1999) conceptualizes this goal as a process of self-discipline applied to acquiring knowledge in order to live a "life of freedom" (43). He further states that approaching knowledge requires "finding the proper moral and ethical road" (43). He also explains how some Western paradigms seek to acquire knowledge for "its own sake" in order to replicate that which often cannot be reproduced (44). Knowledge within such a theory is therefore restricted by a rigid and absolute code of ethics that disrupts the natural development of different ways of knowing (Battiste and Youngblood Henderson 2000). Deloria explains that the challenge for the academic is "to find the proper pattern of interpretation for the great variety of ordinary and extraordinary experience we have" (46). Getty (2010) explains how the interpretations of meaning made from a Western framework reinscribe dominant power relations, blaming Indigenous peoples for their social reality.

Applying a participatory approach without being grounded in my own culture and without an awareness of my own biases, I realize that I may diminish the chance to put Indigenous concerns, peoples, and systems at the center. "Culture comes from the way that people live together, the way people treat each other and the way they interact with one another" (Anderson 2011, 167). In my conversations with Maria Campbell pertaining to an Indigenous theoretical framework, the theme of traditions of the land became central to my exploration. Her direction was to seek a body of knowledge that came from home, land and methods of living that shaped and informed the manner in which I perceive the world. This process was to ensure that the research remains grounded in who I am and vigilant with respect to the interests of Indigenous peoples. I soon became aware that without this grounding, feelings of insecurity and inadequacy came to the forefront.

Within the inquiry to better understand culture as defined above, the various conversations with my own family continuously led to narratives of the land. The words of my relatives echoed the work of various scholars who invoke culturally based knowledge as the basis of their theoretical frameworks (Anderson 2011; Dorion 2010; Kovach 2009; Kelsey 2008). Robbins and Dewar's (2011) research on traditional Indigenous practices makes reference to how James Louche explains culture as informed by land. They quote him, stating (2011, 13):

> With respect to the *land*, knowledge flows from the land and this is expressed in differences and diversity throughout Aboriginal grounds. In contemporary society, this break with the land is the single most important factor in health problems among Aboriginal peoples. *Language* is how knowledge is encoded. The belief among Elders is that Aboriginal language developed organically from the land. *Relationships* need to be strengthened (whether it is relationships between people and the land or people and institutions). It is difficult to enter into a healthy relationship with others if you are not strong in your identity, language, medicine, etc.

While struggling to understand more fully my own relationship to the culture and land (both cognitively and spiritually), I was not surprised at what I heard from Clayton Cheechoo, a kind and wise man who worked with the youth at the John Delaney Youth Center in Moose Factory. During one of our conversations, he felt that perhaps I was in Moose Factory to learn something about myself and to find something I was missing in my life. I nodded, once again comforted by the permission to be vulnerable and transparent. As our sharing continued, he offered a perspective that would shape a culturally based approach to research. Clayton steered me toward his Cree worldview, sending me this email:

> We as Indigenous peoples were given a Sacred Law from the *Shamundoo* (meaning God in Cree), for harmony to be in this world. We (The Peoples) are equal to Nature, not above or below, to control or disrespect that sacred law, is what is happening today as we see it unfold. That every Nation throughout Mother Earth was given a Prayer, Song, and a place to Live (Homeland) within Mother Earth. The first "fire" was given as a gift from *Shamundoo* which we call The Sacred Fire, (*Pii-mattisiun*), meaning life in Cree. We (Indigenous) live in two worlds today, the first is the sacred law and the second the economic law that controls all life today as we know it. These two worlds create a deep conflict within the Indigenous Peoples on Mother Earth, [forcing] us to Decide which of the two will be guiding US in this world today (Nature or Money) for the harmony that was given as a Gift (Life). Each person on mother earth is given a choice, by *Shamundoo*, it is up to us (Humanity), how we weave the Braid of Life (*Pii-matissuin*).

Later, reflecting on our conversations, I realized that Clayton is a living example of a humanistic approach to participating in one's life. The worldview as expressed above asserts the interconnected nature of research and culture, the challenges we face and the choices we are being called to make as researchers to honor the sacred laws of the land.

When the process of coming to knowledge is absent of self-actualization, then "knowledge exists apart from human beings and their communities" (Deloria 1999, 44). For Deloria (1999), knowledge risks standing alone, campaigning on its own behalf. Getty (2010) explains that "traditionally research studies of Aboriginal Peoples' lives that have been conducted by Western academics have examined the formers' lives from a colonial perspective rather than recognizing their Indigenous worldviews, or ways of viewing life and the world around them" (5). Although much of the literature provides extensive guidelines to engage communities to participate in the ownership of the research, in many respects there is little evidence to show which stakeholder groups influence decision making (Cargo et al. 2003; Riecken et al. 2005).

Situating Knowledge in Participatory Research

A participatory mode of research within Indigenous thought seeks a deeper inquiry to examine the process of situating relationship and our human relatedness as a central component. How do I see myself in relationship to the community? Who am I being in this research? Where do I come from? Why is this important? Subjectivity is one of the fundamental principles of participatory research. From an Indigenous epistemological ground, Ermine (1995) explains subjectivity as the "inward space where the real power lies" (108). From this posture, participatory research seeks to legitimize Indigenous ways of thought, learning, relating, and communicating as contributing to the production of knowledge. Separating knowledge from its source results in a power imbalance as knowledge becomes detached from the person's existence. Without recognition of the influence of subjectivity, researchers may further sustain dichotomies through the generations (Fyre 1998; Varcoe et al. 2011). Fyre explains how the "categories such as 'white' or 'indian' are not 'natural' divisions, but rather are products of history and politics" (21). Dichotomies were introduced with assimilation strategies, and more specifically, reinforced in research (Fyre 1998). In the literature about the James Bay Cree way of life, Preston (2002) describes how dichotomy is not appropriate in Cree culture, "but rather an artifact of Western and other cultures" (157). He further explains how the Cree worldview distinguishes the difference in types of relationship, rather than seeing themselves as separate (Preston 2002).

Subjectivity engages the researcher to recognize him- or herself as a part of the research and as part of the community (Wilson 2008). It is through relationship with community that I am able to decolonize within myself the etchings of a divided mindset. By doing so, I am able to delve deeper to untangle my own preconceptions of participatory research. At the University of Ottawa's first Aboriginal Research Committee meeting, Kim Anderson, Métis Cree scholar and mentor, asked us to deeply consider the research team's interest in working with Indigenous communities. I took her guidance to heart and began to go within and ask myself "why?" "Why is this research study important to me?" This resulted in asking the community why the initial research study I had intended to do was important. Their responses redirected the purpose and objective of the research project. Unknowingly, I had implied that my research interests were also theirs. As I got out of my own way, the research question offered itself through an old man's story. His story had to do with deeply rooted memory that spoke of the connection between young and old that was grounded in land through grandmothers' songs. While digesting his personal story for over a year, I could better imagine the function of research as service to communities' values and needs.

Kim Anderson's wisdom has inspired me to invite researchers, students, or development practitioners to reflect on the same "why" question. Most are unsure of a response that will satisfy their action. I understand that it can be a challenge to put a voice to this question out of the fear of being perceived as an undercover cop and reinscribing power relations. Yet I am consoled by knowing that the space in between each breath and thought invites our humanity to be remembered. I, too, continue to seek the answer to "why" with respect to my own research interests. Maria Campbell explained that this requires looking back into my own life history, method of living, norms, and cultural values.

The quality of self-inquiry or self-knowing within a participatory methodology is often mentioned in the literature (Chilisa 2011). It is an aspect of decolonizing the self from within and knowing where we come from in terms of "our spiritual order." This is important to consider, as Castellano (2004) points us to "the class of prevailing norms of Western research" that dictates participatory research (98). She argues that research that is governed by outside researchers "has been instrumental in rationalizing colonialist perceptions of Aboriginal incapacity and the need for paternalistic control" (102–3). The exposure of ill-defined relationships embedded in colonial practices confirms Smith's (1999) argument that participatory language assumes that the value of participating in research will be legitimized as an act of service "for the greater good of Aboriginal peoples" (2). Smith demands that research as a service be based on the voices and experiences of the people themselves. As such, she and other scholars call researchers to counter dominant power relations by holding sacred the stories of Indigenous peoples (Anderson 2011; Wilson 2008).

According to Kemmis and McTaggart (2000), dominant relations of power are challenged when the community thinks about "where they are now, how things came to be that way, and from these starting points, how, in practice, things might be changed" (573). Turner (2006) strongly suggests that an important step to altering paternalistic power dynamics is for communities to establish clarity around how Indigenous knowledge is to be used in legal and political discourse. Mainstream models often have limited application in meeting the holistic realities of Indigenous peoples.

Simpson (2001) argues that participatory research led by outside community researchers represents a modern-day trend to hide "whiteness" and to appropriate knowledge without doing the heavy lifting to acquire this knowledge. Simpson (2001) advocates for Indigenous researchers and communities to conduct research on their own terms, using their own theories, methodologies, philosophies, and epistemologies. From my conversations with scholars and from the literature, it would appear that the guidance of Elders and community can provide additional clarity in terms of what this practically looks like for both Indigenous and non-Indigenous scholars. What we know is that this process does not come without its own discipline and rigor, as Simpson (2001) and many other scholars describe their own personal decolonization and healing process toward renewal of cultural knowledge at the center of our everyday living. Simpson (2001) advocates for a process of critical self-inquiry by the non-Indigenous researcher as a way to challenge the often accepted dominance within institutions.

Horowitz, Robinson, and Seifer (2009) further suggest that collapsing notions of objectivity is vital for researchers to embody an empathetic and humble perspective toward local practices and knowledge. For Smith (1999), it is imperative within decolonization strategies that researchers be "concerned with having a more critical understanding of the underlying assumptions, motivations, and values which inform research practices" (21). If they can achieve this, Butler (2004) explains how researchers can play a role to facilitate a research process that is sensitive to community priorities and respectful of local notions of progress and success. In turn, this challenges dominant relations of power as knowledge is fostered from within the community itself. Turner's (2006) insights offer consideration to the participation tension that researchers often allude to in participatory research. He points to the embedded colonial norms within the communities' everyday lives. As a result, he says, "colonization is not intellectualized in the communities," rather, "it is embedded in the everydayness of indigenous life: language, religion, sexuality, art, philosophy, and politics" (109). This entrenched reality is often deeply misunderstood by researchers. Failure to understand the historical and local context of the impacts of historical trauma can reinscribe researchers' power to define the issues, jeopardize the partnership, and unknowingly lead to misinterpreting cultural knowledge (Chilisa 2011).

Structure and Knowledge

Scholars argue for a deeper understanding of the social and political context in which the imbalance of funding bodies is constructed (Briggs and Sharp 2004; Castellano 1993; Manderson et al. 1998). This has augmented the one-sided scrutiny most often dictated by institutions. Castellano (1993) discusses how the current structural deficiency has created a need for third parties to mediate between the state and Indigenous communities. This approach, she suggests, "devolves responsibility to community institutions" (150). Within these circumstances, the third parties in question, either researchers, businesses, or governmental organizations, have been valorized as most responsible in the dissemination of findings, the accountability of fund management, and in achieving the desired government outcomes. In this context, participatory research can represent a mere conduit between the academy and the community.

The larger dilemma for the researcher is attempting to find a language that bridges both the academic and the community, so as not to begin to categorize the local episteme according to one's assumptions and academic jargon (Chilisa 2011; Kovach 2005). This has provoked questions related to ownership of research and its use outside the local context (Chilisa 2011). Categorizing and misinterpreting local knowledge can be one of the ways in which participatory research reinscribes power imbalances. As such, conveying the importance of fluidity, relationality, and conceptualizations of identity is vital to transforming methodological homogeneity in research (Battiste and Henderson 2000; Colorado 1988; Kovach 2005). I would further add that being adept in listening with "three ears" can disrupt the hierarchy of knowledge and moral order (Wilson 2008).

For many Indigenous scholars, reclaiming cultural identity, oral traditions, and storytelling situates local epistemology as foundational to the production of knowledge within research (Anderson 2011; Battiste 2000; Castellano 1993, 2004; Kovach 2005). The participatory process suggests that the subject(s) of inquiry be subjective, self-directed, and organized based on the commitment of the social group (McTaggart 1994). For Parker (1993), such an approach becomes a useful intervention strategy that calls for desire to change through action. The use of words such as "intervention" implies the involvement of an outside party; in this case the researcher would assume the role of "external change agent" (Parker 1993, 9). Varcoe, Brown, Calam, Buchanan, and Newman (2011) argue that the assumed role of change agents legitimizes academic researchers as more knowledgable than the community itself in finding solutions. "Underlying assumptions also may suggest that such efforts are inherently 'good' for Aboriginal peoples, with little attention paid to how such strategies constitute another form of colonization" (Varcoe et al. 2011, 211). Kemmis and McTaggart (2000) warn against the disguise of participatory research as social activism. They (2000) argue that "this can be another form of deception and manipulation" couched in the practice of participatory research (568). Although ongoing dialogue is a central theme in the literature, it is suggested that the voice of researchers, not only in the academic writing and interpretation of the knowledge, but also in the dialogue itself, remains the dominating authority (Reicken et al. 2005; Strong, Israel, Schulz, and Reyes 2009; Varcoe et al. 2011).

Chilisa (2012) advocates for a participatory approach that is transformative for all parties. She suggests a shift in thinking from a "deficit based inquiry" to an "appreciative inquiry" (243). This approach, she argues, can effectively change the mindset of both the researchers and the community members (2012). With a shift in focus from conventional participation as coresearchers, the research infrastructure is constructed outside Western research frameworks (Chilisa 2012). Varcoe, Brown, Calam, Buchanan, and Newman (2011) attest that "without critical attention to underlying presumptions conveyed by research conventions, even research [that] purports to be decolonizing in intent can re-inscribe rather than resist and replace colonizing practices" (212). Using a collective approach to participatory research rather than an individuated approach challenges, according to Minkler (2005), the homogenous rubber-stamp measurements legitimizing scientific proof as solitary truth.

The integration of local epistemology can reconceptualize the traditional relationship between the researcher as the expert and the researched as subservient. With this integration, the privileged position of the researcher can momentarily be neutralized, and the interaction transformed into a "democratic dialogue," blurring the lines between the dichotomous relationship of researcher and community (Fyre 1998; Reicken et al. 2005). Yet according to Parker (1993), the logistics—or rather "spiral of steps" to defining the problem, assembling the key players, communicating the process, and disseminating the data—are ultimately led by the researcher. Some of the literature has identified this positioning as venturing close to reinscribing power relations and undermining community ownership, decision making, and knowledge transfer solely within a Western context. To address these concerns, a space of respectful dialogue between academic researchers and the community is important to disrupting polarities. Reciprocity, respect, responsibility, and relationship are interrelated at the center of Indigenous principles

(Kovach 2005). Being grounded in cultural protocol is a means to create such spaces and to live according to these principles. Maria Campbell, Métis Elder and educator, explained how our sources of knowledge come directly from the relationships that are made.

Anderson (2011) points out that "it takes much longer to build the types of relationship that oral history requires than validation of research through Western-based theories" (20). This is another example of the points of tension that destabilize the Western viewpoint of progress. Within these points of tension, we can begin to redefine from an Indigenous perspective the characteristics that produce knowledge. Furthermore, the practice of reciprocal models of relationship can begin to crystallize when conducting research with Indigenous peoples themselves, rather than about Indigenous peoples. Although these efforts are identified as central to overcoming power differentials, they do not negate the need to take responsibility for the history nor do they negate the manner in which "contemporary society reinforces (dichotomy)" (Fyre 1998, 22).

Indigenous methodologies are not only significant as a methodological tool but also as a unique form of expression, representing the act of engaging in relationship within a decolonizing framework (Chilisa 2012). Kovach (2005) states that the community-based research approach is a Western methodology intended "to counteract the heinous reputation of Western research in Indigenous communities" (13). Decentering methodological approaches from mainstream to Indigenous epistemological understanding can challenge dominant power relationships when research is done as a ceremony (Wilson 2008). The principles of circle consciousness, which Frye (1998) describes, allow for a participatory approach to nourish a new point of balance within ourselves and to our research practice.

There is a growing body of literature that demonstrates the manner in which scholars have effectively applied the participatory research approach to their community research through an Indigenous framework (Anderson 2011; Lavallee 2009; McBee 2012; Reicken et al. 2005). From their stories, I have learned that participatory research calls for ongoing fluidity and complicity, as both the researcher and the community will situate themselves differently at different points in time (Cargo et al. 2003). In attempting to affect social realities, a renewed orientation toward collaborative research is to reach "the larger context of regional community networks, intersocietal relations and institutional development so that local participatory action may be completed and enhanced" (Castellano 1993, 154). For Castellano, the successful integration of participatory research requires a balance of both internal and external structures. Boundaries are not fixed between knowledge systems.

Concluding Thoughts: Beyond a Colonial Participatory Paradigm

The rethinking of participatory research with Indigenous peoples will most likely continue for decades. I am grateful for the opportunity to be part of these early stages of discussion within the context of a doctoral program. I have come to recognize our voice as Indigenous peoples not as an inclusion or exclusion in regard to the "other." Rather, it is about participating equally in society in the ways we know best.

It is evident that participatory ethics must go beyond a normative set of guidelines to help outside researchers politely manoeuvre their way through Indigenous communities. Consulting and including Indigenous voices, images, and knowledge merely as ingredients to the mixing bowl of research findings can undermine the subtleties of local historicity, conditions, and wisdom (Battiste 2000; Briggs and Sharp 2004). Challenging power relations comes with scrutiny: not of the other but of ourselves. Accordingly, the need to reflect cultural subtleties in ethical and scientific thought is paramount to the co-creation of research efforts.

Much of the literature suggests a respect for the wholeness of Indigenous knowledge systems and the wholeness of Indigenous peoples themselves. At one point on my journey, I wondered, *whoever said we were broken*? It was a moment of awareness that emerged after a fasting ceremony. Somewhere in my consciousness I had come to believe we were broken as a people, and that I needed to be repaired. The knowledge, the prayers, and the experiences that emerged out of ceremony revealed otherwise. Accordingly, Alfred's work (2005) calls for the engagement of the wisdom of the traditional knowledge, values, language, and infrastructure of the people themselves. The historical neglect of Indigenous knowledge as connected to communal and personal well-being has led to the proliferation of knowledge-making in the Western sense.

It would seem that the participatory mode of research is maturing, both intellectually and spiritually. The ebbs and flows of the relationship between research and action, researcher and community, and intellect and heart have the potential to define the varying boundaries among power relations in research. We simply need to remain open to ways of being with one another; perhaps it is the way in which our ancestors taught us. There is a growing scholarship to help us determine the ways in which we can redirect participatory research and community development into a new kind of power; a kind of power that Bishop describes as emerging from a place of "compassionate understanding of one's moral position" (quoted in Denzin, Lincoln, Smith 2008, 11). The teaching that continues to guide my research journey is that a script does not work where real life is.

JANICE CINDY GAUDET (Métis) is a PhD candidate at the University of Ottawa and Faculty of Health Sciences, School of Human Kinetics.

Note

I give thanks to the people of Moose Cree First Nations Community in Moose Factory, Ontario, Canada. Their generosity and willingness to be a part of my PhD journey has opened new pathways to the rethinking of participatory research. I further appreciate the funding received from Social Science and Humanities Research Council that made travel to Moose Factory possible.

Bibliography

Anderson, K. 2011. *Life Stages and Native Women: Memory, Teachings, and Story Medicine.* Winnipeg: University of Manitoba Press.

Barnhardt, R., and A. O. Kawagley. 2005. "Indigenous Knowledge Systems and Alaska Native Ways of Knowing." *Anthropology and Education Quarterly* 36, no. 1: 8–23.

Battiste, M. 2000. *Reclaiming Indigenous Voice and Vision.* Vancouver: University of British Columbia Press.

Battiste, M., and J. Youngblood Henderson. 2000. *Protecting Indigenous Knowledge and Heritage: A Global Challenge.* Saskatoon: Purich Publishing Ltd.

Beck, P., A. L. Walters, and N. Francisco. 2001. *The Sacred: Ways of Knowledge, Sources of Life.* Tsaile, Ariz. Navajo Community College.

Bishop, R. 1998. "Freeing Ourselves from Neo-Colonial Domination in Research: A Māori Approach to Creating Knowledge." *International Journal of Qualitative Studies in Education* 11: 199–219.

———. 2005. "Freeing Ourselves from Neo-Colonial Domination in Research: A Kaupapa Māori Approach to Creating Knowledge." In *The SAGE Handbook of Qualitative Research,* 3rd ed., ed. N. K. Denzin and Y. S. Lincoln, 109–38. Thousand Oaks, Calif.: Sage Publications.

Brave Heart, M. Y. H. 1998. "The Return to the Sacred Path: Healing the Historical Trauma and Historical Unresolved Grief Response among the Lakota." *Smith College Studies in Social Work,* 387–568, no. 3.

Briggs, J., and J. Sharp, 2004. "Indigenous Knowledges and Development: A Postcolonial Caution." *Third World Quarterly* 25, no. 4: 661–76.

Butler, C. 2004. "Researching Traditional Ecological Knowledge for Multiple Uses." *Canadian Journal of Native Education* 28, nos. 1, 2: 33–48.

Cargo, M., L. Levesque, A. MacAuley, A. McComber, S. Desrosiers, T. Delormier, L. Potvin, with the Kahnawake Schools Diabetes Prevention Project Community Advisory Board. 2003. "Community Governance of the Kahnawake Schools Diabetes Prevention Project, Kahnawake Territory Mohawk Nation, Canada." *Health Promotion International* 18, no. 3.

Castellano, M. B. 1993. "Aboriginal Organizations in Canada: Integrating Participatory Research." In *Voices of Change: Participatory Research in the United*

States and Canada, ed. P. Park, M. Brydon-Miller, B. Hall, and T. Jackson, 145–55. Westport, Conn.: Greenwood Publishing Group.

———. 2004. "Ethics of Aboriginal Research." *Journal of Aboriginal Health* 1: 98–114.

Chilisa, B. 2012. *Indigenous Research Methodologies.* London: Sage Publications.

Colorado, P. 1988. "Bridging Native and Western Science." *Convergence* 21, no. 2/3: 49–69.

Deloria, V., Jr. 1991. "Commentary: Research, Redskins, and Reality." *American Indian Quarterly* 15, no. 4: 457–68.

———. 1999. *Spirit and Reason.* Colorado: Fulcrum Publishing.

Dorion, L. 2010. *Opikinawasowin: The Lifelong Process of Growing Cree and Métis Children.* Master of Arts—Integrated Studies. University of Athabasca, Alberta.

Denzin, N., Y. Lincoln, and L. T. Smith. 2008. *Handbook of Critical and Indigenous Methodologies: Introduction.* Thousand Oaks, Calif.: Sage Publications.

Ermine, W. 1995. "Aboriginal Epistemology." In *First Nations Education in Canada: The Circle Unfolds,* ed. M. Battiste and J. Barman, 101–12. Vancouver: UBC Press.

Fitznor, L. 2006. "The Power of Indigenous Knowledge: Naming and Identity and Colonization in Canada." In *Indigenous Peoples' Wisdom and Power: Affirming Our Knowledge through Narratives,* ed. J. E. Kunnie and N. I. Goduka, 51–76. Burlington, Vt.: Ashgate.

Fletcher, C. 2003. "Community-Based Participatory Research in Northern Canadian Aboriginal Communities: An Overview of Context and Process." *Pimatziwin: An International Journal on Aboriginal and Indigenous Health* 1: 27–61.

Fyre, J. G. 1998. *Circle Works: Transforming Eurocentric Consciousness.* Halifax: Fernwood Publishing.

Getty, G. A. MN, RN. 2010. "The Journey between Western and Indigenous Research Paradigms." *Journal of Transculture Nursing* 21, no. 1: 5–14.

Goulet, J. W. 1998. *Ways of Knowing, Experience, Knowledge, and Power among the Dene.* Lincoln: University of Nebraska Press.

Holmes, L. 2000. "Heart Knowledge, Blood Memory, and the Voice of the Land: Implications of Research among Hawaiian Elders." In *Indigenous Knowledges in Global Context,* ed. G. J. Sefa Dei, D. Goldin-Rosenberg, and B. L. Hall, 37–53. Toronto: University of Toronto Press.

Horowitz, C., M. Robinson, and S. Seifer. 2009. "Community-Based Participatory Research from the Margins to Mainstream: Are Researchers Prepared?" *Circulation* 119: 2633–42.

Jackson, T. 1993. "A Way of Working: Participatory Research and the Aboriginal Movement in Canada." In *Voices of Change: Participatory Research in the United States and Canada,* ed. P. Park, M. Brydon-Miller, B. Hall, and T. Jackson, 47–64. Westport, Conn.: Greenwood Publishing Group.

Kelsey, Penelope Myrtle. 2008. *Tribal Theory in Native American Literature.* Lincoln: University of Nebraska Press.

Kemmis, S., & R. McTaggart. 2000. "Participatory Action Research." In *Handbook of Qualitative Research,* 2nd ed., ed. N. K. Denzin and Y. S. Lincoln, 567–605. Thousand Oaks, Calif.: Sage Publications.

Kovach, M. 2005. "Emerging from the Margins." In *Research as Resistance: Critical, Indigenous, and Anti-Oppressive Approaches,* ed. L. Brown and S. Strega, 19–36. Toronto: Canadian Scholars' Press.

———. 2009. *Indigenous Methodologies: Characteristics, Conversations, and Texts.* Toronto: University of Toronto Press.

Ktunaxa, M. A. Sam. 2011. "An Indigenous Knowledges Perspective on Valid Meaning Making: A Commentary on Research with EDI and Aboriginal Communities." *Social Indicators Research* 103: 315–25.

Larkin, L., B. Strong, A. Israel, A. Schulz, A. Reyes, Z. Rowe, S. Weir, and C. Poe. 2009. "Piloting Interventions within a Community-Based Participatory Research Framework: Lessons Learned from the Healthy Environments Partnerships." *Progress in Community Health Partnerships* 3, no. 4: 327–34.

Lavallée, L. F. 2009. "Practical Application of an Indigenous Research Framework and Two Qualitative Indigenous Research Methods: Sharing Circles and Anishinaabe Symbol-Based Reflection." *International Journal of Qualitative Methods* 8, no. 1: 21–40.

———. 2007. *Threads of Connection: Addressing Historic Trauma of Indigenous People through Cultural Recreational Programming.* PhD diss., University of Toronto, Canada. Publication No. AAT NR28105.

Loppie, C. 2007. "Learning from the Grandmothers: Incorporating Indigenous Principles into Qualitative Research." *Qualitative Health Research* 17, no. 2: 276–84.

Louis, R. P. 2007. "Can You Hear Us Now? Voices from the Margin: Using Indigenous Methodologies in Geographic Research." *Geographical Research* 45, no. 2: 130–39.

Manderson, L., M. Kelaher, G. Williams, and C. Shannon. 1998. "The Politics of Community: Negotiation and Consultation in Research on Women's Health." *Human Organizations,* Summer 1998: 57, 2.

McBee, G. 2013. *Learning from Nature-Based Indigenous Knowledge: A Trail to Understanding Elders' Wisdom.* PhD diss. University of Victoria, British Columbia.

McTaggart, R. 1994. "Participatory Action Research: Issues in Theory and Practice." *Educational Action Research* 2, no. 3: 313–37.

Minkler, M. 2005. "Community-Based Research Partnerships: Challenges and Opportunities." *Journal of Urban Health: Bulletin of the New York Academy of Medicine* 82, no. 2, Suppl. 2: ii3–ii12.

Minkler, M., and N. Wallerstein. 2003. *Community-Based Participatory Research for Health.* San Francisco: Jossey-Bass.

Mountz, A. I., R. Miyares, R. Wright, and A. Bailey. 2003. "Methodologically Becoming: Power, Knowledge and Research Team." *Gender, Place & Culture: A Journal of Feminist Geography* 10, no. 1: 29–46.

Nicholls, R. 2009. "Research and Indigenous Participation: Critical Reflexive Methods." *International Journal of Social Research Methodology* 12, no. 2: 117–26.

Parker, P. 1993. "What Is Participatory Research? A Theoretical and Methodological Perspective." In *Voices of Change: Participatory Research in the United States and Canada,* ed. P. Park, M. Brydon-Miller, B. Hall, and T. Jackson, 2–19. Westport, Conn.: Greenwood Publishing Group.

Postnikoff, H. 2005. "Coming Full Circle: Applying A Nuu-chah-nulth Worldview in Community-Based Research." University of Victoria. Paper prepared in partial fulfillment of course requirements.

Riecken, T., T. Strong-Wilson, F. Conibear, C. Michel, and J. Riecken. 2005. "Connecting, Speaking, Listening: Toward an Ethics of Voice With/in Participatory Action Research." *Qualitative Social Research* 6, no. 1: Art. 26.

Robbins, J., and J. Dewar. 2011. "Traditional Indigenous Approaches to Healing and the Modern Welfare of Traditional Knowledge, Spirituality, and Lands: A Critical Reflection on Practices and Policies Taken from the Canadian Indigenous Example." *The International Indigenous Policy Journal* 2, no. 4.

Strong, L., B. Israel, A. Schulz, and A. Reyes. 2009. "Piloting Interventions within a Community-Based Participatory Research Framework: Lessons Learned from the Healthy Environment Partnership." *Progress in Community Health Partnerships: Research, Education, and Action* 3, no. 4: 327–34.

Simpson, L. 2001. "Aboriginal Peoples and Knowledge: Decolonizing Our Processes." *Canadian Journal of Native Studies* 21, no. 1: 137–48.

Sioui, G. 1992. "For an Amerindian Autohistory: An Essay on the Foundations of a Social Ethic." Quebec: McGill–Queen's University Press.

Smith, L. T. 1999. *Decolonizing Methodologies: Research and Indigenous Peoples.* New York: Zed Books.

St. Denis, V. 1992. "Community-Based Participatory Research: Aspects of the Concepts Relevant for Practice." *Native Studies Review* 8, no. 2: 51–74.

Taiaike, T. 2005. *Wasāse: Indigenous Pathways of Action and Freedom.* Peterborough: Broadview Press.

Turner, D. 2006. *This Is Not a Peace Pipe: Towards a Critical Indigenous Philosophy.* Toronto: University of Toronto Press.

Wesley-Esquimaux, C. 2009. "Trauma to Resilience: Notes on Decolonization." In *Restoring the Balance: First Nations Women, Community, and Culture,* ed. G. Guthrie Valaskakis et al., 13–34. Winnipeg: University of Manitoba Press.

Wilson, S. 2008. *Research Is Ceremony: Indigenous Research Methods.* Winnipeg: Fernwood.

Varcoe, C., H. Brown, B. Calam, M. Buchanan, and V. Newman. 2011. "Capacity Building Is a Two-Way Street: Learning and Doing Research within Aboriginal Communities." In *Feminist Community Research,* ed. G. Creese and W. Frisby, 210–31. Toronto/Vancouver: UBC Press.

MICHAEL SNYDER

Imagine Lennon as Choctaw Code Talker: Indigenized Beatles in LeAnne Howe's *Miko Kings*

CHOCTAW POET, playwright, and novelist LeAnne Howe published her third book, *Miko Kings: An Indian Baseball Story*, in 2007. This engaging and insightful novel tells of a Choctaw and Sac and Fox writer from Ada, Oklahoma named Lena Coulter, who in 2006 attempts to uncover the lost story of the Miko Kings, an early twentieth-century Indian Territory baseball team. As Lena's knowledge deepens, she works at unraveling a mystery to explain why the team's star pitcher, Hope Little Leader, who is Choctaw, becomes involved with gamblers and "throws"—that is, deliberately loses—a baseball game in October 1907. This is no ordinary ballgame: it is a symbolically charged contest upon which a great deal is at stake. For this Indigenous team's opponents are none other than Custer's old gang, the Seventh Cavalry, and the game occurs shortly before Indian Territory is swallowed up by Oklahoma statehood, during a period in which the Curtis Act of 1898, which imposed allotment policy upon the so-called Five Civilized Tribes, had been put into effect and was taking a toll on Choctaw tribal communalism.

Lena Coulter is prompted to undertake her investigation upon discovering a mailbag full of old documents cached in the wall of her Ada home. She begins to peruse these documents, which in turn spurs her to research a broad array of materials in order to recover this piece of Choctaw and Indian Territory history. As the Choctaw author D. L. Birchfield states, "Choctaw history must be pieced together from many different sources."[1] Lena subsequently experiences visitations from Ezol Day, the brilliant niece of the Miko Kings' co-owner, Henri Day. A prodigy, Ezol has unlocked secrets of language, time, and space that allow her to counsel Lena. Ezol's ability to move freely in time becomes a metaphor of traditional Choctaw experiences of temporality as conjoining the past, present, and future at any given moment.[2] The reader comes to see Ezol Day as the true author of the story as she guides Lena's quest and composition, asking her questions, and offering her clues. In a Choctaw or Chahta sense, Ezol serves as the "metaphorical *iti fabassa*, the center pole of the story of *Miko Kings*, ever-in-motion, connecting multiple worlds at once," Howe explains in an essay collected in *Choctalking on Other Realities*.

One perplexing task that Ezol Day assigns Lena Coulter is to "find John Lennon" and to "find out what happened" to him.[3] Thus begins a chain of symbolic associations between the Indigenous, in particular the Choctaw, and Lennon and The Beatles that extends across much of the novel. To some readers, the significance of the Lennon and Beatles references remains nebulous, as though the reader is "looking through a glass onion," to quote a song Lennon penned for The Beatles.[4] To others, the mystery of the Fab Four's presence in the novel has even seemed a red herring or a missing puzzle piece. Howe seems to be "Choctaw code talking" in her engagement of Lennon and The Beatles, and without many clues, we must attempt to crack the code by viewing the novel in a Choctaw context as much as possible. LeAnne Howe herself acknowledged the novel's intriguing lacuna in conversation and wrote in an e-mail to the author, "John Lennon is the missing chapter!"[5] In our endeavor to make sense of the concatenation of baseball, Beatles, and Natives in Howe's rich novel, we are led to engage further related topics, gender diversity and same-sex desire, which are important in both the novel's project of Choctaw historical recovery and in John Lennon's life.

If John Lennon is "the missing chapter," with metaphorical pages left blank, it is left to the reader to locate meaning in these references in co-creation with the author. As the reader and Lena scramble for clues, attempting to connect points into a meaningful constellation, unsure to what degree the associations are intended or valid and to what extent they are a product of "paranoid reading," we come to resemble Oedipa Maas, the questing heroine of Thomas Pynchon's sophomore novel *The Crying of Lot 49*, which featured its own Anglophile mop-top band, The Paranoids.[6] I want to argue that, rather than being a red herring or even a colonialist "British Invasion," the Lennon-Beatles connection underscores at least one of the novel's most cogent Indigenous themes, "to make a dovetail joint" with Choctaw traditional religion, to quote again from The Beatles' "Glass Onion." Reflecting on The Beatles as Englishmen, given the Choctaws' historical experience of colonialism in North America (see Debo's *The Rise and Fall of the Choctaw Republic*), the tribe has never been especially fond of Englishmen, which makes the author's and characters' allusions to and engagement of The Beatles even more striking. For example, a character in *Shell Shaker* thinks to himself that "feeding off the misery of Indians has always been their greatest joy . . . Choctaws never liked the English."[7]

One key to understanding this rhetorical link is the traditional Chahta reverence for Hashtali, a life-giving sun god "whose eye is the Sun," Howe writes.[8] Ultimately, Howe indigenizes The Beatles and Lennon's prescription that we "imagine" otherwise, to aid her project of reimagining and rewriting Choctaw history. With a little help from her friends, Howe's imagining of

Choctaw history furthers "the ideologies that contemporary Native critics propose as the objectives of American Indian literatures: sovereignty, decolonization, and survival," as critic Patrice Hollrah explains in her discussion of teaching Howe's novel *Shell Shaker*.[9]

While LeAnne Howe arguably engages "Choctaw code talking" as a literary and rhetorical strategy, the heroic World War I–era Choctaw Code Talkers are not discussed in *Miko Kings*. This trope, however, is one that LeAnne Howe deploys with aplomb throughout her corpus. In *Shell Shaker*, Dolores remarks, "You have to understand a lot of codes to be Choctaw . . . we're all Code Talkers . . . so much goes unspoken."[10] In *Evidence of Red,* the poem "Still Code Talking" suggests that the notion of Choctaw code talking can refer to literary or rhetorical language that encodes a blunter message to colonizers who have betrayed the tribe.[11] In this vein, D. L. Birchfield even implies that the ability of Choctaws to code talk might potentially represent a threat to United States settler–colonial hegemony.[12]

Similarly, in *Miko Kings,* like a DJ, Howe spins a platter of Choctaw-Beatles Code Talking, an encrypted interweave of the tribal and the Fab Four, plus the great game of baseball, empowering her project of reimagining Choctaw history and advocating for tribal sovereignty. One of the novel's claims is that American Indians invented baseball. Making this rhetorical move, Howe positions Indigenous peoples in their rightful place as progenitors, co-creators, or key influencers of many classically "American" things, which are assumed by many to be of European origin. (Another major example is the United States Constitution, influenced by the Constitution of the Iroquois Confederacy.) Tribal ball games were important for social organization and tribal diplomacy. D. L. Birchfield imagines the original Choctaws of ancient times being divided into "groups of a few dozen people, because that was about what it took to have a good ball team."[13] In discussing tribal ball games, Howe further suggests in the essay "Embodied Tribalography" that "it may be time to consider the role of game-play as a progenitor of Choctaw political culture."[14] Along with noting the similarities between Indigenous games involving sticks, balls, and bases, and the fact that unlike most Western sports, baseball has no limit in time, Howe stresses that baseball, like stomp dances, moves in a counterclockwise motion, against the usual Euro-American pattern.[15] In "Embodied Tribalography," Howe writes of reflecting on "the motion of water and wind in the Northern Hemisphere. This may explain why Natives in the Southeast dance counterclockwise and would create an Indigenous ballgame played counterclockwise, mimicking or expressing water flow, tornado, and hurricane winds."[16]

Likewise, in the vinyl era, some rock bands included backwards musical or verbal messages on their LPs which could only be deciphered by manually spinning the record *counterclockwise*. This mysterious practice, later dubbed "backmasking," like so many other trends, was innovated by The Beatles, who recorded several backwards musical and vocal tracks on their songs, including "Rain," "I'm So Tired," and "Revolution #9." In unlocking these secret messages, as one's finger traces a little circle on the record label, one resembles a wizard casting a spell, as The Beatles were pictured in their film *Magical Mystery Tour*. I use this image as an emblem of my hermeneutics, approaching the novel from a different direction, tapping into underground rivers of history, in an attempt to enter into one of the novel's most compelling mysteries.

In part, LeAnne Howe engages The Beatles and Lennon to gesture toward and indigenize Lennon's activism, the ways in which he used his fame to give voice to social justice concerns, linking the power of popular culture and celebrity with forms of resistance and expressions of sovereignty on behalf of Native communities. Plus, on a formalist level, the novel's copious references to The Beatles, especially to the lyrics of their song "Because" and the album on which it appeared, *Abbey Road*, serve as a cultural time marker, signaling an intermediate temporal setting of 1969 between the crucial 1907 ballgame and the 2006 present of Lena's quest. The massive commercial and critical success of *Abbey Road* registered the rising power of the counterculture and the antiwar movement, a time during which "even the Indians in Ada are going to protest the Vietnam War."[17] Usually promoters of various forms of love in their music, The Beatles had positioned themselves against the Vietnam War early on. In August 1964 Lennon cleverly remarked, "all of our songs are antiwar songs."[18] In 1965 John Lennon spoke out against the Vietnam War specifically on behalf of the band to a reporter.[19] In 1968, Lennon penned what can easily be read as an anti–Vietnam War song for The Beatles, "The Continuing Story of Bungalow Bill," which parodies an "all-American, bullet-headed, Saxon mother's son" whose passion is to go "deep into the jungle" and kill. "The children asked him if to kill was not a sin," Lennon sings, and the satirical lyrics are highly suggestive, even if Bungalow Bill's target is tigers.[20] During 1969, the year in which *Abbey Road* was released, John Lennon and Yoko Ono embarked on a series of media events to agitate for peace, including their famous Bed-Ins. Back in Ada, Oklahoma, in 1969 former Miko Kings' pitcher Hope Little Leader is now an elder nicknamed "No Hands" due to the loss he suffered after an act of vengeance for deliberately losing the 1907 ballgame against the Seventh Cavalry. Little Leader is a resident of Elms Nursing Home, where he drifts between the present and the past of his glory days as a hero of the pitching mound.

For LeAnne Howe, the mound itself is of great symbolic and cultural importance, linked to Indigenous roots because first, the Choctaws and other Southeastern tribes were, and in some ways still are, mound builders, as

Howe has stressed. In *Miko Kings*, Ezol tells Lena about the ancient Choctaw game of "base-and-ball": "From the mound, the pitcher was the embodiment of the center pole that could access the Middle, Upper, and Lower Worlds."[21] Moreover, the mound is linked to a traditional story of how the Choctaws received corn from Ohoyo Chishba Osh, "woman who stretches way back," discussed by Howe in an essay published in *Pre-Removal Choctaw History: Exploring New Paths*. Howe notes that one version of the story links Ohoyo Chishba Osh to the Great Spirit of the Choctaws, and stresses that this Great Spirit was often in pre-assimilation times called Hashtali, the eye of the sun.[22] In her essay "The Story of America," Howe elucidates: "from the hunters' initial gift of sacred food to the Unknown Woman, Choctaws and other southeastern tribes received the gift of corn. Today we celebrate Green Corn Ceremony in midsummer to mark the coming of the future: corn, our ancient food cache."[23] According to Angie Debo in *The Rise and Fall of the Choctaw Republic*, the Choctaws' "recognition of the sun . . . as a universal deity seems to have been a native conception."[24] Reinforcing this link, as an Indian School student and already a gifted pitcher, Hope Little Leader is chastised by an assimilationist teacher for offering corn to "*Hashtali*, the eye of the sun, the one who watches over all Choctaws."[25] She views such traditional Choctaw religious practice as akin to devil worship. Toward the end of the novel, Ezol seems to be linked to the woman who brings corn, Ohoyo Chishba Osh, when she appears in "a corn-colored linen dress."[26] Ezol, in her time traveling and guidance of the story, is indeed a powerful and generous "woman who stretches way back."

Throughout the novel, Howe builds concatenations between Lennon, his signature composition "Imagine," Indian Territory, and baseball to forward her project of historical reimagining and recovery. "The Bases Are Loaded," like other chapters, begins with an epigraph evoking "another echo of baseball's childhood memory in *Anompa Sipokni*, Old Talking Places." In this epigraph, while riding the rails, Hope Little Leader claims that "freedom smoked from [his] fingers." A "Hobo" wants to know how long Hope's fingers and arms were. "Like this," Hope replies. "The Hobo" exclaims, "Imagine that!" as though he has seen something defying quotidian reality.[27] This imperative to "imagine" invokes the utopian ballad composed by a man who has become a symbol of peace and social justice activism, John Lennon. Making the connection to Lennon more robust, what immediately follows at the beginning of chapter three is the sound and lyrics of "Because," Lennon's transcendent paean, played "over and over" again on the PA system of the Nursing Home in Ada.[28] The lyrics of "Because" resonate deeply with the Choctaw elder Hope Little Leader, and we learn later that one of Hope's two nurses—both Native ballplayers—is a twenty-three-year-old Comanche named, yes, John Lennon.

The imperative to "imagine" is invoked again by the Miko Kings' player-manager George "Blip" Bleen (and George Harrison, of course, is the Spiritual Beatle) who is "gifted at inspiring the men. He tells them to imagine the plays *before* they happen."[29] Similarly, in his essay "The Man Made of Words," Kiowa author N. Scott Momaday writes: "Our best destiny is to imagine, at least, completely, who and what, and *that* we are. The greatest tragedy that can befall us is to go unimagined."[30] Howe stresses time and again the need to reimagine the past from a Choctaw point of view, serving her ideological project of decolonization and tribal sovereignty. Ezol Day, who theorizes the dynamic interweaving of language, time, and space, writes in her diary: "that we can speak it, makes it possible to imagine" (158).

Ezol's name, which, as noted in the novel, has roots in *isolé*, or isolation (161), recalls Lennon's solo song "Isolation" from the *John Lennon / Plastic Ono Band* album. It contains a lyric that could serve as a message from Ezol to her oppressive teachers at the Hampton Normal School for Blacks and Indians: "I don't expect you to understand / After you've caused so much pain." Then, as though imbued with Ezol's cosmic but sad wisdom accrued from being able to traverse time freely, Lennon continues, "But then again, you're not to blame / You're just a human, a victim of the insane."[31]

Before proceeding further into the tribally-specific connections between Lennon and Choctaws, let us widen the scope in order to highlight some historical moments that more broadly connect these two things that at first glance seem to have little to do with each other: The Beatles and American Indians. In *Miko Kings*, Lena Coulter in 2006 is at first stumped by Ezol's directive that she find out "what happened" to John Lennon. This kind of question raises our own inquiries based on images or associations we may have of Lennon. For example, what happened to the spirit of John Lennon, "a dreamer," a warrior of sorts who waged peace and agitated for social justice?[32] Or, the question of "what happened" to Lennon may suggest controversy over Lennon's death and whether it was truly only the result of the madness of a lone gunman, a "crazed fan." What would Lennon have gone on to do had he lived? How might the 1980s have been different had Lennon continued to re-emerge into political activism, as he gave signs of doing prior to his murder? Such questions parallel the novel's larger project of Lena recovering the history of the Miko Kings baseball team, and by implication Choctaw history generally, and addressing the many larger contextual questions surrounding it. Lena explores the question, and with Ezol's help, imagines its answer: how would history be different had Hope Little Leader not "thrown" the 1907 game against the Seventh Cavalry? In her attempt to fulfill Ezol's task, Lena scours the library to discover a link between Lennon and American Indians, thinking that Lennon may have met a Native baseball player while living in

New York City.[33] Connecting The Beatles and baseball is not at first easy, but the Fab Four did spend a good deal of time in the mid-1960s on diamonds (a bit like Lucy in the Sky), in major league baseball stadia, after being lowered down from the sky like gods—or like Lucy (see Lewisohn). Lena finds no connection but finally realizes that since Ezol knew about John Lennon in 1907, she must have *already* been traveling back and forth in time before then.[34] Therefore at this point the Beatle connection is perhaps dismissed by Lena as a red herring, but the reader knows, as Stephen Stills of Buffalo Springfield sang in "For What It's Worth": "There's something happening here. What it is ain't exactly clear."[35] Although rarely noted in biographies or Beatle books, several historical connections can be made between John Lennon in particular and American Indians.

In the early 1970s, during the height of Lennon's radical period, zestfully undertaken with his partner, the conceptual artist and avant-garde musician Yoko Ono, he became interested in Native American activism and Red Power and sought means by which to bring attention to their causes. According to eyewitness Mark Mahal, on Sunday, October 10, 1971, the day after Lennon's thirty-first birthday, John, Yoko, and Seneca activist and spiritual leader Oren R. Lyons Jr. stepped into a limousine parked at a Syracuse, New York hotel and sped south to the Onondaga reservation. John and Yoko had been in Syracuse for the opening of Ono's transgressive art exhibit *This Is Not Here* at the Everson Museum, with Lennon acting as guest artist, followed by a star-studded birthday jam session in John's honor.[36] Oren R. Lyons Jr., Faithkeeper of the Turtle Clan of the Onondaga and Seneca Nations of the Haudenosaunee Confederacy, moved to Onondaga in 1970 and became involved in the burgeoning Red Power movement. John and Yoko visited the reservation to participate in a sit-in protest against the U.S. government and New York Governor Rockefeller, whose employees had entered the reservation without asking permission to widen Interstate 88, which runs through the Onondaga Reservation. This demonstration was part of a month-long protest movement organized by Tadodaho Leon Shenandoah, who was the Faithkeeper of the Eel Clan of the Onondaga Nation.[37]

Lennon made his sense of alliance with indigenes of North America clear. Speaking to the Indigenous protesters in the presence of media, John stated, "Everybody knows your people have been robbed and slaughtered since the Europeans moved in here. I'm very surprised that, in an area like Syracuse with so many universities and so many students . . . talking about peace and love and radicalization . . . that there doesn't seem to be very many of them helping you around here," reports biographer Jon Wiener.[38] Lennon was calling attention to oppressed people right under the nose of a supposedly progressive academy, chiding students and leftist radicals to ally themselves with local Indigenous struggles for sovereignty. Granted, John and Yoko were wealthy, privileged celebrities, but it seems they participated at some risk to themselves. Prior to the protest, when John had asked civil rights activist Suzan Shown Harjo over the telephone what was the worst that could happen, she replied, "well, you could be killed." "Oh, OK, just so I know," replied Lennon.[39] The tragic Kent State shootings of May 1970, in which National Guardsmen shot and killed four student protesters and injured nine more, was then a recent memory.

Perhaps Lennon felt the need to participate in a radical demonstration that would back up his rhetorical fire from a month earlier. Lennon had used the television medium to agitate during an appearance with Yoko Ono on *The Dick Cavett Show*, asking the host, who had given Lennon an album of Sioux music on their previous meeting, how interested he was in the "Red Revolution, and power for the Red Indian." Lennon wanted to know "what are American people doing for the Indian" and stated that Natives were ill-served and neglected by the government and economically exploited. "First [Euro-Americans] take the land, and then they make movies about taking the land," Lennon quipped, adding that as a boy, he and his Liverpool friends rooted for the Indians when they saw Western movies. Intent on making an impact on viewers, Lennon persisted: "What's going on with the Indians? Don't they really legally own the land? . . . People think there's only a few Indians left but there's millions of them on the continent of America . . . and one day they're going to be asking for their rights. I wouldn't be surprised if they weren't standing next to the Black people too. I reckon it's give now or die later," Lennon warned as the TV studio audience murmured. Relevant to Howe's appropriation of Lennon's imperative to "imagine" otherwise, Lennon had just released the *Imagine* album, and in fact, the promotional film for the song "Imagine" was debuted on this episode of *The Dick Cavett Show*.[40]

A Native connection to Lennon and The Beatles closer to Indian Territory and the Choctaw Nation is found in the late guitarist Jesse Ed Davis, of Muskogee Creek, Seminole, and Kiowa ancestry, who was born in Norman, Oklahoma, dropped out of the University of Oklahoma, and started his music career in Oklahoma City. John Lennon met Jesse Ed Davis in December 1968 when they performed separately in the never-shown television special *Rock and Roll Circus*, which featured The Rolling Stones; Davis was at the time a sideman for the blues musician Taj Mahal. Backstage, when John Lennon started belting out Elvis Presley and Carl Perkins songs, Davis joined in on guitar leads and Lennon, an old-school Rocker, was deeply impressed by Davis's ability to play the solos and licks note-for-note.[41] Davis played alongside Tulsa music icon Leon Russell, recorded many studio sessions with stars such as Willie Nelson, and in August 1971 backed up George Harrison for *The Con-

cert for Bangladesh alongside Ringo Starr. (It was rumored that John Lennon would appear at the concert but he didn't make it.) After playing on a Bob Dylan single, in the mid-1970s Jesse Ed Davis played sessions, including some tasty slide guitar work, for John Lennon on two albums: *Walls and Bridges* (1974) and *Rock 'n' Roll* (1975). Moreover, Davis played on Harry Nilsson's album *Pussy Cats* (1974), which was produced by Lennon, who also served as a guest artist on the record, and he recorded three solo albums in the 1970s. Davis, who struggled with his own demons and addictions, got to know Lennon at his best and worst. Lennon biographer Philip Norman writes that during Lennon's so-called "Lost Weekend" period in Los Angeles when he was separated from Yoko Ono, drummer Jim Keltner and Jessie Ed Davis "were called on to restrain John one night when the cocktail of vodka and 100-proof rock 'n' roll unlocked all his pent-up anguish over Yoko, and he went literally berserk."[42]

Returning to Lennon's connection to *Miko Kings*, it is helpful to have these historical connections in mind when considering how the song "Because" resonates so profoundly with the elder Choctaw ex-pitcher Hope Little Leader. "Because" is a pantheistic hymn, or in Howe's words, "a tender reverie" that praises the wind that is high, the sky that is blue, the world that is round. It speaks of natural elements or forces that are timeless, old and new.[43] Our attention is directed upward, to the sky, or far into outer space to envision that roundness of the world. After quoting most of the lyrics of the song that someone is playing over and over, including, "because the wind is high, it blows my mind,"[44] Howe writes, "The melody echoes . . . and circles high above his head like vague sighing of wind. Hope Little Leader knows something about the paths of prairie wind and the influence it can have on a baseball. A good pitcher must make friends with the cross-currents of summer."[45] Lennon and Little Leader are both deeply sensitive to these forces of nature in a manner that a Christian might call "pagan."

The Beatles' masterful late album *Abbey Road* is alluded to specifically, and nearby songs on Side Two of the record continue this theme of devotion and attention to the natural world, in particular the worship of the sun. The crosswalk on *Abbey Road*'s iconic cover can, in LeAnne Howe's vision, be seen as a transatlantic bridge between The Beatles and Choctaws. In the novel we learn that Hope Little Leader makes an unusual, rapid up-down motion before he fires the ball across the plate. It is gradually revealed that Hope is actually praying to Hashtali, the Choctaw god of the sun. Hope Little Leader's Uncle Ahojebo was a ball player who gave to his nephew Hope a symbolic red baseball. Ahojebo also made the prayerful up-down motion.[46] The movement of the baseball from the hand of Hope Little Leader to home base mimics the movement of the sun across the sky and thus the motion of Hashtali (who sometimes is said to ride a vulture, a scavenger animal, suggesting the cosmic cycle of life and death). As Hope listens to "Because" and its unquoted lyric, "because the sky is blue, it makes me cry,"[47] he reflects: "The young men love the world so round, the sky so blue—that's how he once felt. He looks skyward; a white ceiling of clouds is above him. Just then, the red ball that his uncle Ahojebo gave him is in his eye."[48] The way Howe phrases it, the sunlike red ball is connected with the eye, again suggesting the uncle's and nephew's reverence for Hashtali, the eye of the sun. Hope reflects, "Ahojebo used to twirl his arm so fast that when he set the ball free it flew *up, up, up*, into the heavens and disappeared. How did the singers know that this feat made him cry?"[49] Hope's prayer empowers him to throw preternatural pitches that rupture the space-time continuum. Ezol, with special understanding of time and space, during a game once sees Hope disappear from the mound altogether as a blinding light flashes. "Time had moved backward and then forward," Ezol notes in her diaries.[50]

So too did The Beatles offer praise and prayers to the sun, linking them with the traditional Choctaws. Early on they vowed, "I'll Follow the Sun."[51] "So we sailed into the sun," Ringo Starr sang in "Yellow Submarine."[52] Later, The Beatles were sighted "sitting in an English garden, waiting for the sun" in "I Am the Walrus," written by John.[53] The sun-worshipping songs reached a climax on *Abbey Road*, whose title itself connotes the spiritual: "Here Comes the Sun,"[54] and "Sun King," in whose presence "everybody's happy, everybody's laughing."[55] These latter songs seem to exist almost solely to praise the life and warmth-giving powers of the sun. The Beatles' musical anticipations of the arrival of the sun, also heard on *Revolver*'s "Good Day Sunshine,"[56] recall a line from Howe's first novel *Shell Shaker*, when it is said of Adair Billy that "it had been bred into her that the first seconds of sunlight carry messages from Hashtali to the people."[57] The Beatles' continual praise and longing for the sun is part of their non-Christian or "pagan" spirituality. John's irreverence toward Christianity was suggested in his controversial remarks to the British journalist Maureen Cleave: he remarked, "Christianity will go. It will vanish and shrink," and noted that The Beatles were "more popular than Jesus now; I don't know which will go first—rock 'n' roll or Christianity."[58] The later dissemination of these remarks originally printed in a London newspaper sparked Beatle bonfires throughout the Deep South of the United States.

For Paul McCartney, and to a lesser extent John, the spiritual interest in the sun is linked with what inside sources have revealed to be a fascination with the "occult" and ancient Egyptian cosmologies. The sun symbolism of the protective Eye of Horus and The Eye of Ra might be likened to the Choctaw deity Hashtali, whose eye is the sun and is referred to as "the Choctaw's source of power."[59] LeAnne Howe notes this Egyptian connection in a piece from *Evidence of Red* when she hears devout Muslims praying as she stands outside a mosque in Jerusalem: "When I hear the prayers . . . I am sure he is praying to the Sun, just like Choctaws once prayed to Hashtali." She ventures to a vendor, "It looks like you are praying to the sun, especially with your palms turned up to the sky. The Egyptians once worshipped the sun God, RA. Since the Hebrews and Egyptians once lived together, maybe your religions rubbed off on each other."[60] Incidentally, the ancient Egyptians revered beetles, the scarab beetle, and associated the ball of dung it rolled with cosmic forces moving the sun across the sky. Khepri was a beetle-headed god of the rising sun subordinate to Ra.

In most ways, Hope Little Leader is a Lennonesque character. If Lennon waged peace with music, Hope sings warrior songs to steel himself against his oppressive educational environment.[61] As his name suggests, he is a leader to the team, just as Lennon was the acknowledged leader of The Beatles, and as a prodigious pitcher, he is the hope of his team and by extension the Native people of the region. Hope's relationship with dusky Justina Maurepas is taboo at the Hampton Institute for Indians and Blacks and subject to censure, resembling the maligned love affair and marriage between the Englishman John Lennon and the Japanese Yoko Ono, with World War II not far in the past. Moreover, Hope's connection to Lennon is underscored by his having a Comanche nurse named John Lennon who croons along with "Because" as it plays repeatedly over the loudspeaker.

But the Comanche Lennon seems to embody but one half of the Lennon mythos: the tough, masculine warrior—emblematized by young, leather-jacketed, Rocker John—yet a thoughtful warrior who is also a healer. He tells Hope, "You and I, we're together on the warpath. Right? We're fighting diabetes *and* John Wayne movies, right?"[62] This is the masculine side of Lennon shaped by Liverpudlian working-class roots, the tough, sardonic side. Comanche Lennon is against the Vietnam War, but he has enlisted in the Army so that he might have more choice in where he is stationed, figuring it is better than being drafted. He participates in Comanche ceremonies to prepare. He reckons that the reason the United States is losing the war is because they don't yet have the Comanches on their side.[63]

The yin to Comanche John Lennon's yang, Kerwin Johnston, Hope's other nurse, protests the Vietnam War while wearing a woman's dress, calling for personal freedom along with freedom from war and violence. Apache and Choctaw, Kerwin Johnston represents the contrasting side of Lennon, his *anima*, or feminine principle, to use Jung's term. Kerwin also allows Howe to gesture toward the rise of the Gay Liberation movement, which was stoked by the Stonewall Inn riots a few months earlier in 1969. "I just thought it was a good time to protest for personal change, while we're protesting against the

Vietnam War. Power to the People, man," Kerwin quotes John Lennon to John Lennon, while donning a polka-dot dress and a bright orange wig.[64] While Comanche Lennon bristles at Kerwin's dressing in women's garb, today Kerwin might be called a two-spirit, but in the tribally specific context he is an *Ohoyo Holba*, meaning "like a woman but not." Hope Little Leader, understanding Kerwin in a traditionally Chahta way, tells him that "In the old days, *Ohoyo Holba* was a respected person. They were givers who had multiple kinds of powers inside them. That's why a man would put on a woman's dress. By wearing the dress he was showing the world that he was in a state of grace ... a man without limitations."[65] It is noted that Kerwin possesses healing powers that are linked to this role. We might recall that the hairstyle The Beatles favored was considered extremely long and disturbingly feminine when they were launched to fame in 1963–64, and their trademark Cuban-heeled Chelsea boots were derided as "fruit boots." Along with wearing the clothes of another gender, Kerwin prefers men sexually.

Correspondingly, Beatle John Lennon also had a repressed side that might be called queer or bisexual; several incidents point to this. John loved deeply the artist Stuart Sutcliffe, an early member of The Beatles, whose tragic death at age twenty-one devastated him. Also, Lennon shared a sexual experience with The Beatles' closeted gay manager Brian Epstein in Spain.[66] Moreover, according to Philip Norman, who interviewed Yoko Ono, Lennon held deep feelings of affection for his songwriting partner Paul McCartney, unrequited feelings that even Ono was aware of.[67] Unfortunately, although Lennon experienced homosexual desire, he was also prone to fits of "homosexual panic," a concept discussed by Eve Kosofsky Sedgwick,[68] bursting out in violence against suggestions that he was gay. Sadly, Lennon was not able to reconcile his tough, working-class sense of masculinity with his more sensitive, homoerotic side, which is why Howe is right to split the Lennon character into two Native ball-playing characters, Kerwin and John. In June 1963, Lennon brutally attacked Bob Wooler, a Liverpool disc jockey who was a supporter of the Beatles, when Wooler made a jest about Lennon going on "honeymoon" with Brian Epstein.[69] Interestingly, Lennon seems to have felt desire for his Native American sideman, Jesse Ed Davis. Twice Lennon kissed his guitarist on the mouth, only to dole out appalling violence upon him afterward. Following a drunken studio session recording the *Rock 'n' Roll* album in which John got in a fight with producer Phil Spector, outside the Los Angeles studio, John Lennon ran over to Davis and "gave Jesse Ed a passionate kiss on the mouth," according to biographer Albert Goldman. "Not to be outdone, Jesse Ed grabbed John and kissed him back," Goldman writes. Lennon screamed a homophobic slur and "knocked Jesse flat on his ass," according to Goldman.[70] Amazingly, this was not the last time that Lennon would kiss, then assault his sideman. Goldman includes a lengthy account from Davis narrating how a drunken Lennon, after being ejected from the Troubadour Club, with his fellow revelers destroyed a friend's apartment, then wrestled with Jesse Ed Davis. Lennon restrained Davis into a Nelson hold, and then, Davis told Goldman, "he started to kiss me on the mouth! He was laughin' and kissin' me on the mouth . . . then he stuck his *tongue* in my mouth. God! So I *bit* him. Bit him on the tongue."[71] Lennon then knocked out Jesse Ed with an ashtray. So we see that there were at least two John Lennons, and the dark side that violently repressed his same-sex desire did not mesh with the popular view of the peace-loving activist. Thus Kerwin Johnston and Comanche Lennon are the yin and yang of John Lennon, and as opposed but complementary forces, they experience friction. For example, the masculine Lennon is angry at Kerwin for cross-dressing, declaring that he is going to scare the elders, not realizing that the elders seem to have special intimations about such non-Western, multiple-gender traditions, as Hope Little Leader demonstrates.

Hope's name is allegorical in that the Miko Kings team represented a hope for Indian Territory Natives, that they could run things their way successfully, exercising sovereignty, and represent tribes as cultural diplomats, diplomacy being a traditional role of ball games. Choctaw co-owner of the team Lonnie Johns truly believes in the deeper purpose of the team, its role of promoting tribal diplomacy and pride. He along with others was able to imagine this team and make it a reality. Oddly enough, scramble *Lonnie Johns* and one finds that he too "is John Lenon [sic]." The hope of the Miko Kings team, and thus by extension Native Americans of the Indian Territory, is crushed when Hope Little Leader is corrupted by greed, giving in to the temptation of instant wealth, betraying the team and the Native community. Thus Custer's bunch, the Seventh Cavalry, wins and Oklahoma statehood quickly follows on the heels of this symbolic defeat. But with the aid of an indigenized Lennon and Beatles, Lena is able to reverse this historical trauma, restoring hope for Choctaw sovereignty and survivance.

As Lena Coulter acquires a depth of knowledge, her project becomes not only to learn the obscured history of this team and divine what fate befell it, but additionally to glean Ezol's lessons of language, time, and space to imagine and rewrite a new narrative history for Choctaws and other Indigenous peoples, re-visioning a new ending of the story in which Hope is imbued with great power by Hashtali, his prayer rewarded, and he hurls the winning pitch to change the destiny of Choctaws, Chickasaws, Creeks, Seminoles, and other Indian Territory tribes.[72] The discovery and rewriting of Choctaw history are not limited to historians; as D. L. Birchfield argues, if one wants to be a student of Choctaw history, one should read "Choctaw literary practitioners, such as . . . LeAnne Howe."[73] The Beatles and John Lennon in particular played a symbolic role as spiritual allies or inspiration aiding this project of imagining and re-visioning the Choctaw past to imagine a better future, serving the ends of Choctaw decolonization and tribal sovereignty. "We are what we imagine ourselves to be," concludes N. Scott Momaday.[74]

MICHAEL SNYDER is professor of English in the Division of English and Humanities, Oklahoma City Community College.

Notes

I wish to thank Thomas Hanna, who was a student in my Native American Literature course at Oklahoma City Community College, for calling my attention to the link between Ezol Day and the Lennon song "Isolation" and recalling the link between Jesse Ed Davis and John Lennon in a short paper he wrote for the class. I want to show gratitude to LeAnne Howe, who graciously spoke with me at length about my project at the 2013 NAISA conference in Saskatoon. Thanks also go to Pamela Stout, professor of English at Oklahoma City Community College, who helped me edit this manuscript and made helpful suggestions for revision.

1. D. L. Birchfield, *How Choctaws Invented Civilization and Why Choctaws Will Conquer the World* (Albuquerque: University of New Mexico Press, 2007), 295.
2. LeAnne Howe, *Miko Kings: An Indian Baseball Story* (San Francisco: Aunt Lute, 2007), 37–39, 164.
3. LeAnne Howe, *Choctalking on Other Realities* (San Francisco: Aunt Lute, 2013), 192. Howe, *Miko Kings*, 127, 46.
4. The Beatles, "Glass Onion," *The Beatles* [*The White Album*] (Apple, 1968).
5. Leanne Howe, email to the author, October 3, 2013.
6. Thomas Pynchon. *The Crying of Lot 49* (Philadelphia: Lippincott, 1966).
7. LeAnne Howe, *Shell Shaker* (San Francisco: Aunt Lute, 2001), 53.
8. Ibid., 7.
9. Patrice Hollrah, "Decolonizing the Choctaws: Teaching LeAnne Howe's *Shell Shaker*," *American Indian Quarterly* 28, no. 1/2 (Winter/Spring 2004): 84.
10. Howe, *Shell Shaker*, 145.
11. LeAnne Howe, *Evidence of Red* (Cambridge, U.K.: Salt, 2005), 89.
12. Birchfield, *Choctaws*, 57.
13. Ibid., 10.
14. Howe, *Choctalking*, 192.
15. Howe, *Miko Kings*, 43–44.
16. Howe, *Choctalking*, 174.
17. Howe, *Miko Kings*, 59.
18. Quoted in Geoffrey Giuliano, *The Lost Beatles Interviews* (New York: Plume, 1996), 38.
19. Giuliano, *Lost Beatles*, 68.
20. The Beatles, "The Continuing Story of Bungalow Bill," *The Beatles* [*The White Album*] (Apple, 1968).

21. Howe, *Miko Kings*, 39.
22. LeAnne Howe, "Ohoyo Chishba Osh: Woman Who Stretches Way Back," *Pre-Removal Choctaw History: Exploring New Paths*, ed. Greg O'Brien (Norman: University of Oklahoma Press, 2008), 34.
23. Howe, *Choctalking*, 19.
24. Angie Debo, *The Rise and Fall of the Choctaw Republic* (Norman: University of Oklahoma Press, 1934), 6.
25. Howe, *Miko Kings*, 62.
26. Ibid., 219.
27. Ibid., 48.
28. Ibid., 49.
29. Ibid., 54.
30. N. Scott Momaday, "The Man Made of Words," in *The Remembered Earth: An Anthology of Contemporary Native American Literature*, ed. Geary Hobson (Albuquerque: University of New Mexico Press), 167.
31. John Lennon, "Isolation," *John Lennon/Plastic Ono Band* (Apple, 1970).
32. John Lennon, "Imagine," *Imagine* (Apple, 1971).
33. Howe, *Miko Kings*, 127.
34. Ibid., 127.
35. Buffalo Springfield, "For What It's Worth," *Buffalo Springfield* (Atco, 1966).
36. Mark J. Mahal, "This Is Not Here," in LENNONOLOGY, ed. Chip Madinger, http://www.lennonology.com.
37. Patrick O'Waterman, "Tadodaho Leon Shenadoah," *Water Man Spouts* (January 10, 2005), http://h2oman.blogspot.com/2005/01/tadodaho-leon-shenandoah.html.
38. Jon Wiener, *Come Together: John Lennon in His Time* (New York: Random House, 1984), 175.
39. Suzan Shown Harjo, "Rewriting the Lies," in *My Soul Looks Back in Wonder: Voices of the Civil Rights Experience*, ed. Juan Williams (New York: AARP/Sterling, 2004), 190.
40. "John Lennon—On Revolution and Native Americans," online video from *The Dick Cavett Show*, 1971, https://www.youtube.com/watch?v=sRq1mp4VArA.
41. Albert Goldman, *The Lives of John Lennon* (New York: Bantam, 1989), 560–61.
42. Philip Norman, *John Lennon: The Life* (New York: HarperCollins, 2008), 720.
43. Howe, *Miko Kings*, 49.
44. The Beatles, "Because," *Abbey Road* (Apple, 1969).
45. Ibid., 49.
46. Ibid., 49, 218.
47. The Beatles, "Because."
48. Howe, *Miko Kings*, 49.
49. Ibid., 49.
50. Ibid., 160.
51. The Beatles, "I'll Follow the Sun," *Beatles for Sale* (Parlophone, 1964).

52. The Beatles, "Yellow Submarine," *Revolver* (Parlophone, 1966).
53. The Beatles, "I Am the Walrus," *Magical Mystery Tour* (Parlophone, 1967).
54. The Beatles, "Here Comes the Sun," *Abbey Road* (Apple, 1969).
55. The Beatles, "Sun King," *Abbey Road* (Apple, 1969).
56. The Beatles, "Good Day Sunshine," *Revolver* (Parlophone, 1966).
57. Howe, *Shell Shaker*, 41.
58. Maureen Cleave, "How Does a Beatle Live? John Lennon Lives Like This," *London Evening Standard* March 4, 1966, rpt. in *The Mammoth Book of The Beatles*, ed. Sean Egan (London: Constable and Robinson, 2009), 104.
59. Howe, *Miko Kings*, 218.
60. Howe, *Evidence*, 55–56.
61. Howe, *Miko Kings*, 63.
62. Ibid., 59.
63. Ibid., 88.
64. Ibid., 60.
65. Ibid., 89.
66. Norman, *John Lennon*, 310.
67. Ibid., 669. Intriguingly, John's dynamic with Paul caused insiders at Apple Records to jokingly refer to Paul as "John's Princess," punning on the brand of sports car owned by members of the band.
68. Eve Kosofsky Sedgwick, *Epistemology of the Closet* (Berkeley: University of California Press, 1989), 19.
69. Norman, *John Lennon*, 310.
70. Goldman, *Lives*, 564.
71. Ibid., 576–77.
72. Howe, *Miko Kings*, 218.
73. Birchfield, *Choctaws*, 297.
74. N. Scott Momaday, "A First American Views His Land," *The Man Made of Words: Essays, Stories, Passages* (New York: McMillan, 1998), 39.

Special Forum
Perspectives on the Israeli-Palestinian Conflict from Indigenous Studies

JEAN M. O'BRIEN AND ROBERT WARRIOR

Introduction: Indigeneity, Palestine, and Israel

THE ONGOING POLITICAL and military conflict between Israelis and Palestinians has, over the past year, made academic politics matters of public scrutiny in the United States and other places in ways reminiscent of the "culture wars" of the late 1980s and early 1990s. Most prominently, in December 2013 the membership of the American Studies Association voted decisively to endorse its elected leadership's resolution to support the call from Palestinian civil society to engage in boycotts and divestment campaigns against academic and cultural institutions supported by the state of Israel.

The Asian American Studies Association had unanimously joined that same academic boycott campaign many months before, though it was ASA's resolution that captured the attention of media in the United States, Israel, Middle Eastern Arab nations, and other places. Simultaneous with ASA's decision, the elected council of the Native American and Indigenous Studies Association (the sponsoring association of this journal) announced its own resolution in support of the academic boycott of Israeli institutions, with NAISA's resolution being the result of a multiyear process involving a group of members circulating a petition and requesting action from the council.

The political ramifications of these academic associations and some others joining the boycott campaign have been debated and discussed in many forums. Indeed, whatever one's position on the political stakes of the boycott campaign, the Israeli occupation of Palestinian lands in the West Bank and Gaza has surely been more widely discussed inside and outside of the academy than ever before.

In the midst of the sometimes heated discourse over the academic boycott campaign, *NAIS* received the two scholarly essays published here, and we have decided to present them in a special forum to highlight perspectives that two scholars in Native and Indigenous studies are bringing to bear on the variegated scholarly issues indigeneity prompts in relation to Israel and Palestine. In his contribution to the forum, Eric Cheyfitz examines the parallels between exceptionalist nationalism in the United States and modern Israel, analyzing the ways in which indigeneity undergirds, but also troubles, the deployment of nationalist discourse. Steven Salaita, on the other hand, sets out a scholarly agenda in which he works through the process by which Palestine has come to prominence in some quarters of American Indian studies and, in similar ways, in Indigenous studies more generally.

We know that many other perspectives on Israel, Palestine, Zionism, and related topics exist among scholars working in Native and Indigenous studies. The fact that these two essays came our way independently from each other and made it successfully through peer review made it compelling to us to present them together in this highlighted way. Salaita and Cheyfitz accepted our invitation to respond briefly to each other's essays, and we appreciate their willingness to do so on short notice.

Taken together, these essays and responses allow us to participate in the scholarly work we believe these issues demand. We think it says something salutary about our field, our association, and this fledgling journal that these accomplished scholars have found Native and Indigenous studies to be an academic location from which to address these vital and entangled topics.

JEAN M. O'BRIEN (*White Earth Ojibwe*), University of Minnesota
ROBERT WARRIOR (*Osage*), University of Illinois, Urbana–Champaign

Note

Please note that this forum went to press in March 2014 and has not been revised since August 2014, except to correct Steven Salaita's affiliation.

ERIC CHEYFITZ

The Force of Exceptionalist Narratives in the Israeli–Palestinian Conflict

There has been a turn, for many people, in recognizing that Manifest Destiny was a horror, and the supposed "exceptionalism" or "idealism" of American "foreign" policy—these first inhabitants from whom the land was stolen were long not treated as having American "rights," as foreigners—will not survive this evidence. We have come to a turning point in our society, where we might recognize the truth of what was done and resolve to go forward, as best we can, as a serious, multiracial society in which the stories of each person are acknowledged and the dark history which still afflicts us rejected.
—ALAN GILBERT, JOHN EVANS PROFESSOR AT THE UNIVERSITY OF DENVER, 2014

But it's hard sometimes, letting go of the stories you think you know.
—PAMELA J. OLSON, *FAST TIMES IN PALESTINE: A LOVE AFFAIR WITH A HOMELESS HOMELAND* (2013)

MY INITIAL INTEREST in the Israeli–Palestinian conflict comes from the fact that I am a Jew and one of my daughters and three of my grandchildren are citizens of Israel. But this personal connection is deeply embedded with my intellectual, scholarly, and political interest in the conflict. In this last connection, I am a member of both the American Studies Association (ASA) and the Native American and Indigenous Studies Association (NAISA) and a supporter of the resolutions published by both groups, following that of the Asian American Studies Association (AAAS), in solidarity with the 2005 call by Palestinian civil society for an academic boycott of Israeli institutions of higher education.[1] These nonbinding resolutions, it should be stressed, are focused not on individual scholars, but on Israeli academic institutions because of the complicity of these institutions with Israel state policies in Gaza; the West Bank, including East Jerusalem; and the Golan Heights. These policies, which impose martial law on the Palestinian territories and are in violation of international law, interdict the academic freedom and human rights of the Palestinians.

As the title suggests, this essay focuses *neither* on American nor Israeli exceptionalism *per se* but on how the intersection of the two narratives results in the historical denial by both nation-states of the actual history of the Israeli–Palestinian conflict—the way in which American exceptionalism reinforces that of Israel is a particular focus. As I argue, this denial, which erases the Palestinian narrative of the conflict, makes a just resolution of the conflict impossible. We should remember in what follows that nations are narratives that rationalize, or idealize, the material force of the state. That is what is implied in the formation of the *nation-state*, a synthesis of rhetorical and material power. The state, then, requires the narrative of the nation to cover its tracks. The nation is the state's alibi.

The Israeli–Palestinian conflict has been continual, at least in the formal sense, since 1917. In that year the Balfour Declaration was proclaimed in a letter from British Foreign Secretary Arthur J. Balfour to Lord Rothschild:

> His Majesty's Government views with favour the establishment in Palestine of a national home for the Jewish People, and will use their best endeavours to facilitate the achievement of this object, it being clearly understood that nothing shall be done which may prejudice the civil and religious rights of existing non-Jewish communities in Palestine, or the rights and political status enjoyed by the Jews in any other country.[2]

The Declaration is manifestly a colonial document. Edward Said notes,

> That is the declaration was made (a) by a European power, (b) about a non-European territory, (c) in flat disregard of both the presence and the wishes of the native majority resident in that territory, and (d) it took the form of a promise about this same territory to another foreign group, so that this foreign group might, quite literally, *make* this territory a national home for the Jewish people.[3]

The British transferred their colonial project in Palestine to the UN in 1947, which, without the agreement of the over 700,000 Palestinians living there or any of the Arab states in the region, partitioned the country in 1947. This led to the Arab–Israel war of 1948, which commenced with the "ethnic cleansing"[4] by Israeli forces of approximately 750,000 Palestinian residents of what became the state of Israel. In violation of international law, Israel formally instituted its colonial regime at the end of the 1967 war with the occupation of the West Bank, including East Jerusalem; the Golan Heights; and the Gaza Strip, from which Israel formally withdrew in 2005 but which the UN still regards as occupied territory because of the Israeli siege of Gaza.

I have made it my business as I am able, particularly since the 2008 Israeli attack on Gaza, to study the history of the conflict, which intersects with my field of expertise, the field in which I have published and taught for close to thirty years, that of the history of U.S. imperialism, beginning and continuing into the present moment with the displacement of Native Americans from their lands. Simply put, the United States is literally built on stolen Indian land. Along these lines, let me begin with some comments from Moshe Dayan, which I find in *The Iron Wall*, Avi Shlaim's book on the history of the Arab–

Israeli conflict, and which provide a direct link to the two exceptionalist narratives that focus this essay.

Dayan, Chief of Staff of the Israeli Defense Forces (IDF) from 1953–58, gave the funeral oration for Ro'i Rotberg, "a young farmer from Kibbutz Nahal-Oz who was murdered by Arab marauders in April 1956." In the course of the oration, Dayan admits, surprisingly perhaps, that the Israelis have no "cause . . . to complain about [the Arabs'] fierce hatred for us" because "they sit in their refugee camps in Gaza, and before their eyes we turn into our homestead the land and villages in which they and their forefathers have lived" (101). Embedded in this frank admission of a land grab is the fact of the ethnic cleansing of the Israeli portion of Palestine during the Arab–Israeli war in 1948. Thus, Dayan continues, we "should demand [Rotberg's] blood not from the Arabs but from ourselves. . . . a generation of settlers, [who] without the steel helmet and the gun barrel . . . will not be able to plant a tree or build a house" (101). In his funeral oration, then, Dayan announces quite bluntly and even proudly the fact of Israeli settler colonialism buttressed by Israeli weaponry. Underlying his words is an inescapable image of settlers circling the wagons (an image that uncannily foretells the construction of the current security wall between the West Bank and Israel). In commenting on Dayan's oration, Shlaim connects the dots linking the image to its origin in the forging of U.S. settler colonialism:

> [Dayan's] funeral oration epitomized the stark philosophy of the "Arab fighter," that is, the equivalent of what Americans used to call the Indian fighter, a type common to the second generation of settlers in a country where newcomers are forced to fight the native population. His instinctive feeling that Israel was doomed to live in continual warfare and the grim outlook that followed from it made him the symbol of a whole generation of Israeli activists or "Arab fighters." (101–2)

As someone who has focused his energies on writing and teaching the history of U.S.–American Indian conflict, what catches my attention is the parallel Shlaim draws between the Arab and the Indian fighter, between the United States and Israel as settler societies. In his book *Image and Reality of the Israel–Palestine Conflict*, Norman Finkelstein draws the same parallel:

> In fact, many in the enlightened West came to view displacement of the indigenous population of Palestine as inexorable concomitant of civilization's advance. The identification of Americans with Zionism came easily, since "the social order of the Yishuv [Jewish Community in Palestine] was built on the ethos of a frontier society, in which a pioneering settlement model set the tone." To account for the "almost complete disregard of the Arab case" by Americans, a prominent British Labour MP, Richard Crossman, explained in the mid-1940s: "Zionism after all is merely the attempt by the European Jew to build

his national life on the soil of Palestine in much the same way as the American settler developed the West. So the American will give the Jewish settler in Palestine the benefit of the doubt, and regard the Arab as the aboriginal who must go down before the march of progress."[5]

As Dayan makes clear in his funeral oration, a settler society is based on the forcible displacement of an Indigenous population: "we [the settlers] turn into our homestead the land and villages in which they [the Indigenous people] and their forefathers have lived." Typically, the settlers operate within a narrative that justifies this violence. In the cases of both American Indians and Arabs, that narrative is racist, the narrative of a superior civilization, that is, a Western one, displacing an inferior, or non-Western, one. According to Shlaim, Theodor Herzl (1860–1904), "the father of political Zionism" (2) "viewed the natives as primitive and backward. . . . He thought that as individuals they should enjoy full civil rights in a Jewish state but he did not consider them a society with collective political rights over the land in which they formed the overwhelming majority. . . . At the time of [the] issue [of the Balfour Declaration], the Jewish population of Palestine numbered some 56,000 as against an Arab population of 600,000, or less than 10 percent" (4, 7). As Shlaim notes (and I quote him here at length because his characterization of Zionism as a nationalist movement is germane to my analysis, which follows):

> The Zionist movement, which emerged in Europe in the last two decades of the nineteenth century, aimed at the national revival of the Jewish people in its ancestral home after nearly two thousand years of exile. . . . Zionism was in essence an answer to the Jewish problem that derived from two basic facts: the Jews were dispersed in various countries around the world, and in each country they constituted a minority. The Zionist solution was to end this anomalous existence and dependence on others, to return to Zion, and to attain majority status there and, ultimately, political independence and statehood. . . . Modern Zionism...was a secular movement, with a political orientation toward Palestine. Modern Zionism was a phenomenon of the late nineteenth-century Europe. It had its roots in the failure of Jewish efforts to become assimilated in Western society, in the intensification of antisemitism in Europe, and in the parallel and not unrelated upsurge of nationalism. If nationalism posed a problem to the Jews by identifying them as alien and unwanted minority, it also suggested a solution: self-determination for the Jews in a state of their own in which they would constitute a majority. Zionism, however, embodied the urge to create not merely a new Jewish state in Palestine but also a new society, based on the universal values of freedom, democracy, and social justice. (1–2)

Nationalist narratives (we could call them "myths") are always founded on contradictions that are then forgotten. In this case, the Jewish nationalist movement, Zionism, is itself founded because the Jews have been historically marginalized by Western nationalism. Nationalism is conceived as the antidote to nationalism. Jewish racism toward the Arabs is itself a reaction to or a transference of Western anti-Semitism. Racism is conceived as the antidote to racism. That is, the tendency here is to adopt the very forms of oppression from which one is seemingly in flight, which requires a forgetting, repression, or sublimation of one's history. Israeli apartheid in the West Bank and Gaza is the answer to the ghettoization of the Jews in nineteenth- and twentieth-century Europe. One must note here that Zionism is a Western European Jewish movement and so, implicitly, Arab, African, and Asian Jews are assimilated (i.e., forgotten) in this Western stereotype, though given the way political power has been historically concentrated in the hands of Western European Jews in Israel, the figure of the Jew as Western has a particular political force. What I am referring to here as a forgetting, repression, or sublimation of history goes by the name of exceptionalism. I define exceptionalism as a mode of imagining a history outside of history, as a way of reading history ahistorically in order to create a coherent narrative—one that appears to be without contradiction—that we call *The Nation*.[6] In particular, the exceptionalist mode functions to deny the violent displacement of Indigenous peoples by settler-colonialism.

Nadia Abu El-Haj, born in New York of mixed U.S./Christian and Palestinian/Muslim heritage, analyzes an important aspect of such displacement in her book *Facts on the Ground: Archaeological Practice and Territorial Self-Fashioning in Israeli Society*.[7] But before I arrive at a discussion of her book, a brief history of Abu El-Haj's tenure travails is in order because it is illustrative of the way the Israeli exceptionalist narrative has been wielded against scholars who have called it into question. The case of Dr. Norman Finkelstein, whose professionally esteemed publications are critical of Israeli state policy in Palestine, comes immediately to mind not only in its own right but also because I cite his work throughout this essay as a critique of Israeli exceptionalism. After a positive vote for tenure and promotion by the political science department at DePaul University, the university administration denied Finkelstein tenure and subsequently struck a deal with him compelling his resignation from DePaul in 2007. Under intense pressure from pro-Israel supporters, the administration's action was clearly politically motivated.[8]

Nadia Abu El-Haj is professor of anthropology at Barnard/Columbia, who was granted tenure in November 2007 in a climate of controversy over her book. According to Wikipedia:

> On August 7, 2007, an online petition against the professor was started by Paula Stern, a 1982 Barnard alumna who lives in the Israeli settlement of Ma'aleh Adumim.
>
> In response to Stern's petition, in late August a petition supporting Abu

El-Haj was initiated by Paul Manning, a linguist in the anthropology department at Trent University in Peterborough, Canada.

By the time Barnard announced that it had granted Abu El-Haj tenure, in November 2007, 2,592 people had signed the anti-tenure petition and 2,057 had signed the pro-tenure petition.[9]

On a website posted by the Deny Abu El-Haj Tenure Committee, who identify themselves as "a committee of Barnard and Columbia graduates who have never stopped caring about our alma mater," we find the following characterization of her book:

> *Facts on the Ground* is best understood as a postmodernist effort to deconstruct the existence of the ancient Hebrew kingdoms and nullify the connection between modern Jews and the ancient Hebrew people. Put simply, for Abu El-Haj, if you can deny the ancient Jewish connection to the land of Israel, you can delegitimize the current Jewish presence there. This, and not truth and research, is her goal.
>
> In *Facts on the Ground*, Abu El-Haj asserts that the ancient Israelite kingdoms are nothing but a "pure political fabrication" and "a tale best understood as the modern nation's origin myth." Despite all evidence to the contrary, Abu El-Haj puts forth the notion that the ancient Jewish presence in the Land of Israel is not a matter of history, but a mere "belief," a "tale or historical myth," and that Herodian Jerusalem was "not a Jewish city," it was "inhabited primarily by 'other' communities."[10]

In an article posted on the online edition of *Reason Magazine*, "The Case of Nadia Abu El-Haj," Jesse Walker, following an article by Richard Silverstein in *Tikun Olam* online suggests that the case against Abu El-Haj is made through the misrepresentation of her book, largely through both quoting from it out of context and misstating certain facts (Abu El-Haj does speak Hebrew, *contra* her opposition, and she does reference numerous sources that the opposition claims she ignores).[11]

In point of fact, *Facts on the Ground* does not deny "the ancient Jewish presence in the Land of Israel." Rather, it raises questions about the way, with the central help of the discipline of archaeology, the post-1948 nation of Israel projected onto an ethnically heterogeneous past, including Jews and Arabs, a history of a continuous and cohesive Jewish–Israeli history, which claims indigeneity over and against historical facts to the contrary. That is, in arguing for the relationship between nationalist ideology and archaeology, what *Facts on the Ground* questions is an *exceptionalist* Israeli–Jewish history. Among her points of focus, Abu El-Haj elaborates a colonialist process of translation that effects "the generation and designation of Hebrew names upon the geographical and historical knowledge contained within the land's known Arabic terms and names" so that the Arab (even if a *misnomer*) no longer occupied the category of native. That which was understood to be indigenous was, *by definition*, Jewish. Therefore, so too were Hebrew names, even if they had to be revived and substantiated on the landscape, via their "redemption." Settler nationhood had arrived, and the land's indigenous population had been *ideologically*, not just physically, displaced. (94–95)

While the field of Native American Studies has been busy deconstructing American exceptionalism at least since the publication of Vine Deloria Jr.'s *Custer Died for Your Sins* in 1969—a deconstruction that since the 1970s has been ongoing and intensifying in the related fields of American Studies, African American Studies, Asian American Studies, and Latino/a Studies—the exceptionalist mode of dehistoricizing history remains a driving force in U.S. political life as witnessed, to take a current and highly visible example, by Barack Obama's March 18, 2008 repudiation (in his Philadelphia speech on race) of the Reverend Jeremiah Wright's two controversial sermons: the 2003 sermon *Confusing God and Government* delivered a month after the U.S. invasion of Iraq and the sermon delivered in 2001 shortly after the 9/11 attacks, *The Day of Jerusalem's Fall*.[12] In both of these sermons Reverend Wright offers in rhetoric reminiscent of his biblical namesake, the Jewish prophet Jeremiah, a quite accurate recitation of U.S. history, which commences with the genocide of American Indians, who as members of Native nations remain a formally colonized population in the United States under the jurisdiction of federal Indian law, a kind of civil equivalent to the martial law that governs Palestinians in the occupied territories. While Israel is practicing a full-blown nineteenth-century colonialism in the Palestinian territories, U.S. American Indians, who became U.S. citizens by Congressional fiat in 1924, are living under what I have termed elsewhere a "(post)colonial" regime.[13] That is, when U.S. American Indians are in "Indian country" (the legal term for all federally controlled Indian space in the United States, including most reservation land)[14] they are living in a space the sovereignty of which is subordinated to the U.S. Hence, as they were defined in the 1831 Supreme Court case of *Cherokee Nation v. Georgia*, Indian nations remain "domestic dependent nations." It is worth noting in this respect that had they been enacted both the Oslo (1993–95) and Camp David II (2000) accords would have created the Palestinian state as a "domestic dependent nation" of Israel.[15]

It is within his unexpurgated version of U.S. history and his prophetic critique of it that Wright in his *Confusing God and Government* sermon proclaimed "God damn America," a sentence the mainstream media and the politicians it serves proceeded to take out of context in order to condemn the Reverend Wright and, through guilt by association, Barack Obama, which prompted Obama to repudiate Wright. In both sermons, the voice of Jeremiah

Wright sums up the U.S. position in the history of Western imperialism and colonialism from the Romans to the present, reminding his congregation that the United States was built on stolen Indian land with stolen African labor. While the Reverend Wright makes clear in the sermons that this history of theft is not the whole of U.S. history, he also makes clear that it is the ground of that history, a damned history, and that if the United States is to be redeemed with God's blessing, it must first own the historical grounding from which it springs and change its history to one of social justice. Until America focuses on that trajectory, as Wright acknowledges it has at certain moments in its past, God will not bless but damn America as God damned the Jews for their violations of the law of social and economic justice in the time of Jeremiah. Wright's voice is clearly biblical, the voice of his namesake; and in *Confusing God and Government* to remind his congregants of the origin of his voice, just before he reminds them that "God never fails," he asks them to "Forgive him for the 'God Damn,' that's in the Bible Lord. Blessings and cursing is in the Bible, it's in the Bible." Jeremiah's "God damn America!," then, is not simply a condemnation of America, as politicians, including most conspicuously Barack Obama, and the media played it for the public, but a Judeo-Christian call to the United States to live up to its ideals (its ideology). What could be more exceptionally American?

In particular, in the Philadelphia speech Obama felt compelled to distance himself from the notion, articulated forcefully by Wright, that the United States itself is complicit in a history of state terrorism and that within this history, as Wright notes in *The Day of Jerusalem's Fall*, is U.S. "support [. . . for Israeli] state terrorism against the Palestinians." But in spite of official denial, this history is manifest in Indian removal and genocide. It is manifest in slavery, Jim Crow, old and new (the mass incarceration of black men).[16] It is manifest in the involvement of the United States in the genocide of Native Guatemalans from the 1960s through the 1980s (representative of a brutal interventionist policy throughout Latin America in the Cold War period).[17] It is manifest in the U.S. collaboration in the Indonesian genocide of 1965,[18] the preemptive wars in Vietnam and Iraq, the ongoing war in Afghanistan and in contravention of the Geneva conventions the institution of such sites of torture and the suspension of civil liberties as Abu Ghraib and Guantanamo Bay. The Obama administration's institution of drone warfare is the most recent manifestation of this ongoing imperial history. American exceptionalism grounds itself in the denial of American imperialism so that the United States can continue to represent itself without contradiction as the "New World" of democratic promise, just as Israel represents itself as the only democracy in the Middle East as it enforces an apartheid regime in the Territories. No one to date has been able to run for national office in either country outside of the confines of exceptionalist ideology. Obama articulates this ideology in his 2009 inaugural address when he evokes typical heroic images of westward expansion and settlement without once mentioning the Native bodies dead and displaced as a result of this settlement or the ongoing Native resistance to it:

> In reaffirming the greatness of our nation, we understand that greatness is never a given. It must be earned. Our journey has never been one of shortcuts or settling for less.
>
> It has not been the path for the faint-hearted, for those who prefer leisure over work, or seek only the pleasures of riches and fame. Rather, it has been the risk-takers, the doers, the makers of things—some celebrated, but more often men and women obscure in their labor—who have carried us up the long, rugged path towards prosperity and freedom.
>
> For us, they packed up their few worldly possessions and traveled across oceans in search of a new life. For us, they toiled in sweatshops and settled the West, endured the lash of the whip and plowed the hard earth.[19]

Here is the paean to settler colonialism with a brief metonymic reference to slavery, which does not oppose it to American exceptionalism but absorbs it in the mythos and thereby neutralizes it. At the same time, I would argue, no substantive change is possible in the polity without a national recognition and critique of the national exceptionalist myth.

So while certain historians in both the U.S. and Israel have been rewriting history against the exceptionalist myth,[20] these histories have not registered significantly in the sphere of national political action. What we have at the present juncture is the intersection of these two exceptionalist histories and their reinforcement of each other. In this respect, it is important to emphasize, both exceptionalisms have a common origin in the Old Testament narrative of the Jewish journey to the " promised land."[21] The Puritan sects that in the first half of the seventeenth century invaded and settled in the northeast coast of what would become the United States imagined themselves in their writings as repeating the sacred journey of the Jews, as being God's "chosen people," "a light unto the nations," "a city upon a hill."[22] The Indians, who were already settled in the Americas, the Arabs who were already settled in Palestine, were projected as a temporary impediment to God's plan, a savage test from God. In his 1836 oration, "Eulogy on King Philip" (the Wampanoag sachem Metacomet), the Pequot minister William Apess rewrote this providential history from an Indigenous point of view, which, with Montaignesque irony, cast the Indians as the true Christians, extending kinship and thereby hospitality to all, and the Puritans as the savages. Writing in his memoir *Journal of an Ordinary Grief* (1973) of the Nakba (the Palestinian narrative of the catastrophe of ethnic cleansing in 1948), the Palestinian poet Mahmoud Darwish rewrites Israeli exceptionalist history with his own sense of irony:

> The Israelis used the exit as an excuse to claim we had no attachment to our homeland and were therefore not worthy of one if we could so easily leave it behind. But they deceive only themselves when they believe their own claims, for they supplemented the prevailing rumor that the exit was temporary with guns and daggers that gave the Arabs a strong incentive to leave. They offered them the following option: either death or departure for a few days. Emptying Palestine of its Arab inhabitants was not an emergency measure imposed by circumstances, but part of an ongoing Zionist strategy before the establishment of the state, during the [1948] War, and after. They carried out this strategy violently with their weapons, and justified it on religious grounds from the example of Joshua Son of Nun and the text "The Day of the Lord is a day of terror." And they justified it on secular grounds from their own practices. . . . And in all the villages they occupied afterward they gathered the inhabitants in the main square and made them stand in the sun for several hours. Then they chose the handsomest young men and shot them dead in front of the other villagers in order to force them to leave, in order to let the news of the massacre spread to villages not yet occupied, and to purge their repressed historical resentment.[23]

What buttresses Israeli exceptionalism and seems to lend it an unassailable legitimacy is the narrative of the Holocaust. But as Norman Finkelstein argues in his book *The Holocaust Industry*, it was not until the 1967 Arab–Israeli war that either the Holocaust or Israel became important to American Jewish life and to America:

> From its founding in 1948 through the June 1967 war, Israel did not figure centrally in American strategic planning. As the Palestinian Jewish leadership prepared to declare statehood, President Truman waffled, weighing domestic considerations (the Jewish vote) against State Department alarm (support for a Jewish state would alienate the Arab world). To secure U.S. interests in the Middle East, the Eisenhower Administration balanced support for Israel and for Arab nations, favoring, however, the Arabs.[24]

But, Finkelstein continues, "Then came the June war. Impressed by Israel's overwhelming display of force, the United States moved to incorporate it as a strategic asset. . . . Military and economic assistance began to pour in as Israel turned into a proxy for U.S. power in the Middle East" (20). This strategic direction has only intensified in the post–9/11 world as the West reimagined itself in opposition to what it understood as a barbarous Islam (a reversion in a way to an old colonialist vision or simply a continuation of that vision).

Following the 1967 war, Finkelstein notes, "To protect their strategic asset, American Jewish elites 'remembered' the Holocaust. The conventional account is that they did so because, at the time of the June war, they believed Israel to be in mortal danger and were thus gripped by fears of a 'second

Holocaust.' This claim does not withstand scrutiny"(24). What Finkelstein argues is that although Israel clearly had military superiority in both the 1948 and 1956 wars, it was more vulnerable, isolated from the international community, in both, whereas "Israel quickly proved to be far less vulnerable in 1967 than in its independence struggle," where it "suffered 6,000 casualties. . . . Israeli and American leaders knew beforehand that Israel would easily prevail in a war with the Arab states. This reality became strikingly obvious as Israel routed its Arab neighbors in a few days" (25).[25]

Memories of the Holocaust did not reemerge at a time of Jewish vulnerability, then, but precisely at a time of Jewish or, more specifically, Israeli strength, at a time when Israel expanded imperially to include the West Bank, Gaza, and the Golan, a prelude to the expansion of settlements that continues to the present moment. Thus, Finkelstein concludes, "Once ideologically recast, The Holocaust (capitalized as I have previously noted) proved to be the perfect weapon for deflecting criticism of Israel" (30) at a time when Israel was embarking on clearly imperial ventures. Further the capitalization of "The Holocaust" points to its exclusivist or exceptionalist construction:

> Two central dogmas underpin the Holocaust framework: (1) The Holocaust marks a categorically unique historical event; (2) The Holocaust marks the climax of an irrational, eternal Gentile hatred of Jews. Neither of these dogmas figured at all in public discourse before the June 1967 war; and, although they became the centerpieces of Holocaust literature, neither figures at all in genuine scholarship on the Nazi holocaust. On the other hand, both dogmas draw on important strands of Judaism and Zionism. (41–42)

This framework effectively places "The Holocaust" outside history and thus outside the processes of historical analysis. It is not a catastrophe to be understood in comparison with other holocausts (the Native American, the Armenian, the genocide in Rwanda, for example). It is not to be understood—indeed, it cannot be understood, as is commonly asserted—it can only be viewed with awe. Indeed, its very designation as "*The* Holocaust," implicitly erases, denies, or subordinates other holocausts, as Ward Churchill has argued.[26] Within this context, Jewish suffering becomes unique—who would dare to suggest that the suffering of the Palestinian people under Jewish occupation compares in any way to the suffering of the Jewish people under the Nazis?—and to suggest otherwise, even if one is careful to note that the Jewish holocaust and the Nakba are not equivalent, is a form of anti-Semitism. The exceptionalist structure of "*The* Holocaust," then, becomes *sui generis* a justification for the state of Israel no matter what suffering the state may have caused and be causing the Palestinian people. And just as the exceptionalist structure of "The Holocaust" rules out other holocausts, so the exceptionalist structure of Israeli history, which is structured by "The Holocaust" narrative, rules out competing or contradictory narratives, specifically the narrative of the Nakba.

In March 2004 I gave a paper, "The Force of Translation in the Foundation of U.S. Federal Indian Law," at the Justice Across Cultures conference at the International Center for Ethics, Justice, and Public Life of Brandeis University. Presenting at the same conference was Omar M. Dajani, a professor of law at the University of the Pacific. Dajani had "served as senior legal advisor to the Palestinian negotiating team from 1999 to 2001 while working in the Palestinian Territories" and as such was present at the Camp David negotiations in 2000, which failed to produce a settlement between Israel and the Palestinians. Concerning this failure, which in the U.S.–Israeli narrative is blamed on the intransigence of the Palestinians, Dajani remarks:

> the single thing that is most likely to bring peace; i.e., an unequivocal commitment by Israel to end its military occupation of the West Bank, Gaza Strip, Golan Heights, and Shebaa Farms and return those lands to Palestinians, Syrians, and Lebanese . . . has not yet been offered.
>
> Americans tend to say, "Oh, Arabs and Jews have been fighting forever and will continue to fight forever." Not true. This is a recent conflict with (primarily) a territorial focus. Although Israel offered to return much of the West Bank and Golan Heights in 2000, it insisted at the time on retaining 5–10 percent of the West Bank and the Golan Heights' frontage on the Sea of Galilee. One may say that the Palestinians were inflexible for turning down the offer, but would Americans accept to cede 5–10 percent of our own country to a foreign power particularly if it included New York and San Francisco and the Mississippi River? There is tremendous opportunity for peace, but it must include an end to the occupation. That is the critical issue.[27]

Of the Camp David negotiations, citing "Robert Malley, a key American negotiator," Finkelstein reports: "Although accounts of the [Ehud] Barak [Israeli prime minister at the time] proposal significantly differ, all knowledgeable observers concur that it 'would have meant that territory annexed by Israel would encroach deep inside the Palestinian state' (Malley), dividing the West Bank into multiple, disconnected enclaves, and offering land swaps that were of neither equal size nor equal value" (*Image and Reality*, xxi). What Dajani told me at the conference was that at the start of the negotiations in 2000 the Palestinians wanted to present a narrative, their narrative, of the conflict; but that the U.S. and Israeli negotiators were not interested in listening; they wanted instead, simply, to get down to the facts on the ground.[28] The problem to this approach is that the facts on the ground cannot be separated from the narratives in which they are embedded; and up and into the present moment the narrative that has dominated the conflict is the Israeli exceptionalist narrative, reinforced by its imbrication, as I have tried to suggest, with the narrative of American exceptionalism. Both of these narratives are driven by an ideology of manifest destiny that is fundamentally deaf to the narrative of an autonomous Palestinian state on the West Bank and Gaza.

Indeed, as the U.S.'s quixotic quest to revive peace negotiations between Israel and Palestine began again in late 2013, the Israeli prime minister, Benjamin Netanyahu, asserted that "'the real key to peace,' 'the minimal requirement' and 'an essential condition'" is "that the Palestinians recognize Israel as a Jewish state," a demand the Palestinians refuse precisely because it institutes the Israeli exceptionalist narrative as authoritative. As *The New York Times* reports, "At its heart, it is a dispute over a historical narrative that each side sees as fundamental to its existence."[29] Until the United States and Israel are willing to listen to and hear the Palestinian narrative, I believe the conflict will continue. This narrative necessarily includes the legitimacy of Hamas, based both on its popular victory in the 2006 parliamentary elections and now on its governance of Gaza, but a narrative that at present must imagine the reconciliation of Hamas and the Palestinian Authority on the West Bank.[30] Further, I would argue that the U.S.'s inability or refusal to hear the Palestinian narrative is intimately linked to its inability/refusal to hear the narrative of Native American genocide, which it has never officially acknowledged. In the case of both countries, the acknowledgment of these "other" narratives is necessary if historical trajectories are to be redirected toward social justice. For one is either a prisoner of one's historical narrative or liberated by it.

At present, both the United States and Israel are prisoners of their exceptionalist narratives. This captivity is summarized in a blog dated December 22, 2013, by Richard Falk, at the time UN Special Rapporteur on the situation of human rights in the Palestinian occupied territories since 1967:

> Israel has evidently not perceived such a conflict-resolving outcome [even under the favorable conditions of the Oslo or Roadmap guidelines] as being in its national interest, and has not been given any sufficient incentive by the United States or the UN to scale back its ambitions, which include continuous settlement expansion, control over the whole of Jerusalem, denial of Palestinian rights of return, appropriation of water and land resources, intrusive, one-sided, and excessive security demands, and an associated posture that opposes a viable Palestinian state ever coming into existence, and is even more opposed to give any credence to proposals for a single secular binational state.

Falk notes that "this unreasonable diplomatic posture . . . attains plausibility only because of Israel's disproportionate influence on the intermediary mechanisms and its own media savvy in projecting its priorities." A significant part of this "media savvy" I would say is the way the Israel government manipulates its exceptionalist narrative so that, as Falk remarks, "Palestine and its leadership is mainly blamed for the failures of the peace process to end the conflict by a mutually agreed solution." Without access to the media, particularly the mainstream U.S. media where the Palestinian voice is silenced, the Palestinian narrative cannot be heard with the result that the Israeli narrative becomes the *only* narrative. Consequently, "Israel's extreme unreasonableness in relation to resolution of the conflict," buttressed "by . . . U.S. partisanship" appears reasonable.

Within this context, where the irrational appears rational, Falk notes that "the American Secretary of State, John Kerry," who is fronting the U.S. peace initiative, can make "the gross disparity in position and capabilities of the two sides" appear symmetrical by referring to the "painful concessions that both sides would have to make if the negotiations are to succeed." Among its other effects, such talk erases Israel's continual violation of international law and Palestinian human rights beginning with the 1967 occupation of Palestinian territory and the institution of its ever-expanding settlement program. Given this "gross disparity" in power, Falk questions the use of "the language of conflict" to describe the facts on the ground. But while Israel may be winning the material war, Falk remarks, "this perception is deeply misleading because it overlooks what might be called the other war, that is, the Legitimacy War that the Palestinians are winning, and given the history of decolonization, seems to have a good chance of controlling the political outcome of the struggle."[31] Along these lines, it would appear that the international community is increasingly listening to a Palestinian narrative, which calls into question Israeli exceptionalism. This Palestinian narrative is reflected, for example, in the Boycott, Divestment, and Sanctions movement, instituted in 2005 by a significant number of organizations in Palestinian civil society.

The asymmetry of power to which Falk refers engineers the erasure of the Palestinian narrative by the exceptionalist narratives of the United States and Israel. Nowhere is this erasure more evident than in Obama's erasure in his Philadelphia speech of Jeremiah Wright's rewriting of the exceptionalist narrative of U.S. history:

> But the remarks [of Wright] that have caused this recent firestorm weren't simply controversial. They weren't simply a religious leader's effort to speak out against perceived injustice. Instead, they expressed a profoundly distorted view of this country—a view that sees white racism as endemic, and that elevates what is wrong with America above all that we know is right with America; a view that sees the conflicts in the Middle East as rooted primarily in the actions of stalwart allies like Israel, instead of emanating from the perverse and hateful ideologies of radical Islam.

Within the U.S. exceptionalist narrative, racism is not "endemic." We are to forget, for example, the continuing discrepancies in wealth between African American, Latino, and Native communities and the rest of the United States and the concomitant discrepancies in incarceration rates. Likewise, within the exceptionalist narrative, Israel plays no part in triggering the "conflicts of the Middle East," which are solely instigated, apparently, by "the perverse and hateful ideologies of radical Islam." Obama plays the "good Arab, bad Arab" (derivative of the "good Indian, bad Indian") card here in exonerating an exceptional Israel.

If it is true, as Falk suggests, that while losing the current "conflict" (if we can call it that), the Palestinians are winning "the Legitimacy War" and thus "given the history of decolonization . . . have a good chance of controlling the political outcome of the struggle," then we can ask what form this outcome will take. To this question at this moment I can offer only the following.

During the first Gulf War, when I was teaching at Southern Methodist University in Dallas, Texas, I was invited by a local temple to speak about the state of affairs in the Middle East. My talk focused on the fact that in espousing the Western position, the Jews seemed to have forgotten the narrative in which we were originally a Middle Eastern people, living in both comity and conflict with the ancestors of present-day Arabs, in which, after the destruction of the Second Temple by the Romans, we were dispersed, many of us into a Christian Western Europe that marginalized us through exile, torture, forced conversion, and finally the six million murders of the Nazi holocaust, a holocaust to which the United States along with the rest of the West was largely a passive observer, and in which the Palestinians played no part. In light of this other narrative, which is certainly powerful but unexceptional (unexceptional because shared with the histories of other peoples), I suggested to the congregation that Israel should and could reimagine itself not as a proxy of the West but as a Middle Eastern state that because of its diasporic histories could act as legitimate mediator for peace and justice in the region. But for this other narrative to take hold, and at the present moment it seems quite fantastic, Israel must first acknowledge the narrative of Palestinian liberation from Israeli bondage.

ERIC CHEYFITZ is Ernest I. White Professor of American Studies and Humane Letters at Cornell University.

Notes

An earlier version of this essay appeared in *Notes on Palestine/Israel* 3 (Spring 2012): 4–12, published by Cornell Students for Justice in Palestine. A version of the essay was also given as The A. D. White Invitational Lecture at Cornell University, February 5, 2014. I would like to thank Timothy Murray, the director of the Society, and Brett de Bary (interim director) for affording me this opportunity.

1. It should be noted the AAAS and ASA resolutions have been endorsed by a vote of the membership, while the NAISA resolution is at the moment endorsed only by the Council of the organization.

2. Avi Shlaim, *The Iron Wall: Israel and the Arab World* (New York: Norton, 2001), 7. Further citations from this book will be in the body of my text.

3. Edward W. Said, *The Question of Palestine* (1979; New York: Vintage Books, 1992), 15–16.

4. This is the formal term used by Ilan Pappe in his book *The Ethnic Cleansing of Palestine* (Oxford, U.K.: Oneworld Publications, 2007). Avi Shlaim points in the direction that Pappe takes without exactly going that way: "Although the wording of Plan D [the Israeli plan of expulsion, which Pappe also references] was vague, the objective was to clear the interior of the country of hostile and potentially hostile Arab elements, and in this sense it provided a warrant for expelling civilians. By implementing Plan D in April and May [of 1948], the Haganah thus directly and decisively contributed to the birth of the Palestinian refugee problem" (31).

5. Norman G. Finkelstein, *Image and Reality of the Israel–Palestine Conflict*, 2nd ed. (1995; London: Verso, 2003), xiv–xv. Brackets in the original.

6. I have used this formulation of American exceptionalism in my essay "Disinformation: The Limits of Capitalism's Imagination and the End of Ideology," which will appear in *boundary 2* 41, no. 3.

7. Nadia Abu El-Haj, *Facts on the Ground: Archaeological Practice and Territorial Self-Fashioning in Israeli Society* (Chicago: the University of Chicago Press, 2001). Further citations from this book will appear in the body of my text.

8. For a discussion of the pro-Israeli attacks on Finkelstein, Abu El-Haj, and others see Eric Cheyfitz, "The Corporate University, Academic Freedom, and American Exceptionalism," *South Atlantic Quarterly* 108, no. 4 (Fall 2009). Parts of that essay have been incorporated in this essay.

9. http://en.wikipedia.org/wiki/Nadia_Abu_El_Haj.

10. http://www.nadiaabuelhaj.com/. This website and hence these exact quotes no longer exist. However, the petition to deny Abu El-Haj tenure, which contains the charges against her represented in these quotes, can be found at http://www.petitiononline.com/barnard/petition.html.

11. Jesse Walker, "The Case of Nadia Abu El-Haj," http://reason.com/blog/2007/08/18/the-case-of-nadia-abu-el-haj.

12. Barack Obama, "We the People, in Order to Form a More Perfect Union," March 18, 2003, at http://www.nytimes.com/2008/03/18/us/politics/18text-obama.html?pagewanted=all; Jeremiah Wright, "Confusing God and Government," April 13, 2003, at http://www.blackpast.org/2008-rev-jeremiah-wright-confusing-god-and-government; "The Day of Jerusalem's Fall," September 16, 2001 at http://blakfacts.blogspot.com/2008/03/day-of-jerusalems-fall.html.

13. See Eric Cheyfitz, "The (Post)Colonial Construction of Indian Country: U.S. American Indian Literatures and Federal Indian Law," in *The Columbia Guide to American Indian Literatures of the United States since 1945*, ed. Eric Cheyfitz, 1–124 (New York: Columbia University Press, 2006).

14. See Title 18, Section 1151, of the U.S. Code.

15. On the Oslo accords, see Finkelstein, *Image and Reality of the Israel–Palestine Conflict,* 172–83. I will discuss the Camp David II further along.

16. See Michelle Alexander, *The New Jim Crow: Mass Incarceration in the Age of Colorblindness* (New York: New Press, 2010).

17. See "Guatemala Memory of Silence: Report of the Commission for Historical Clarification Conclusions and Recommendations (1999)," established through the Accord of Oslo on 23 June 1994 (Prologue). See in particular "Conclusions," sections 13–14, 31–33.

18. See Andre Vltchek, *Indonesia: Archipelago of Fear* (London: Pluto Press, 2012). Kindle Edition, locations 776–958.

19. Barack Obama, "Inaugural Address," January 20, 2009, at http://www.nytimes.com/2009/01/20/us/politics/20text-obama.html?pagewanted=all. No pagination.

20. Shlaim and El-Haj are clearly examples of counterexceptionalist narratives in the case of Israel. In the United States case, see for example: Richard Drinnon's groundbreaking *Facing West: The Metaphysics of Indian-Hating and Empire Building* (New York: New American Library, 1980). The Donald Pease/Amy Kaplan anthology *Cultures of United States. Imperialism* (Durham, N.C.: Duke University Press, 1993) was instrumental in constructing a counterexceptionalist narrative.

21. See Robert Allen Warrior, "Canaanites, Cowboys, and Indians: Deliverance, Conquest, and Liberation Theology Today," *Christianity and Crisis* 49, no. 12 (September 11, 1989), 261–65. In this essay, Warrior provides a succinct critique of the Exodus narrative in order to argue that whereas the narrative provides a basis for the liberation theology of traditionally underrepresented communities it cannot do so for Indigenous peoples, precisely because Jewish liberation is predicated on the displacement (ethnic cleansing, genocide) of an Indigenous people, the Canaanites.

22. The urtext in this case is John Winthrop's address to Puritan settlers, "A Model of Christian Charity."

23. Mahmound Darwish, *Journal of an Ordinary Grief*, trans. Ibrahim Muhawi (New York: Archipelago Books, 2010), 18.

24. Norman G.Finkelstein, *The Holocaust Industry: Reflection on the Exploitation of Jewish Suffering*, Second Paperback Edition (2000; New York: Verso, 2003), 17–18. Further citations appear in the body of my text.

25. It should be noted that Shlaim and Finkelstein have very different interpretations of Israel's motives for its preemptive strike starting the Six-Day War. For Shlaim, it was "a defensive war" on Israel's part (242), while for Finkelstein "Israel's overarching aim was to extirpate any and all manifestations of Arab 'radicalism'—i.e. independence and modernization" and it also offered Israel an opportunity to fulfill its territorial destiny" (*Image and Reality*, 143).

26. Ward Churchill, *A Little Matter of Genocide: Holocaust and Denial in the Americas, 1492 to the Present* (San Francisco: City Lights Books, 1997).

27. These remarks were formerly posted on a website that no longer exists. But in a personal communication with me Professor Dajani has confirmed that they are his words and given me permission to publish them.

28. Personal communication with Omar Dajani in which he affirmed this statement and gave permission to publish it.

29. Jodi Rudoren, "Sticking Point in Peace Talks: Recognition of a Jewish State," *The New York Times*, January 1, 2014 at http://www.nytimes.com/2014/01/02/world/middleeast/sticking-point-in-peace-talks-recognition-of-a-jewish-state.html?_r=0.

30. As of June 2014, such a reconciliation has tentatively taken place. But its implementation in the face of Israeli resistance remains to be seen.

31. Richard Falk, "Northern Ireland and the Israel/Palestine 'Peace Process,'" at *Global Justice in the 21st Century*, http://richardfalk.wordpress.com/2013/12/22/northern-ireland-and-the-israelpalestine-peace-process/.

STEVEN SALAITA

Inter/Nationalism from the Holy Land to the New World: Encountering Palestine in American Indian Studies

THIS ESSAY EXPLORES the conditions rendering Palestine, as both symbolic and living space and site of conflict, of interest to the field of American Indian studies (a broad field with degrees of overlap with Indigenous studies, Pacific Island studies, ethnic studies, and so forth). Numerous factors have contributed to this phenomenon, all of which illuminate valuable contexts of decolonial scholarship and advocacy. Understanding the conditions leading to what I term inter/nationalism (described below) among Natives and Palestinians offers crucial insight into the scholarly and material possibilities of American Indian studies and a variety of amenable fields. In particular, Native–Palestinian inter/nationalism forces us to assess the viability of, and the ethical questions inherent to, the scholarly imperatives of national liberation and its aftermath.

I mainly focus on American Indian studies rather than on the more general Indigenous studies not as an overt political decision, but because this article is largely limited to North American nations. When I examine other areas of the world, I try to offer appropriate nomenclature, though all taxonomical terms used to describe Indigenous peoples are somehow contested (including the term "Indigenous"). Indeed, one of my goals is to undermine the mechanical analyses of naming, which produce conversations fundamentally entrapped in the dictates of colonization, thereby impeding the invocation of more pressing questions. This goal is not intended to demean the importance of various modes of identification; rather, I suggest that naming usually consigns us to the realm of symbolism at the expense of the intricate matters of liberatory dialogue and practice that render naming so complex and difficult in the first place—a situation arising from the peculiar juridical and discursive conventions of colonial practice.

With the term "inter/nationalism" I emphasize action and dialogue across borders, both natural and geopolitical—not the nationalism of the nation-state, but of the nation itself, as composed of heterogeneous communities functioning as self-identified collectives attached to particular landbases (something I explore more fully below). Inter/nationalism is a way to compare nationalisms, to put them into conversation, but also to examine how the invention and evolution of national identities necessarily rely on international dialectics. An interesting conversation that has developed recently in American Indian studies is the role of Palestine in the field, which forms the nucleus of this project. I am not merely interested in elucidating the processes by which Palestine has become a topic of interest in American Indian studies, although I will do that, but also in exploring the implications of incorporating Palestine into the field and the comparative possibilities that exist when it happens.

I have discussed this topic before. My book *The Holy Land in Transit* was published in 2006, but I compiled most of the research for it in the early 2000s. In the book, I look at some of the ways colonial discourses in North America and Palestine arise from the same moral and philosophical narratives of settlement, examining how modern Palestinian and Native literatures incorporate and react to those discourses. Back then, there was good source material, some of which I had to mine from old documents, but the comparison of Palestine and Native America was pretty undeveloped. Ward Churchill had done some comparative analysis, as had Norman Finkelstein, neither especially strong.[1] Robert Warrior had long before published his classic essay "Canaanites, Cowboys, and Indians"[2] and the American Indian Movement had released numerous statements in support of Palestinian nationhood.[3]

Thus I was not bereft of materials, but over the past few years, comparison of Natives and Palestinians has reached a level of sophistication and complexity I never could have imagined in 2006. Before I sort out what is happening in these comparisons, let me take a look at some of the reasons comparison of Natives and Palestinians has increased in recent years. I believe there are three primary factors, each with its own set of contradictions and subtexts:

1. The proliferation of blogs and social media where people are able to argue, inform, share, and theorize, however superficially (or, in some cases, with sophistication). These platforms lend themselves to all sorts of comparisons, usually for the sake of rhetorical persuasion. The benefits and detriments of social media to activism and scholarship are wide-ranging and much contested, so it is difficult to quantify exactly how influential new media have been on the proliferation of comparison among Natives and Palestinians. Social media platforms, however, document the extent to which the comparison has entered into the consciousness of a certain demographic: that of the intellectual engaged in public discourse around decolonization.

2. Palestine scholars and activists have increasingly been using the language of indigeneity and geocultural relationships to describe the political,

economic, and legal positions of Palestinians. For instance, the 2007 United Nations Declaration of the Rights of Indigenous Peoples, which ultimately binds no state to legal recrimination, has caused significant trepidation among the Zionist right, who see the application of the document to Palestinians as a delegitimization of Israeli claims to the Holy Land.[4] A noteworthy feature of the Palestinian claim to indigeneity, made largely at grassroots levels, is the effect an Indigenous positionality has on statehood bids as facilitated by the Palestinian Authority. Through claims to indigeneity, Palestinians reject the neocolonial processes of state diplomacy in favor of decolonial narratives of global scope. The appropriation of such language is a rhetorical act meant to situate—rightly, based on considerable evidence—Palestinian dispossession in a specific framework of colonial history rather than as an exceptional set of events brought forth by ahistorical circumstances. The language also identifies a perceived sociohistorical familiarity with other dispossessed communities, in this case North American indigenes. The declaration that Palestinians are not merely native or original but *indigenous* to the land colonized by Israel, not a completely new phenomenon but one growing in frequency, alters a number of crucial factors of Palestinian strategies of decolonization, in particular the relationship of human rights organizations with international law, the comparative possibilities in fields such as ethnic and Indigenous studies, and both intellectual and physical deployment of Palestinian nationalism into transnational spaces.

3. The most important reason for the proliferation of comparative discourses is the Boycott, Divestment, and Sanctions movement (BDS). Boycott of Israeli institutions or of the state itself has a long, albeit uneven, history in the Arab world. When I discuss BDS, I have in mind a specific call for cultural and academic boycott issued by nearly 200 organizations representing Palestinian civil society.[5] Thus BDS is not a governmental or corporate initiative, but neither is it spontaneous or organic, for it arises from a long history of decolonial advocacy on an international scale. Space limitations disallow even a broad history of BDS. Narrowly, it can be identified as an initiative of Palestinian civil society to pressure the Israeli state to comply with international laws against colonialism and military occupation, using nonviolent methods of resistance as opposed to traditional diplomatic and dialogic strategies that have repeatedly failed (peace talks, for example, or multicultural programming). Numerous Native writers and activists have taken up or support BDS. The participation of American Indian studies scholars in BDS, best exemplified by NAISA's "Declaration of Support for the Boycott of Israeli Academic Institutions," brings to the movement a worldly orientation that it otherwise lacks and without which it would be intellectually and experientially circumscribed.[6] (I use "worldly" in a Saidian context, as a mode of

engaging cross-border discourses that counteract the provincialism of colonial monologues.) The role of American Indian studies in BDS is performative (that is, critical to many central questions of the field) and not reflexive (or uninterested in appeasing racialized appeals to credibility). For many Native scholars, BDS is another element in the complex process of realizing Indigenous national aspirations.

Other reasons for the increase in comparisons of Natives and Palestinians include the ascension of Palestine as a test case of one's decolonial/leftist/scholarly credibility; the success of the Palestinian national movement in convincing greater numbers of people around the world to support or even identify with its cause (aided by increased Israeli belligerence and its dissemination in alternative media); the growth of Arab American studies, a field to which Palestine is central, in the academic spaces of ethnic studies, where it has encountered American Indian and Indigenous studies; and the increased emphasis in American Indian and Indigenous studies on transnational and comparative methodologies, which has led scholars from the Pacific, North America, and South America to Palestine both intellectually and physically. We can read the expanding geographies of American Indian studies as a means of grounding Native nations into their own liberatory spaces (geopolitical and intellectual) as a precursor to, or prerequisite for, engaging Palestine. The topographies of Indian Country become the groundwork of a global decolonial project.

This piece is not meant to be a part two of *The Holy Land in Transit*. Rather, I conceptualize it as a synthesis of important comparative trends in American Indian studies and subsequently an analysis of the many roles Palestine plays in the development of ethics, innovations, and debates in American Indian studies, with a particular interest in theories of decolonization. Before I enter into these analyses, I offer a final qualification, one that highlights the limits of inter/national work. While there is much to support the effectiveness of comparative scholarship and to support intercommunal approaches for theory, activism, service, and pedagogy, there are problems inherent in comparing cultural practice rather than examining contexts of intellectual and historical interchange across the restrictive categories of academic labor and the physical constraints of geopolitical borders. I am wary of moves that, even inadvertently, compartmentalize the complexities of formal and informal cultural practice into comprehensible phenomena sorted within the taxonomies of Western epistemology. I would suggest, then, that it is a mistake to orient comparative scholarship around the ceremonial or the spiritual and look instead at sets of historicized encounters made in the past or that have the potential to happen in the future.

The New New Canaan

American Indian studies has recently discovered Palestine at an institutional level—scholars in the field are now producing systematic analyses of Palestine as a geography of interest (and in some ways crucial) to our understanding of decolonization in North America. In what ways does the presence of Palestine in the field shape and define its limits and possibilities? What are the terms and frameworks for useful comparative scholarship? Are there material politics at stake in comparing North America and Palestine?

There are identifiable conditions in which Native scholars have taken up the issue of Palestine. Those conditions accommodate complicated sites of material politics (by which I mean economic systems, activist communities, electoral processes, educational paradigms, and modes of resistance). In accessing those sites, recent scholarship has aspired to relationships that go beyond theoretical innovation by concomitantly emphasizing the practices and possibilities of decolonization.[7] If early settlers conceptualized North America as a New Canaan (evidenced by the numerous towns across the United States named Canaan or New Canaan), then the role Israel plays in current American imperial practices extends the metaphor by using the immutable legitimacy of its colonial enterprise as further justification for the permanence of a federal United States under whose ultimate jurisdiction Indigenous nations will remain. America thus becomes a New Canaan all over again, invigorated by the emergence of a nation-state atop the original Canaan.

Although North America was settled by different national groups, colonization of the so-called New World has been infused with a particular biblical narrative of salvation, redemption, and destiny. Settlers assumed the role of Joshua crossing the river Jordan into the Promised Land, where God commanded them to exterminate the Indigenous populations and establish for themselves a beatific nation on a land of milk and honey underused and unappreciated by the natives.[8] The English, Puritans most specifically, were the most avid proponents of this view, but vast geographies of North America were overwhelmed by settlers and missionaries animated by Godly purpose. Even in acknowledging the variegated, often conflicting, narratives of New World settlement, multitudinous sources illustrate that from its earliest moments, the United States has been beholden to a holy-land ethos, articulated in various ways throughout the enterprise of European settlement.[9] The mutual ideology underlying the relationship of North America and the Holy Land encompasses a teleology of divine fulfillment that must occur through the creation of beatified nations.

As such, the emergence of Zionism in Europe in the late nineteenth century entered a dialectic with the project of American settlement whose implications persist in the close relationship between the United States and Israel, apparent in military aid, security cooperation, and foreign policy. It is actually in the complex discursive and psychological spaces of ideology, however, that the two states most closely align. The relationship is built through particular articulations of belonging that codify national identity into the mythologies of colonial domination and military conquest. Both Israel and the United States are relentlessly exceptional—and they are exceptional, ironically, only together.

Through identification and assessment of those connections, scholars in American Indian studies have recently made important advances in inter/national analysis. For instance, there has been much reflection on the relationship of Zionism with global systems of imperialism, militarization, plutocracy, and the neoliberal economies that undercut Indigenous self-determination in numerous parts of the world. American support for Israel illuminates the breadth of actors and actions involved in the continued occupation of Native lands in North America. Israel's conduct in the world, beyond its mistreatment of Palestinians, affects the health and economies of Indigenous communities worldwide, Indian Country among them.[10]

Two interesting things arise from these advances in inter/national analysis. The first is the transformation of Native peoples from complex political subjects into metaphorical objects of decolonial credibility. Indians have become actors in the rhetorical battlegrounds of the Israel—Palestine conflict, wherein they comprise an imagined subject position of ontological verisimilitude to which both Zionist Jews and Palestinians aspire. Many with an interest in the Israel—Palestine conflict recognize in Indians a sort of moral authority on the subject of dispossession with which they seek to be associated, a thoroughly problematic but lucid phenomenon, one that informs the moral and historical parameters of Holy Land discourse. As a result, appeals to Native authority become inscribed in the very language of Israeli settlement and Palestinian decolonization.

For Palestinians, such appeals to Native authority as a way to accrue decolonial legitimacy are inherently anachronistic: neither Zionists nor anti-Zionists need to be correct for anything to change in our understanding of Palestine, not to mention our understanding of North America (which gets trivialized and dehistoricized in this type of situation). Indeed, the historical dispossession of Indians has often resembled, and in some instances has more than resembled, the mistreatment of Jews, particularly in Spain on the eve of Columbus's voyage and in Eastern Europe after the industrial revolution. But these realities do not preclude Palestinian dispossession from also resembling that of Indians. In fact, Palestinian dispossession also often resembles historical Jewish dispossession; that the Palestinians' current oppressors self-identify as Jewish does not in any way diminish this simple fact of history. Thus the crude comparisons made for the sake of rhetorical expediency stop short of analyzing the historical, economic, and discursive forces that inform the American–Israeli alliance and bind Natives and Palestinians to the same anticolonial polity.

The second thing that comes out of these advances in inter/national analysis is what we learn about the practice of American Indian studies as an academic enterprise that exists beyond the corridors of academe, by which I mean the element of the field, not always consistent but omnipresent, that compels its participants to practice communal engagement and pursue social justice (to use an old-fashioned term, one that might interchange with human rights, sovereignty, self-determination, liberation, and so forth). This ethic, in contradistinction to the traditional notion of scholars as practitioners of an objective vocation, is apparent in the mission statements of numerous academic departments. The Native American and Indigenous Studies program at the University of Texas, for example, is "particularly concerned with scholarship and intellectual exchange that contributes to the economic, social, and political advancement of indigenous peoples."[11] Likewise, American Indian Studies at the University of Arizona, which explores "issues from American Indian perspectives which place the land, its history and the people at the center," makes clear its emphasis: "American Indian Studies promotes Indian self-determination, self-governance, and strong leadership as defined by Indian nations, tribes, and communities, all of which originated from the enduring beliefs and philosophies of our ancestors."[12] Similar professions of material engagement and commitment to self-determination are common. Such is the case in Palestine studies.

The interest in Palestine in American Indian studies accords with its central questions concerning the limits and practice of self-determination, the discursive and ethical imperatives of decolonization, and the methodological complexities inherent in contrapuntal readings of history. Critique of American empire and imperialism in the field has produced comparative analyses of Indians with other racial and religious minorities (or with colonized majorities). Of particular concern is an expansionist Israel not only funded by the United States but claiming to be a modern incarnation and proud conserver of American manifest destiny. American elites and rank-and-file Christians simultaneously conceptualize Israel not merely as a worthy recipient of U.S. patronage, but as an indivisible component of American cultural identity. Barack Obama made clear this bond in his 2012 America Israel Public Affairs Committee [AIPAC] speech: "The United States and Israel share interests, but we also share those human values that Shimon spoke about: a commitment to human dignity. A belief that freedom is a right that is given to all of God's children. An experience that shows us that democracy is the one and only form of government that can truly respond to the aspirations of citizens."[13]

Comparison of the United States and Israel is particularly germane around the concept of values, a term Obama emphasized in his AIPAC speech. Less than a year after that speech, when former U.S. Senator Chuck Hagel faced scrutiny as Obama's choice as Secretary of Defense because of his supposed hostility to Israel (an accusation with no basis in fact),[14] Hagel responded to criticism by proclaiming, "America's relationship with Israel is one that is fundamentally built on our nations' shared values, common interests and democratic ideals."[15] Values, of course, are unstable things—unreliable, too, because they are invested with so many explicit and implicit demands and coercions. In this case, as Hagel's passage indicates, there is a longstanding discourse of shared values between the United States and Israel that mutually implicates Natives and Palestinians as premodern and unworthy of liberation.

What are those values? Democracy. Modernity. Industriousness. Freedom. Nobility. Humanity. Compassion. Natives and Palestinians not only lack these qualities, but actively seek to undermine them. American values arise not only from an expansionist capitalism but also from the redemptive mythologies of Israeli colonization, a fact that has led numerous people in American Indian studies to question the divinity of Zionism's heroic narratives and to explore how the current situation of Palestinians under military occupation lends understanding to Native reinterpretations of those American values. As J. Kehaulani Kauanui notes,

> The politics of indigeneity bring much to bear on critical analyses of Israeli exceptionalism, as it is bolstered and bankrolled by an American exceptionalism that denies the colonization of Native North America. Comparative examinations of Israeli settler colonialism in relation to questions of occupation, self-determination and decolonization within the framework of international law demand ethical consideration by Native American and Indigenous Studies scholars.[16]

While the inclusion of Palestine in American Indian studies tells us much about the shifting possibilities of Palestine studies, particularly its uneasy relationship with Middle East studies, it also illuminates (or reinforces) a particular set of commitments in American Indian studies. Such is especially true of the material politics of decolonization and their role in the formation of certain liberationist ethics to which many practitioners of American Indian and Indigenous studies adhere. The analysis of Palestine in American Indian studies forces us to continue exploring the cultures and geographies of indigeneity.

Here the issue of Palestine continues to prove instructive. In the culture wars of Israel—Palestine there is much chatter about the matter of indigeneity. In fact, it is the central moral basis for claims of geographic and cultural ownership in the so-called Holy Land, a reality illuminated by former Canadian MP Irwin Cotler when he proclaimed, "Israel is the aboriginal homeland of the Jewish people across space and time. Its birth certificate originates in its inception as a First Nation, and not simply, however important, in its United Nations international birth certificate."[17] Cotler's claim is noteworthy for numerous reasons. By appropriating the language of Indigenous peoplehood ("aboriginal," "First Nation"), Cotler positions Israel, against available historical evidence,[18] as a presence dating to antiquity and a beneficiary of exceptional juridical standing based on a specific legal categorization.

Although conceptually Cotler articulates a variant of the Zionist claim of Jewish ownership of Palestine, his specific language arises from an approach quite outside the commonplaces of Zionist discourse, which has largely focused on historical grievance (particularly European anti-Semitism), promissory narratives (God granted the land to Jews), and the inevitability of ingathering the diaspora (we were here in the past and thus have a right to be here in the present). In Cotler's argument, these commonplaces recede to assumptions as a more dramatic form of reasoning emerges, that of Israel as predecessor to the very existence of Palestinians, who become the conquerors, the foreigners, the aliens, the strangers. This argument rejects historical evidence of Palestinian dispossession and instead consigns them to the status of aggressor, stewards of their own suffering. Less obviously, it also disenfranchises Indigenous peoples in North America by subordinating their claims of nationhood into the logic of Western conquest. Cotler offers one example of the ability of Western multicultural practice to appropriate anything at its disposal in order to buttress an imperial power structure, for his pronouncement offers nothing to indicate that he would support a level of autonomy for Indigenous peoples similar to that enjoyed by the Israeli state.

Indeed, countless Zionists have employed the language of indigeneity—"*Jews* are indigenous to the land"—to explain the settlement of Palestine throughout the twentieth century or to rationalize the current settlement of the West Bank. Palestinians in return often rely on the same language of indigeneity to counter Zionist claims or to assert a moral narrative of belonging. When Zionists and Palestinians lay claim to indigeneity, they are not merely being technical. The term "indigenous" is infused with numerous connotations about access, belonging, biology, culture, jurisdiction, and identity. Indigeneity is not simply a moral entitlement, but a legal and political category. To access that category is to be positioned as steward and legatee of a particular territory. Thus the appropriation of the language of Indians inherently recognizes Indians as the rightful indigenes of North America—a recognition made infrequently by politicians and commentators—and simultaneously appropriates Natives into an extraneous debate whose conduct invalidates their agency. The debate invalidates Indian agency because it rarely visualizes Natives as members of living communities engaged in the work of decolonization or even in the work of survival. When a person says "Jews are the Indians of the Holy Land," the statement affixes Indians into a specific historical posture that renders them rhetorical but not legal or contemporaneous claimants against colonization. This is so because the claim is fundamentally statist, referencing a particular history to support an argument of the present. The referenced history does not make it into the present. The argument it informs already occupies that space.

Further evidence that this sort of move invalidates Indian agency is available in the language of the rhetoric itself. One need only read major forums of debate—*The New York Times, Washington Post, Slate*, the *Huffington Post*, and even social media such as Facebook and Twitter—to notice the extent to which visions of the American past bear upon the matter of Palestine. Because it remains locked in the past, Indian dispossession is frequently used to rationalize Palestinian dispossession. As Laila Al-Marayati observes, "Today, most Americans do not believe that the decimation and expulsion of entire Indian tribes in response to 'terrorist' attacks against wagon trains was justified. But, as one caller to a syndicated radio program suggested, since we're not about to give anything back to the Indians, why should the Israelis be expected to return stolen land to the Palestinians?"[19]

Unlike the Jews-as-Indians argument, this one acknowledges Indian disenfranchisement (again, only in the past), but forestalls any possibility of reparation. Yet exactly like the Jews-as-Indians argument, the goal is to justify the original sins of Zionism and the current settlement of the West Bank. This time the Palestinians become Indians and both communities end up consigned to an unfortunate-but-inevitable antiquity overwhelmed by the progress of a linear history, another powerful example of how a colonial ethos allows people to own history without being responsible for it. The common wisdom and common sense of this argument arise from a settler logic of divine possession and democratic entitlement whose values—the hegemony of its assumptions—render conquest a permanent feature of modern American consciousness. Zionism has adopted this consciousness in its desire to normatize—that is, to render normative—garrison settlement and military occupation. For Zionists, colonization is permanent even as it happens—in many ways before it has even taken place, for the ideologies of modernity underlying expansionist worldviews emphasize the progress of a distinct state culture with a neoliberal economy and a militarized infrastructure. The idea of returning land to Indians is crazy, indeed, as crazy as the idea of allowing Palestinians to remain on theirs.

The Indian interventions into these debates are of special interest. Much of the scholarly and political opposition to Zionism moves beyond moral displeasure at the behavior of Israel and its American sponsor, concerning itself instead with broader questions of power and meaning. What does it mean to confront a state whose presence, ipso facto, ensures legal and territorial dominance of its Indigenous communities and its legitimization as a permanent arbiter of its subjects' destinies? In the interrelated narratives of colonial permanence in the United States and Israel, we have a profound set of circumstances within which to explore this question. Answering the question from a perspective that does not take it as a point of fact that the United States and Israel are permanent has an added benefit of delegitimizing the state, but its primary function is to imagine a future outside of the notion that displacement and disenfranchisement must necessarily be permanent simply because they succeeded.

I would emphasize that despite an abundance of American–Israeli interactions—military, economic, diplomatic, cultural, historical, religious—the relationship of the two states is most profound at a level of discourse and ideology. In fact, a manifest Holy Land ethos has played an enormous role in the development of American society, both physically and philosophically. As Tim Giago notes in highlighting the interconnectedness of Natives and Palestinians, "The early settlers believed it was God's will (Manifest Destiny) that the heathens be driven from the land. It was God's will that the land be settled and populated by white Christians. They looked upon the indigenous population as a mere obstacle to be slaughtered or removed."[20] That ethos predates the creation of Israel, but also presupposes it. In this sense, the ancient Israel of the Old Testament was realized not through modern Zionism but in the settlement of North America.

Steven Newcomb explores these phenomena in his book *Pagans in the Promised Land*. He notes that "when dominating forms of reasoning (categorization) found in the Old Testament narrative are unconsciously used to reason about American Indians, Indian lands metaphorically become—from the viewpoint of the United States—the promised land of the chosen people of the United States."[21] Newcomb's analysis is valuable, though I would question the extent to which reasoning about American Indians as biblical Canaanites is unconscious. The teleology of North America as a new Promised Land is obvious in the early days of European settlement, but even now the inventions of America as a metaphorical Israel, with Indians as a romanticized but ungodly presence, remains common—quite consciously so.

These discursive geographies have traveled continuously between North

America and Palestine. In turn, the geographies of American Indian and Indigenous studies have transcended the restrictions inherent to the nation-state, the quintessential entity of colonization. In so doing, the field challenges the probity of the nation-state as a governing authority and progenitor of social organization. As Duane Champagne notes in the introduction to a comparative collection coedited with Palestinian Ismael Abu-Saad examining the future of Indigenous peoples, "Native struggles within nation-state systems are not simply efforts to gain inclusion or access to citizenship. . . . Native peoples wish to preserve land, economic subsistence and means, and political and cultural autonomy. In many cases, nation-states often find the demands of Native communities threatening, at odds with national policies of integration and assimilation."[22]

I want to explore some of the ways this inter/national Indigenism raises important questions and portends future directions in American Indian studies, but first let me return to one of the concrete phenomena bringing Natives and Palestinians into conversation, for it reveals with striking clarity the factors that endow the conversations with ethical and intellectual power. I primarily speak of Boycott/Divestment/Sanctions (BDS). The issue has initiated tremendous interchange among Native and Palestinian scholars, activists, and so-called cultural workers (creative writers, musicians, actors, and so forth). Natives are well represented in various initiatives to pass boycott resolutions among scholarly associations such as ASA and NAISA, and the endorsers of BDS include dozens of Indigenous peoples from across the globe.[23] More germane is the proactive role Indigenous peoples have assumed on behalf of the issue, to the point that the topic of Palestine has come into debate in Indigenous scholarly and activist communities, a fact in evidence when Muscogee poet Joy Harjo evoked impassioned protest and subsequent debate after announcing a reading (as part of a short-term residency) at Tel Aviv University.[24]

What does it mean for Indigenous people to debate Palestine? And what do Indigenous peoples bring to the debate? There are many possible answers, but an underlying feature of the phenomenon is the existence of Palestine as a sort of metonymy of variegated reactions to North American colonization (or New Zealander or Australian or South African or Algerian colonization). All sites of conflict exhibit unique characteristics, but within certain taxonomies of conquest exist fundamental discursive and martial scenarios, observable and often interrelated. A scholarly and ethical focus on decolonization among Native and Indigenous scholars has produced an impetus to engage in the work of liberating their communities from a type of garrison settlement reinvented and practiced with brute reminiscence of the American past (and, in many ways, the present) by Israel right now in Palestine. This focus can produce material articulation in movements such as BDS, which deterritorialize the vocation of scholarship from the impulses of anthropological objectivity.

Indigenous peoples have not merely latched onto BDS, but have played a central role in forming its ideas, developing its tactics and strategies, and crafting its narratives. The experiences of North American colonization have been seminal in developing more sophisticated understandings of Israeli colonial practices and Palestinian modes of resistance and nation-building. In turn, the analysis of Palestine by Indigenous writers has been seminal in more strongly comprehending American imperialist impulses and iniquitous economic policies, especially the often overlooked matter of current, not merely historical, colonial practices. As Julia Good Fox explains, "As indigenous peoples, we can supplement our local and tribal self-determination activity by setting aside just a few hours to locate and work through an international political or human rights organization that promotes informed solidarity and intelligent mutual support with the Palestinians. In doing so, we can bring to a halt the United States' and Israel's attempt to re-create 'Indian country' in the Occupied Territories."[25]

Returning to the NAISA Declaration of Support for the Boycott of Israeli Academic Institutions, we see that Good Fox's notion of Palestine advocacy supplementing and informing Native nationalism is forming as a disciplinary ethic. Calling Palestinians "Indigenous," the statement proclaims,

> As the elected council of an international community of Indigenous and allied non-Indigenous scholars, students, and public intellectuals who have studied and resisted the colonization and domination of Indigenous lands via settler state structures throughout the world, we strongly protest the illegal occupation of Palestinian lands and the legal structures of the Israeli state that systematically discriminate against Palestinians and other Indigenous peoples.

Of particular interest is the statement's incorporation of Palestine into the everyday practices of American Indian and Indigenous studies, which expands the geographies of Indigenous decolonial movements while situating the physical and symbolic territory of Palestine into a specific disciplinary context.

Befitting of this inter/nationalism, dozens of Palestinian organizations released a statement supporting Idle No More, an aboriginal protest movement in Canada that attracted considerable attention. The statement reads, in part,

> We recognize the deep connections and similarities between the experiences of our peoples—settler colonialism, destruction and exploitation of our land and resources, denial of our identity and rights, genocide and attempted genocide. . . . The struggle of Indigenous and Native peoples in Canada and the United

States has long been known to the Palestinian people, reflecting our common history as peoples and nations subject to ethnic cleansing at the hands of the very same forces of European colonization.[26]

This statement was one of many issued from Palestine in 2012–13.

Of interest in the two passages is their insistence on identifying the practices of colonialism in the present and a profession that working across boundaries increases the odds of mutual liberation. The latter point is both an ethical and strategic proposition, one that does more than just recognize shared historical circumstances. It also recognizes the coalescence of power in this age of militarized neoliberalism across the borders of nation-states. Indeed, the conduct and composition of today's nation-state are fundamentally globalized around military, economic, and technologies alliances that subordinate Indigenous communities across all continents. Any effective decolonization must take those alliances into account.

Assessing Inter/Nationalism

While it might be hyperbolic to say that all Indigenous peoples will have to be liberated simultaneously, it can be observed that a discrete power structure, of which the United States and Israel are primary stewards and beneficiaries, maintains their dispossession. That power structure preserves its existence through pervasive reinvention based on the common sense of divine intendment, which manifests itself at the levels of assumption and praxis in cultural, educational, governmental, and legal institutions. Indigenous struggles for liberation exist at the axis of what it means to contest empire, militarism, and economic injustice. The actions and ideas of today's Indigenous scholars and activists highlight the importance of inter/national theory and analysis, which I consider more carefully in the following paragraphs, paying note to how it encompasses both the ideological and the material.

Inter/nationalism encourages and assesses the play of decolonial narratives across cultures and colonial borders. I divide the term with a slash to reflect not just the political, philosophical, and ethical dialogue intimated by the prefix "inter-," but also to separate "nationalism" from the prefix while keeping the two halves connected in such a way that they create more possibilities in juxtaposition. Inter/nationalism expresses a desire for scholarship to explore broader patterns of discourse and power in our analyses of specific communities and a commitment to the project of nation-building through deep engagement with decolonial paradigms. Whereas "internationalism," without the slash, connotes cosmopolitan modernity or an epistemology of worldly experience, "inter/nationalism," with its typographical emphasis on the complex and volatile term "nationalism," encourages the possibility of putting nationalisms into conversation or, more ambitiously, into collective practice.

I adhere to a notion of nationalism generally accepted in American Indian studies, the one articulated by Jace Weaver, Craig Womack, and Robert Warrior in *American Indian Literary Nationalism*, with Simon Ortiz's thoughts on the subject serving as their foundation.[27] The book's preface declares, "Nationalism is a term on a short list, one that also includes sovereignty, culture, self-determination, experience, and history, that is central to understanding the relationship between the creative expression of Native American literature and the social and historical realities that such expression embodies."[28] This formulation avoids the nationalism of the industrial revolution and of jingoism, patriotism, and imperialism, highlighting instead a descriptive symbol of geography and humanity, the nation, not as constituted in the image of the Western state but in a dynamic structure of discrete, autonomous community. The nation in this scenario is a collective working in the interests of the community itself rather than of corporations and plutocrats. It precedes the nationalism of state-sponsored patriotism.

Nationalism relates to inter/nationalism in varied and important ways. The nation is not an isolated organism. It is a radical entity that survives in relation to the destinies of other nations, especially in this era of decolonization. It was disassembled in the era of poststructuralism but retains profound value to Natives and Palestinians as a subject of cultural practice, not merely as a geopolitical, historical, or discursive entity. Conceptualizing the nation as a subject of cultural practice compels us to consider the implications of peoplehood in the framework of liberation, while tending to the effects on identity when a displaced people endeavors to repossess the autonomies of its precolonial existence.

Beyond the Native and Indigenous support of BDS (a quintessential form of inter/nationalism), examples include the solidarity work among Palestinians and Hawaiians;[29] the participation of Palestine activists in Idle No More; the conjoining of Native and Palestinian scholars in the spaces of critical ethnic studies; the steady migration of Palestine scholars from Middle East studies into various areas of Indigenous studies; the repositioning of Palestinians into the category of Indigenous at the UN and other international governing bodies;[30] and the increasingly common juxtaposition of Natives and Palestinians in all areas of the American and Israeli political spectrums. Each phenomenon provides a strong basis for inter/national scholarship of the variety that both draws from and contributes to the work of decolonization occurring inside and beyond academe. Such analysis enables scholars to reorient emphasis from the state to the nation.

Performing Inter/Nationalism

In closing, I offer a few thoughts about the ethics of performing inter/nationalist scholarship.

In many ways, Palestine has become a test case of one's bona fides in American studies, ethnic studies, and other areas of inquiry—likewise in political and community organizations beyond academe. To be opposed to, say, the invasion of Iraq while simultaneously supporting Israel ensures, at least among a considerable demographic, a loss or weakening of credibility. Anti-Zionism as test case of one's trustworthiness represents the ascension of Palestine into the consciousness of the political and academic left and, more important, into the worldwide collective of Indigenous scholars challenging the structures and mores of academic convention. This ascension of Palestine arises from the recognition, always evident but now common, that Israel is not merely an ally or client of the United States, but a profound component of its imperial practice. To support Israel is to support U.S. Empire; thus other professions of resistance to U.S. Empire come into conflict with their own values in the presence of Zionism.

Any political or methodological commitment as a litmus test is problematic, of course. Those inherent problems notwithstanding, the juxtaposition of Natives and Palestinians represents a deterritorialization of traditional disciplinary areas. In many ways, it makes more sense for Palestine studies and Indigenous studies to be in conversation than Palestine studies and Middle East studies, as Middle East studies encompasses vast geographies in which liberation of Palestine is but a specialized subset and has traditionally accommodated various incarnations of Zionism as well as institutional acceptance of Israel, in its current ethnocentric form, as a permanent reality. Emphasis on territoriality in Native communities, as both cultural geography and national fulfillment, and in American Indian studies, as both intellectual capital and self-determined critique, informs the transformation of Palestine as an object of study from metaphor to site of territorial aspiration.

For scholars serious about better comprehending Palestine's present and working to ensure its very future, American Indian studies offers more groundbreaking and germane critique than do the Cold War–era area studies. In Palestine, American Indian studies participants can access a view of American history as it has been reinvented in the present, wherein the residue of conquest continues in North America through plutocratic governance and the rapid militarization of Native land[31] and functions in Palestine through the old-fashioned use of soldiers, tanks, tear gas, guns, grenades, and armed settlers, a violent continuation of the American legacy of Holy Land myth-making and ostensible reclamation.

Questions arise about the conduct and modalities of inter/national work; those questions will need to be addressed and readdressed as inter/nationalism continues to influence American Indian and Indigenous studies. In order to function optimally, the starting point of inter/nationalist methodologies, in both research and political organizing, must be sincere commitment to solidarity, to use a quaint term, one I prefer to similar possibilities: kinship, fraternity, unity, interconnection, fellowship, alliance (terms that actually describe the relationship between the American and Israeli states). Solidarity, through overused and subsequently attenuated in public discourse, can be distinguished from comparable terms because it implies pursuit of common goals—in this case, a common future—rather than appealing to the abstract tenets of existential amity. Even granting that this distinction arises from my own interpretive preference, the broader point is that whatever we call the practices of inter/nationalism, they are better suited to decolonial aspirations than to cosmopolitan dialogue.

Solidarity requires certain ethical commitments to function. A functional solidarity does not involve appropriation. It does not come with the expectation of reciprocity. It is not quid pro quo. It is not recorded on ledgers. Solidarity is performed in the interest of better human relationships and for a world that allows human societies to be organized around justice rather than profit. It happens with the communities with whom we are in contact—on behalf of the many we have never met.

This ethic is precisely why Palestine has become important to American Indian studies. Without Palestine, after all, North America never would have been colonized, at least not in the way that the conquest occurred. And without that conquest, Israel might have been but a fleeting historical experiment, a new Republic of Ararat or State of Aleppo. Natives and Palestinians, then, have much to discuss. The first order of business is the acknowledgment that both peoples must, of geopolitical necessity, undertake liberation together, and that our scholarship should be an asset toward that goal and not a mere recapitulation of state power.

STEVEN SALAITA is an independent scholar.

Notes

1. Churchill has regularly referenced Palestinians in his writing, most consistently in his book *A Little Matter of Genocide: Holocaust and Denial in the Americas 1492 to the Present* (San Francisco: City Lights, 2001). Churchill largely focuses on the physical violence of the United States and Israel, paying little note to discursive comparison. Finkelstein has a comparative chapter on the

Cherokee and Palestinians in *The Rise and Fall of Palestine: A Personal Account of the Intifada Years* (Minneapolis: University of Minnesota Press, 1996). Though conceptually solid, Finkelstein's comparison is problematic because it overlooks various American Indian sources.

2. See further, Robert Warrior, "Canaanites, Cowboys, and Indians: Deliverance, Conquest, and Liberation Theology Today," *Christianity and Crisis* 11 (September 1989): 261–65. Warrior presented an update of this paper at the 2011 NAISA Conference in Sacramento, examining Natives and Palestinians in comparative context more explicitly than he does in the original essay.

3. Former AIM leader Russell Means once proclaimed, "What the American Indian Movement says is that the American Indians are the Palestinians of the United States, and the Palestinians are the American Indians of the Middle East." See further http://www.counterpunch.org/2009/01/12/russell-means-breaks-the-silence-on-obama/.

4. The UN document is available at: http://www.un.org/esa/socdev/unpfii/documents/DRIPS_en.pdf. For some of the reaction to the document's effects on Israeli hegemony, see Shoshana Bryen, "The Rights of Indigenous People and the Rest of Us," *American Thinker* 8 (November 2013), http://www.americanthinker.com/2012/05/the_rights_of_indigenous_people_and_the_rest_of_us.html; and Joseph Klein, "The UN's Palestinian Rights Covenant," *FrontPage Magazine* 17 (September 2007), http://archive.frontpagemag.com/readArticle.aspx?ARTID=28145.

5. See further, www.usacbi.org.

6. To view the Declaration, visit: http://naisa.org.

7. See further, Waziyatawin, "Malice Enough in Their Hearts and Courage Enough in Ours: Reflections on U.S. Indigenous and Palestinian Experiences under Occupation," *Settler Colonial Studies* 2, no. 1 (2012): 172–89.

8. See further, Perry Miller, *Errand into the Wilderness* (Cambridge, Mass.: Harvard University Press, 1956); and Sacvan Berkovitch, *The Puritan Origins of the American Self*, reissue edition (New Haven, Conn.: Yale University Press, 2011).

9. See further, Hilton Obenzinger, *American Palestine* (Princeton, N.J.: Princeton University Press, 1999).

10. This happens largely through Israel's crucial role in the various modes of neoliberal corruption that dispossess Natives of land and resources. For a synopsis of Israel's neoliberal turn, see Orly Benjamin, "Roots of the Neoliberal Takeover in Israel," *Challenge* (July/August 2008), http://www.challenge-mag.com/en/article__224/roots_of_the_neoliberal_takeover_in_israel. A more specific example can be found in Israel's direct involvement in repression and genocide of Indigenous peoples in Guatemala and El Salvador in the 1980s. For information about this involvement, see Adam Jones, *Genocide: A Comprehensive Introduction*, 2nd ed. (London: Routledge, 2010), 147.

11. See further, http://www.utexas.edu/cola/inits/nais/.

12. See further, http://www.ais.arizona.edu/content/mission-and-core-values.

13. A full video and transcript of the speech can be found at: http://www

.whitehouse.gov/photos-and-video/video/2012/03/04/president-obama-2012-aipac-policy-conference.

14. As a senator, Hagel reliably voted for both pro-Israel and anti-Palestinian legislation. For more information about his voting record and professions of support for Israel, see http://jstreet.org/the-facts-on-chuck-hagel#proisrael.

15. Chemi Salev, "Hagel: 'I intend to expand the depth and breadth of U.S.–Israel cooperation,'" *Ha'arez*, January 15, 2013, http://www.haaretz.com/news/diplomacy-defense/hagel-i-intend-to-expand-the-depth-and-breadth-of-u-s-israel-cooperation.premium-1.494075.

16. J. Kēhaulani Kauanui, "Ethical Questions of Boycotting Israel," in *Shifting Borders: America and the Middle East/North Africa*, ed. Alex Lubin (Beirut: American University of Beirut Press, forthcoming).

17. Irwin Cotler, "The Gathering Storm, and Beyond," *Jerusalem Post*, May 14, 2008, http://www.jpost.com/Opinion/Op-EdContributors/Article.aspx?id=101152.

18. A number of scholarly books have shown that Zionism's claims to an ancient Jewish past in Palestine are largely mythological. See Shlomo Sand, *The Invention of the Land of Israel: From Holy Land to Homeland*, trans. Geremy Forman (London: Verso, 2012); Keith Whitelam, *The Invention of Ancient Israel: The Silencing of Palestinian History* (London: Routledge, 1997); and Eyal Weizman, *Hollow Land: Israel's Architecture of Occupation* (London: Verso, 2012).

19. Laila Al-Marayati, "Will Palestinians Go the Way of Native Americans?" *Los Angeles Times*, April 21, 2002, http://articles.latimes.com/2002/apr/21/opinion/op-almarayati.rtf.

20. Tim Giago, "Israel Could Have Learned Much from Native Americans," *Notes from Indian Country*, August 22, 2005, http://www.nativetimes.com/index.asp?action=displayarticle&article_id=6881.

21. Steven Newcomb, *Pagans in the Promised Land: Decoding the Doctrine of Discovery* (Golden, Colo.: Fulcrum Publishing, 2008), xxii.

22. Duane Champagne and Ismael Abu-Saad, "Introduction," in *Future of Indigenous People: Strategies for Survival and Development*, ed. Duane Champagne and Ismael Abu-Saad (Los Angeles: UCLA American Indian Studies Center, 2003), x.

23. A complete list of signatories can be found at the following site: http://www.usacbi.org/endorsers/.

24. See further Ali Abunimah, "Rejecting Palestinian Calls, Native American Poet Joy Harjo Entertains Apartheid at Tel Aviv University," *Electronic Intifada*, December 10, 2012, http://electronicintifada.net/blogs/ali-abunimah/rejecting-palestinian-calls-native-american-poet-joy-harjo-entertains-apartheid; and Joanne Barker, "Regarding Joy Harjo's Performance at Tel Aviv University," *Tequila Sovereign*, December 10, 2012, http://tequilasovereign.blogspot.com/2012/12/regarding-joy-harjos-performance-at-tel.html.

25. Julia Good Fox, "Stop the Re-Creation of 'Indian Country' in the Holy Land," *Good Fox*, June 3, 2010, http://juliagoodfox.com/indian_country_holy_land/.

26. Hadani Ditmars, "Palestinians and Canadian Natives Join Hands to

Protest Colonization," *Ha'aretz*, January 29, 2013, http://www.haaretz.com/news/features/palestinians-and-canadian-natives-join-hands-to-protest-colonization.premium-1.500057.

27. Ortiz writes, "It is because of the acknowledgment by Indian writers of a responsibility to advocate for their people's self-government, sovereignty, and control of land and natural resources; and to look also at racism, political and economic oppression, sexism, supremacism, and the needless and wasteful exploitation of land and people . . . that Indian literature is developing a character of nationalism." Passage from "Towards a National Indian Literature," in Jace Weaver, Craig S. Womack, and Robert Warrior, *American Indian Literary Nationalism* (Albuquerque: University of New Mexico Press, 2006), 259.

28. Ibid., xv.

29. Francis Boyle offers a useful analysis of comparable Palestinian–Hawaiian claims to sovereign nationhood in a 1993 address in Honolulu; the full text is available at the following link: http://www.freehawaii.org/boyeladd1.html.

30. The Palestinian claim to "Indigenous" status at the United Nations has generally been connected to the Bedouin (traditional, nomadic, tribal communities), though Palestinians have also worked to include the whole of Palestinian society into the category.

31. See further Margot Tamez, "Indigenous Women, Anti-Colonial Histories, and Resurgent Autonomy Movements: The U.S.–Mexico Militarized Zones of War and Occupation," *Works & Days* 57/58. *Invisible Battlegrounds: Feminist Resistance in the Global Age of War and Imperialism* 29, nos. 1, 2 (2011): 281–318.

ERIC CHEYFITZ

Response to Steven Salaita's "Inter/Nationalism from the Holy Land to the New World: Encountering Palestine in American Indian Studies"

STEVEN SALAITA'S ESSAY and mine, "The Force of Exceptionalist Narratives in the Israeli–Palestinian Conflict," certainly intersect, particularly in how we read the way that American and Israeli exceptionalisms buttress each other: how the Puritan "errand in the wilderness" replicates the Jewish trajectory in the Old Testament, for instance. These exceptionalist narratives, as both Salaita and I remark, position Arabs and Indians (to employ two anachronisms) in the place of a "savage" force resisting the "civilizing" project of Euramericans and Jews. And in that sense, however insidious the narratives, they implicitly recognize both Arabs and Indians as being Indigenous (first peoples). Thus Jewish claims to indigeneity ("Jews are the Indians of the Holy Land"), which Salaita engages, are always already contradicted by the Israeli exceptionalist narrative of a late-arriving civilization overcoming a preexisting savagery. In other words, the Israelis can't have their historical cake and eat it too, except by decoupling the historic inhabitants of Canaan, which the Jews invaded, from the present-day Palestinians. And of course that is a claim one hears certain sectors of the Jewish public make: that the Palestinian people are a post-1948 invention. But in that sense, as Shlomo Sand has pointed out, the Jewish people are equally invented, as are, for that matter, all national identities out of political necessity. The Jews-as-Indians, Palestinians-as-Indians arguments that Salaita analyzes point to the contradictions inherent in Jewish–Israeli claims of indigeneity (the Jews are simultaneously indigenous and settlers) while distracting from the colonial situation on the ground (the modern Jews are decidedly settlers on Palestinian lands), just as a U.S. history that consigns Indians to the past distracts from the ongoing colonialism in Indian Country enforced by federal Indian law.

Concomitantly with the essay's work in comparative colonialisms, a crucial question that Salaita's essay asks is this: What are the boundaries, if any, of American Indian studies? Those boundaries, of course, have already been extended in NAISA's very title. The term "Indigenous" brings into the field an ambiguity both promising and dangerous, which threatens the identities of U.S. Native nations at the same time it creates virtual links between these nations and the "inter/national" (the coinage is Salaita's) "Indigenous" community. Because of differing histories of colonial conquest, south of the U.S.–Mexican border "Indigeneity" is a much more flexible term—witness its use to mobilize different social movements in the Bolivian revolution beginning in 2000—than it is north of that border, where it is policed by federal statutes and tribal enrollment rules in both the United States and Canada. Indeed, the Zapatistas have opened up the term to include everyone who identifies with it in the practice of a certain new-left (Indigenous) or anti-neoliberal politics. When Salaita raises the issue of Israeli anxieties about the Palestinians being covered under the UN Declaration on the Rights of Indigenous Peoples, he implicitly raises the question of what peoples exactly the Declaration does cover.

Finally, here are some of the questions implicit in my foregoing comments: Does Salaita's essay succeed in saving the term "nation"—a Western term—from its regressive history of being tied to the form of the nation-state as it is in U.S. federal Indian law? Here it was and is imposed by courts on Native communities in order to translate these communities into a Western regime of property relations as "domestic dependent nations." And if the term "nation" is redeemable, why aren't nations? Or is it only a certain form of the nation, as Salaita tries to redefine the term, that is viable? And where do we find this form in practice? Or is Salaita only projecting a utopian form of the nation as a critique of the nation-state formation? After all, the nation is typically not a material structure but a way of narrativizing the state. Salaita remarks: "To support Israel is to support U.S. Empire." Is he referring here to Israeli state policies that support the occupation or to Israel per se, which is a matrix of conflicting narratives, some militantly opposed to these state policies? Is he referring here to U.S. imperial policies or to the inseparability of the United States—itself a congeries of conflicts—and empire? That is, do we simply want to collapse Israeli state policies with Israel as a nation-state, or U.S. state policies with the United States? And if we do, then do Israel and the United States represent forms of the nation (the nation-state) that are incapable of progressive change, of renarrativization? And if this is what Salaita has in mind, perhaps what we ought to imagine is not other forms of the nation, which inevitably bring with it the structure of the state (witness the ongoing conflicts in Bolivia between "Indigenous" communities and the "Indigenous" central government), but forms other than the "nation," forms modeled on traditional Indigenous governance, like the Zapatista autonomous communities.

ERIC CHEYFITZ is Ernest I. White Professor of American Studies and Humane Letters at Cornell University.

STEVEN SALAITA

Response to Eric Cheyfitz's "The Force of Exceptionalist Narratives in the Israeli—Palestinian Conflict"

I WAS DELIGHTED to read Eric Cheyfitz's "The Force of Exceptionalist Narratives in the Israeli—Palestinian Conflict" and am excited to offer this brief response. This conversation is one that must necessarily continue. It is appropriate for a variety of reasons that it happens in a space of Indigenous reflection and theorization.

I found it of particular value that Cheyfitz begins with analysis of the Balfour Declaration, which, beyond its obvious historical importance, is profoundly interesting as a rhetorical document. It promises a classically humanistic version of coexistence but is simultaneously a promissory certificate of colonial intent, attempting to assuage the anxieties of those its drafters were secretly planning to displace. In these contradictions we find ample opportunity to imaginatively assess the modern history of Palestine. In many ways, the state of Israel has indeed failed to live up to Balfour's discourse. In that most important way, however, the behind-the-scenes conflation of "homeland" with "nation-state," Israel managed to fulfill the declaration's unspoken logic.

It did so in large part through the exceptionalism Cheyfitz so ably explores. Here the colonial discourses of the United States and Israel exist in close proximity, if not in juxtaposition. I am interested in the ways that the Nazi Holocaust helped enact the performance of Israeli exceptionalism, because of the fruitful narratives of religious persecution as a precursor to settler colonization.

One comment that Cheyfitz offers requires, I think, further conversation: "While the field of American studies, within which I include Ethnic and Native American studies." Drawing from my readings of Robert Warrior, Jodi Byrd, Dale Turner, and others, I would argue that it's useful to complicate the positionality of these fields in relation to one another. The move toward disciplinary independence—which is not to preclude interdependence—draws from (and contributes to) a particular narrative of decolonization that deeply informs the material politics of North America and Palestine.

While Norman Finklestein, from whom Cheyfitz draws significant supporting material, has produced important work, I'm fond of the recent writings of Waziyatawin, J. Kehaulani Kauanui, and Steven Newcomb. There is a body of scholarship emerging that more robustly situates itself in decolonial paradigms that Finkelstein either ignores or refuses to engage. Those paradigms are crucial because Natives and Palestinians seek forms of self-determination that move beyond the conventional frameworks of Western human rights or international laws.

Cheyfitz writes movingly in his conclusion of a Jewish presence in the Middle East that is integrative rather than isolated. This vision is one that advocates of decolonization should pursue vigorously, for it provides a model not only for a democratic Palestine but also for the engagement of Indigenous communities in North and South America with the institutions from which they have been excluded and from which they have endured considerable violence. In order for these forms of democratic engagement to become reality, they must, as Cheyfitz notes, disengage themselves from the ethnonationalism of the settler state. This is not an easy or especially realistic task. But I find any scholarly or material aspiration that stops short of this desired result to be unworthy of our time. And I'm quite unmoved by the hegemony of realism.

I hope that our pieces can move beyond conversation with one another and into a broader discussion of what it means to dismantle and recreate the histories of our dispossession. I stand firm in my belief that it won't happen in Palestine unless it happens in North America.

STEVEN SALAITA is an independent scholar.

Notes from the Field

MALINDA TRILLER DORAN

Dickinson College Builds Carlisle Indian Industrial School Resource Center

MORE THAN TEN THOUSAND STUDENTS attended the Carlisle Indian School (CIS) between 1879 and 1918, and each one of them has a story. Over the last century, however, materials documenting the Carlisle experience, including photographs, letters, and the administrative files of the school itself, have been dispersed among various institutions. This scattered historical record makes it a challenge for descendants, scholars, teachers, and students to connect with the lives of the individuals who were affected by the school. The Archives and Special Collections department of Dickinson College has partnered with the College's Community Studies Center to create a website that will bring together and make freely available these widely dispersed materials.

The CIS paper trail currently leads to institutions such as the National Archives in Washington, D.C.; the Cumberland County Historical Society in Carlisle, Pennsylvania; and the Special Collections of Dickinson College. Jim Gerencser, college archivist at Dickinson, had long dreamed of building an online resource that would provide convenient access to digital versions of these resources, regardless of their geographic location. In October 2012, more than 290 individuals gathered at Dickinson for the symposium titled "Carlisle, PA: Site of Indigenous Histories, Memories, and Reclamations." The response to this symposium provided the energy necessary to set a digitization project in motion.

Gerencser collaborated with Susan Rose, professor of sociology and Community Studies Center director, and Malinda Triller Doran, special collections librarian, to develop a plan for an online Carlisle Indian School Resource Center. In spring 2013, the three project leaders secured funding from an Andrew W. Mellon Foundation Digital Humanities grant and Dickinson's Research and Development Committee. Since that time, they have sent four research teams to the National Archives in Washington, D.C., to scan and photograph records located within the Bureau of Indian Affairs Record Group. These teams have scanned the files of four thousand students, which include items such as photographs, correspondence, newspaper clippings, and administrative forms documenting the experience of students while they were enrolled at CIS and after they returned to their homes. One member of the research team also photographed twelve bound ledgers that contain entries documenting events such as the arrival and departure of students and their outing assignments.

Upon their return to Dickinson, members of the research teams have prepared the digital images for presentation on the project website: http://carlisleindian.dickinson.edu. As of July 2014, more than 1,775 student files were available online. Members of the project team have also begun transcribing the contents of the ledger volumes to provide the information they contain as searchable and sortable text.

Gerencser, Rose, and Triller Doran plan to continue adding resources to the CIS website over a period of several years. Additional research teams will scan and upload the remaining student files and ledgers located at the National Archives in order to provide comprehensive access to those resources. Gerencser has also begun to seek partnerships with other institutions that hold materials related to the CIS, such as the Beinecke Library at Yale University, which holds the papers of Richard Henry Pratt, founder of the CIS, and the U. S. Army Heritage and Education Center in Carlisle, Pennsylvania.

The ultimate goal is to provide a searchable database that will facilitate discovery, whether an individual wishes to search for information about a specific student or explore broader aspects of the CIS experience, such as tribal affiliations or outing assignments. The project leaders also anticipate building interactive capabilities into the site that will allow individuals to contribute photographs, family documents, or oral histories. In addition, they plan to work with both Native and non-Native scholars, teachers, and community members to develop teaching and learning materials utilizing the resource center content.

The Carlisle Indian School Resource Center will continue to grow as project staff add new content almost daily. For more information about the project, please contact Jim Gerencser or Malinda Triller Doran in the Dickinson College Archives and Special Collections at cisproject@dickinson.edu or 717-245-1399.

MALINDA TRILLER DORAN is the Special Collections Librarian at Dickinson College.

JOEL T. HELFRICH

Cultural Survival in Action: Ola Cassadore Davis and the Struggle for *dził nchaa si'an* (Mount Graham)

I'm just a little bitty lady. I've never grabbed anyone before. But he [Senator Dennis DeConcini, D-Ariz.] is working for us in Arizona. He doesn't scare me because I know I'm doing the right thing—standing up for my people.
—OLA CASSADORE DAVIS

MOUNT GRAHAM, an ecologically unique mountain range in Arizona, is one of the most written-about and contended over Indigenous sacred sites globally.[1] It is an oasis in the middle of a desert, an exceptional "sky island" ecosystem that possesses the most life zones or biotic communities of any solitary mountain in North America, and the home of at least 18 endemic species, especially the imperiled Mount Graham red squirrel. Mount Graham, or *dził nchaa si'an* ("big seated mountain") in the Apache language, is the only place where Western Apache (Nneé) people collect certain plant and animal resources for use in ceremonials, learn how to live, and go to understand their cosmology—all of which are central to their culture and sovereignty.[2] The landscape that has encompassed the "traditional Western Apache" homeland is diamond-shaped and includes Mount Graham, San Francisco Peaks, the White Mountains, especially Mount Baldy, and the Mazatzal Mountains.[3] A sacred place since "time immemorial" to the Western Apache people, Mount Graham has been a site of struggle since the 1870s when it was removed from reservation lands by U.S. presidential order, but especially since the 1980s as a consortium of international research institutions led by the University of Arizona (UA) has sought astrophysical development opportunities.

The struggle for this mountain has been long and contested. In the early 1980s, UA and its research partners selected Mount Graham as the location for a new generation of telescopes. Soon afterwards, environmental groups not only began to protest and litigate but also to point out the Apache connections to the mountain. In early 1987, Paul Pierce, a Tucson businessman and Director of the Coalition for the Preservation of Mount Graham, wrote to the Coronado National Forest. He pointed out the sacredness of the mountain and its present-day use by Apaches of the mountain: "We have since identified a group of San Carlos Apache people who are still using the high peaks of [Mount Graham] for religious reasons. Evidently this religious use of the mountain is contemporary and has been happening over the last few hundred years," a comment that is supported by ethnohistorical records from approximately 1910 to 1940. Pierce stated that Mount Graham is sacred to members of the San Carlos Apache tribe and was still being used for religious rites. "The proposed development is viewed as potentially damaging to the Apache religion and the ceremonies that take place," argued Pierce. He urged that the Forest Service address the potentially harmful impacts of UA's astrophysical development. However, UA decided habitually to ignore and fight against ecological facts, Apache spiritual and tribal concerns, and its own data regarding the usefulness of its site selection and the limited astrophysical value of the mountain.[4] In the face of legitimate concerns and strong opposition from both environmentalists and Apache people, UA lobbied the U.S. Congress in 1988 in order "to establish an international astronomical observatory on Mount Graham."[5]

UA became the initial academic institution to achieve several dubious firsts regarding U.S. environmental, cultural, religious, and human rights law in its pursuit of astronomical excellence. Before it obtained an exemption from federal environmental and cultural laws, UA was the first university to lobby against the creation of a national wilderness (Mount Graham Wilderness Area) in 1984 and the first university to fight against the listing of an endangered species in 1986.[6] UA obtained the additional recognition of being the first university to lobby and secure not one, but two, precedent-setting congressional exemptions (1988 and 1996) to subvert American Indian cultural and religious protection law, as well as U.S. environmental law; to promote a project whose biological approval was acknowledged to be fraudulent; to fight in court against an endangered animal species; to litigate against traditional American Indian religious practice rights; to require "prayer permits" and then arrest for trespass an American Indian accessing his ancestral sacred ground; to be the only U.S. university in the twentieth century to sue an Indian tribe for its religious beliefs; and to devise a written plan to divide and exploit differences and factions within a sovereign Indian tribe.[7] UA's observatory is also the only observatory protected by police attack dogs.[8] Although UA led the efforts, numerous scientific organizations, including the Vatican, Arcetri Astronomical Observatory (a research arm of the Italian government), Germany's Max Planck Institute, and several universities (Ohio State, Notre Dame, Virginia, and Minnesota), have endorsed UA's actions.

One important Indigenous person at the forefront of much of the struggle for Mount Graham and against UA—led colonial endeavors was San Carlos Apache elder Ola Cassadore Davis. She showed by doing, by her actions, her deeds, her organization and organizing, through her words in public, press releases, letters, and opinion pieces and editorials, that she was an effective leader. Recently, several scholars examined "personal agency in heritage stewardship" through the lens of five leaders of Northern Coast Salish cultural heritage. Their research suggested "four overlapping characteristics of effective leadership in heritage stewardship."[9] Successful heritage stewards are: "1. personally identified with the heritage; 2. clearly serving collective interests; 3. credible in communications within and across social boundaries; and 4. willing to act on personal commitments, even in risky situations."[10] Ola was an effective heritage steward because she possessed all of those qualities. Ola's story is shared here not only as a tribute to her and her work but also as a significant example of a person who can illuminate the importance of heritage stewardship, effective leadership, and "the personal satisfactions and societal benefits stemming from altruistic service to cultural and biophysical heritage."[11]

Examining Ola's life and activist work for Mount Graham can tell Apaches, scholars, and activists a great deal about the significance of resistance in historic preservation and in Indigenous human rights, religious, and environmental justice struggles. Her story illuminates why a life of decolonial resistance is so important. Ola's life and work also suggest how Apaches, especially older, traditional Apaches, are viewed and treated by American Indians, white Americans, and Europeans, and the convergence and collision of Apache and white male European/American culture. Perhaps most significantly, Ola's age and status as an elder—and Apache, as well as white European and American, age norms—arguably played a large role in her successes and the respect that she garnered, as well as having shaped and enabled her amazing later life.

"The medicine men sing about the mountain when they pray, generation to generation, all the way down through the years," stated Ola Cassadore Davis in October 1989, the day before UA and its research partners intended to begin construction on the two-mile access road to the observatory. "They say there is holy water on top of that mountain, and sacred herbs and a burial site," she continued. "To us Apache, it is a very sacred place. It's really important to my people to not have those things (telescopes) built up there."[12] With these words, Ola began her activism full-time.

Ola was sixty-six years old when she made her initial comments regarding Mount Graham to the Tucson media. She spent many years as a housewife raising seven children. Ola had at least sixteen grandchildren and at least eleven great-grandchildren. She had grown up in Peridot, a small settlement on the San Carlos Apache Reservation, approximately thirty miles from Mount Graham.[13] In a family of eleven, Ola was the oldest daughter. She attended the Peridot Lutheran Mission School and then a boarding school in

San Carlos, completing ninth grade.[14] At age eighteen, Ola married. Eventually through a Bureau of Indian Affairs program, she relocated with her first husband and seven children to Dallas, Texas. In the early 1960s, after a divorce, she married her second husband, Mike Davis, a Choctaw from Mississippi. They settled eventually in Tucson where Ola worked as a nurse's aide, having earned a certificate in Skilled Allied Health Services from Pima Community College in 1975.[15]

Early in her life, Ola established a deep connection to, respect for, and relationship with Mount Graham. Her family influenced her greatly. Both her grandfather and father were Apache "clan chiefs," according to Ola, who knew the mountain was sacred and shared that knowledge with her. Her brother, Philip Cassadore, was a spiritual leader, lecturer, radio host, singer, and a key decolonial actor on the San Carlos Apache reservation who also told of the sacredness of Mount Graham during the 1960s, 1970s, and 1980s, and created an organization called Apache Culture History Foundation to work on Apache history and culture concerns.[16]

According to Ola, "Every fall, [she] accompanied her family to camp at the base of Mount Graham. After a day of gathering acorns from the oak trees—which later would be peeled, ground into meal, and used in acorn soup—her father, surrounded by Ola and the other children, talked about the importance of the traditional Apache way." Ola later "recalled that her father said Mount Graham was a sacred place.... She learned that a mountain spirit lives there, and it helps Apaches choose their spiritual leaders. In the spring, the water or 'sweat' of Mount Graham is holy water."[17] Ola spoke of her "grandmother Lena and how she had fled from U.S. soldiers to the sanctuary of Mount Graham. There Lena met the great Chief Cochise who helped heal her bleeding feet." Ola once "recalled how her grandmother had used such plants to cure hepatitis, syphilis, even to prevent pregnancy." Stated Ola, "She was a very powerful medicine lady. She was one of the most important people in my life."[18] Ola became one of the most famous Western Apache people to speak for "the mountains which circle the Apache land," as she put it in her first published letter.[19]

Ola was determined to get involved in the effort to protect Mount Graham.[20] Although Ola was not tall, she had a determined, blue-eyed gaze that was immensely kind and intensely fierce. After her brother Philip's death in 1985, Ola reached out to anthropologist Elizabeth Brandt for help protesting.[21] Brandt had worked with Philip and had known Ola for a long time. Ola then "told the leaders she would pray awhile, before making decision.... For ... months [Ola] prayed."[22] She found her calling after a dream she had.[23] "One night she dreamed her father said, 'It's a hard job. Are you strong enough? Do you really want to do it? It's up to you.'" Ola also spoke with her 107-year-old aunt. "If you decide to do it, don't ever turn back," her aunt told her.[24] "Nobody influenced me but my prayers," said Ola. "My decision came to me through my spirit, my brother's spirit and my father's spirit."[25]

Ola began the fight that she would conduct for the rest of her life, giving herself an education about and against university, state, federal, judicial, and international bureaucracies. Ola reached out to activist Michael D'Amico and the radical environmental group "Earth First! to offer her help in protesting construction."[26] She let it be known that at first "she [had] been nervous about speaking up."[27] Such fears are not unfounded. Even in the present, it is common to hear that many Apache elders fear speaking up and worry about leaving reservation boundaries. Ola took up "the protest in memory of her brother, Philip."[28] In fact, Ola felt her family was helping her "wage the war" against encroachments on Apache sacred lands.[29] To a movement of native and nonnative people, Ola was a highly valued human energy source.[30]

She set to work and initially collected seventy-four signatures on the San Carlos Apache reservation, no easy task for anyone, especially given the size of the reservation and other logistical obstacles. Eventually she was able to, miraculously enough, collect signatures from many important tribal elders and spiritual leaders. During a speech before the University of Minnesota faculty senate years later, anthropologist Keith Basso discussed the signatures that Ola was able to obtain and the importance of her work: "In a document rarely seen . . . , thirteen Western Apache medicine men or spiritual leaders and three female spiritual leaders declared emphatically in a two-word statement the central sacred importance of *dził nchaa si'an*." According to Basso, "The University of Arizona and its friends have dismissed these and other attitudes as mere chaff. They have," Basso explained, "taken numerous steps to discredit the validity of such statements, although . . . on three separate occasions the San Carlos Apache Tribal Council . . . *ratified* . . . the sacredness of Mount Graham and its importance to continuing an Apache way of life" (emphasis added).[31]

Ola started the not-for-profit cultural and religious rights organization called Apache Survival Coalition in 1990. Along with environmentalists, anthropologists, and Apaches, Ola's group sought to halt telescope development.[32] By mid-1990, Ola and Apache members of her organization had already traveled once to Washington to lobby for Apache interests. The delegation met with Congressional staff members and attended Congressional hearings.[33] Soon afterwards, Ola worked to get the San Carlos Apache tribe to pass a unanimous resolution against telescope development on Mount Graham.[34] She was selected by the tribal leadership as the "Mount Graham ambassador, or their spokeswoman, on the issue."[35] The General Accounting Office (now General Accountability Office), the investigative arm of Congress, then suggested the astrophysical development be postponed so that new studies could be undertaken to study the Mount Graham red squirrel.[36] Ola was at the center of this initiative and strategy, as well as others, during her many visits to lobby in Washington and elsewhere. Ola made things happen and organized people, despite the fact that her organization was never able to have the merits of its legal cases heard in court.

Ola regularly appreciated the help she received. In a letter thanking Apaches for their support, Ola wrote, "Because of these activities and new contacts, the Apache people have gained in strength and knowledge. We are now in much better position to protect our rights and to preserve our culture and religion." She acknowledged historical barriers: "The Apache people are learning how to work within the system which has been imposed on us for far too long and which has virtually ignored our religious and cultural rights for years." She also noted that new alliances were being formed. "The environmental community has gradually been learning about Apache culture and traditional respect for the land and sacred places. The Mount Graham issue has played major role in bringing Indian people and white people together," Ola pointed out, "in a working relationship which has trust and understanding. Both groups have responded out of an inner calling and have taken responsibility to save this very special and important mountain for humans and for other forms of life and for nature itself. We cannot help but be strengthened by these collaborations."[37] When the rock band Pearl Jam supported the Apaches, she wrote, "We thank Pearl Jam and their fans for helping us fight for our cultural survival and religious freedom."[38]

Ola was a key reason that Apaches were organizing, that Indigenous peoples and environmentalists were working together, and that they were already finding success. In fact, within the first six months of becoming involved with the struggle, she was already making a name for herself and displaying her abilities as both an organizer and leader.[39] While in Washington, the Apache delegation was rebuffed by a number of politicians. By chance Ola saw Arizona Senator Dennis DeConcini and made the best of the opportunity. "The Indians, new to the lobby game, had been unable to meet with DeConcini and were about to give up when they spotted him walking across a courtyard not far from the Capitol," wrote a reporter. DeConcini "'started shaking hands, and when he got to Ola she grabbed his hand with both of hers and wouldn't let go,' said Robin Silver, a Phoenix doctor and observatory opponent who went along on the trip." Stated Silver, "She had her feet planted and was giving him an earful, and he was trying to pull away. . . . He was being a gentleman. But she wouldn't let him go. Finally, we had to ask her to let loose of him." Although she remembered this event with humor sometime later, her encounter displayed the immense amount of Ola's insistence and her boldness.[40] This was not her last notable run-in with a member of the Arizona delegation.[41] She was not intimidated by any person who held political power. As Ola put it, "I don't care how powerful they are."[42]

The education that Ola learned in her new role as an organizer, nonprofit director, and leader was impressive. She used her newfound skills to challenge UA and its research partners, as well as UA's propaganda machine that always worked to undermine and divide the members of a sovereign tribe.[43] For example, UA put forth opinion-editorials by UA presidents, astronomers, public relations officials, and supportive media. Several Catholic priests at UA marginalized Apache viewpoints and promoted mythmaking and historical revisionism.[44] The UA-financed Booz-Allen Report suggested making "outliers" of Apaches who disagreed with astrophysical development and offer "inducements" to the tribe that should not be seen as "bribes."[45] During her first interview, Ola proclaimed, "We Apache have to learn to fight for our rights."[46] She passed the skills that she acquired on to other Apache leaders and activists. According to Apache Wendsler Nosie, the Mount Graham Coalition—the onetime largest organization of Indigenous and environmental groups in the United States—"was the door for Ola to learn how to fight the system with Mount Graham and in turn Ola was the door to Wendsler [Nosie] and Terry [Rambler, the current tribal chairman of the San Carlos Apache Tribe,] to be able to be as effective as they now are" at organizing, leadership, and politics.[47] "Ola's struggles and all that she did brought education (of politics) to the forefront for all tribes," stated Nosie, chairman of the San Carlos Apache Tribe from 2006 to 2010. "Her passions woke us up as Apaches."[48]

But she had her detractors. Journalist Fergus Bordewich, in his much-discredited work *Killing the White Man's Indian*, attacked Ola cruelly, reading almost without forethought from UA's playbook of dirty tricks.[49] Indeed, from the beginning of her struggle against UA, Ola was belittled and marginalized. UA officials and astronomers asserted she was too late to the "process" and that her voice hardly carried the same weight as the rest of the San Carlos Apache Tribe, nor the San Carlos Apache Tribal Council. UA administrators claimed to be "surprised" that Apaches had any problems with their activities on the mountain.[50] Ola also had some disagreements with other Apaches, although none were permanent nor hampered her message.[51] Indeed, she bristled when her relative, former Tribal Chairman Buck Kitcheyan, lied about Apache opposition (of which he was originally a part) to telescope construction. Kitcheyan also claimed that Ola was "being used" by environmentalists "that reject progress and development."[52] He was later convicted in tribal court on fourteen counts of embezzlement, but not before working to support UA and its plans.[53] The pattern of San Carlos Apache Tribal Council members defending the sacredness of Mount Graham, then going to work for UA, was repeated by Tribal Chairman Harrison Talgo and others.[54]

With meager funds and a high level of intelligence, brinksmanship, and care, Ola regularly fought against ignorance, political machinations, and "UA's vast financial resources" and disregard for U.S. laws.[55] She was indefatigable. As she tersely put it, "UA, accustomed to buying, sliding and suing their way around the laws of [the United States] which were established to protect human rights and our Earth, may never understand that moral issues don't go away."[56] When UA joined a lawsuit "to suppress the religious rights of the Apache people," Ola responded: "If they decide to sue us they will be the first American university to openly and intentionally pursue the course of cultural destruction started by Columbus 500 years earlier. They even named one of the telescopes Columbus which adds to the insult! Do the Vatican and German people [partners in the project] want to be part of a project which is spearheading the cultural destruction of the beliefs of indeginous [sic] peoples?"[57] Stated Ola, "If they were to try to put telescopes on Mount Sinai, the world would be outraged. Just because we have no written Bible, and we don't build shrines at our sacred places, some German astronomers think they can ignore our religious freedom."[58] At a protest on UA's campus where then UA president Manuel Pacheco spoke at the introduction to Native American Recognition Week, Ola stated, "He's not really for Indians. . . . He's just up there to look nice."[59] As Ola put it in 1998, "The money talks for (UA), but not for me. . . . I fight back. If they [UA administrators] get too rude, I get that way myself."[60]

She could be both quick on her feet and able to succinctly sum up the realities for her people. Indeed, when in 2004 the universities of Arizona, Minnesota, and Virginia proposed a series of programs and compensation totaling $120,000 for "the partnership's telescope projects atop Mount Graham," Ola commented that the institutions were "offering cash in exchange for our Apache religion and culture." In response to UA's presentation of the proposal, Ola stated in the Apache language, "You talk to us now, offering bribes of cash in exchange for letting go our defense of our Apache religion and culture." She stated that UA's actions were paternalistic, "something like giving us a little ice cream to quiet us down. . . . Money, like ice cream, does not last," she pointed out, "but our mountain stands there for us and we must stand for our mountain. I would like to see if you all tell us the truth for once, and that the telescopes are to be stopped. . . . They always lie to your face (the U of A)." She exclaimed, "They are lying!" The San Carlos Apache Tribal Council joined the White Mountain Apache Tribal Council in rejecting the so-called Northern Tribes Initiative.[61]

U.S. Congressman Rick Renzi (R-Ariz.) should have known better than to cross Ola. In response to Renzi's outlandish plans to gut the Endangered Species Act and delist the Mount Graham red squirrel, Ola stated, "How would . . . Renzi like to have the hair on the top of his head thinned and parts of his hair chopped out. That's a pretty sacred place to him, I would guess," a direct reference to the Apache belief that plants, trees, and animals are the hair of the mountain, which is a living being.[62] "But he disrespects places that are sacred to us." She reprimanded Renzi: "Congressmen like Renzi would sacrifice sacred places in order that developers can destroy the forests, rivers, mountains and special places of this country. The reason our endangered fish and wildlife animals are now endangered is because [of] unscrupulous developers backed by people like Renzi." As she saw it, "Renzi and the astronomers on Mt. Graham look up at the stars but they don't look down at their feet to see what they have destroyed on the earth beneath them." She articulated the environmental concerns regarding Mount Graham, then stated, "Look at the severely endangered animal like the Mt. Graham Red Squirrel, now down to just a few hundred individuals. . . . Congressman Renzi and Congressman Kolbe and others want to make them go extinct so UA [can] build a city of telescopes on the mountain." She pointed out, "If it hadn't been for the squirrel, UA would have by now built a city of telescopes all over the summit of this sacred mountain."[63] Later, Renzi was convicted of seventeen felony offenses, including conspiracy, wire fraud, extortion and bribery, racketeering, and money laundering for his involvement in a land-swap deal—proof positive of Ola's comments regarding this "unscrupulous" politician.[64]

Ola spoke before church organizations and the general public—indeed, to anyone who would listen—and often to resounding applause. She was never a person to mince words. About the Arizona Congressional delegation, she said, "I'm a voter; I vote. . . . I vote for (Sen. Dennis) DeConcini, I vote for (Sen. John) McCain and (Rep. Mo) Udall. And the time when we really needed their help, they turned their back on us. Instead, they approved those things (telescopes) up there," a direct reference to the Congressional exemption that enabled UA to get a foothold on the mountain. "This is really sickening to think about."

Ola visited colleges across the United States, always traveling with her husband, Mike Davis, the Executive Director of Apache Survival Coalition. She testified before student groups, faculty governing bodies, and religious and community organizations. In 2002, she visited with and spoke to my students at Minnesota. Ola traveled to and throughout Europe several times. During one visit, she met with the President of the Italian Parliament and received extensive media coverage.[65] She initiated lawsuits.[66] She led a number of prayer ceremonies on Mount Graham.[67] She organized and spoke during conferences on sacred sites and religious freedom; one conference she planned included a keynote speech by Vine Deloria Jr.[68] She also helped to organize the 200-mile Mount Graham Sacred Run as part of the "Peace and Dignity Journeys 1992 Spiritual Run" from Alaska to Argentina.[69] The Mount Graham Sacred Run is still carried out each year and ends on Mount Graham. Ola wrote dozens of letters over the years.[70] She spoke during press conferences and to international news organizations such as CNN, radical environmentalists from Earth First!, and during a rock concert.[71] She also worked with other Apaches to obtain several resolutions against telescope development from cities such as Pittsburgh, Pennsylvania, national environmental groups such as the Audubon Society, and organizations such as the National Congress of American Indians.[72] She was on set for the filming of the TNT Channel's *Geronimo* in 1993.[73] Ola even ran at age seventy-three for tribal office.[74] "Most of what was once ours has been taken from us. The telescopes will destroy what little we Apaches have left," Ola said. "They [UA] have broken the laws" such as the National Environmental Policy Act (NEPA) and National Historic Preservation Act, bypassed by the UA-secured Congressional exemption, "that were promised to protect us. We come to court to stop the Mount Graham telescopes which threaten our religion and our cultural survival."[75]

She was outraged by the role of the Vatican, especially the Pope, in the astrophysical development: "He should understand about religion. . . . And that mountain is important to the (traditional) religion of my people."[76] She planned to speak with Pope John Paul II, but was turned away at the eleventh hour so that the Pope's handlers could introduce him to "bought" Apaches, as she put it, who supported the Vatican's plans for astrophysical development. In May 1992, Apaches traveled throughout Germany and Italy in an effort to meet with Vatican officials, as well as members of the astronomical associations affiliated with the telescope project.[77] Led by Ola, "The delegation met with representatives of the German and Italian parliaments, . . . city governments . . . , concerned citizens, [and] religious and cultural groups in Germany, Italy and Holland." Rome, Florence, and other municipalities "passed resolutions asking the Vatican . . . to withdraw from Mt. Graham," but the Vatican's chief astronomer, George Coyne, had the audience with the Pope canceled while Ola was waiting to meet him. Two weeks later the Pope met instead with UA's select group of Apaches and representatives of UA Steward Observatory and the Graham County Chamber of Commerce.[78] Apache Geri Kitcheyan made the trip in the place of her husband, Buck, who was forbidden from traveling by court order.[79]

In 2003, Ola spoke to the University of Minnesota Faculty Senate. Minnesota had joined the telescope project exactly one year earlier amid controversy and protest. Ola said, "I am here . . . as a representative of traditionalists and leader fighting for . . . Mount Graham. . . . What I have heard and seen through my fight to preserve my sacred mountain bring many sadness in my heart. So our Apache people strongly believe in upholding their religion and preserving their Apache culture." After the First Parliamentarian informed her that she had long since "exhausted her time," Ola continued talking at length. In a last attempt to marginalize and silence her, the First Parliamentarian again told Ola that she had "exhausted her time," but that did not deter Ola. She continued, "And it will never be in favor of the telescope project which is destroying their religion and cultural property on Mount Graham. . . . I have more to say, but one minute is not enough." The audience of mostly faculty members, as well as a few students, erupted in applause. It was the only moment during the lengthy faculty meeting that saw the audience applauding.[80]

Her travels to Minnesota where I first met her were many, but not the start of her busy calendar of outreach and action. She participated in numerous public rallies. At a UA Columbus Day protest in 1991, "she held the megaphone with her hair tied back and the rick-rack sewed on to her campdress was dignified in white colors. There were others watching her, astounded by her serious determination, as she publically protested."[81] At times, she was the voice of moderation and dutifully used her skills as a grandmother to diffuse tensions, as when she told the activists at a 1992 Columbus Day demonstration on UA's campus to stop wrestling with police: "I am a grandmother. You should listen to me," she admonished, even as she was "manhandled" by police.[82] She was center stage of various documentaries regarding Mount Graham in particular but also sacred sites generally.[83] She appeared alongside American Indian leaders and medicine men in the 1993 VH-1 "rockumentary" titled *World Alerts: Makoce Wakan: Sacred Earth*.[84] She can be seen in many photographs carrying banners and posters, talking with youthful protestors, and telling crowds of people about her messages from the mountain. She met with Henrietta Mann and Deloria, among many other American Indian dignitaries. In the early 1990s, she addressed 5,000 people gathered at the Cathedral of St. John the Divine in New York City.[85] In 1998, workers in Milan, Italy, who were assembling steel structures for the telescopes on Mount Graham, delayed their construction for months in a show of solidarity with Ola's efforts.[86] She provided testimony to the United Nations' Sub-Commission on Prevention of Discrimination and Protection of Minorities, Working Group on Indigenous Peoples, in 1994 and to the UN Commission on Human Rights in 1999.[87] There was nowhere she would not go and no forum that she would not address for the mountain.

Heritage Steward of the Western Apache People

Ola met all criteria for effective "heritage stewardship." She had personal, familial, and tribal ties to her people and to the landscapes, places, and traditions on and near Mount Graham. Her "embeddedness" within Apache culture helped to promote her to leadership roles, both in the Apache Survival Coalition and within the eyes of members of the San Carlos Apache Tribe.[88] She was an elder who knew and understood her language, history, and culture. Her relatives allowed for traditions to be passed down through generations to her. For Ola, Mount Graham was an extremely personal issue. She would talk regularly and argue forcefully about "my mountain" and "my Mount Graham." She also was willing to sacrifice. "Individuals who set aside personal interests or link such concerns to communal heritage goals are more likely to attract support for their agenda," wrote Welch et al. Ola lived modestly and placed nearly all of her energy and efforts into fighting for what she believed.

Ola networked and worked well with people of various faiths and religious beliefs. She created alliances of Indian tribal governments, faith-based communities, Apaches, and environmentalists. She not only knew about the mountain but also how to navigate white male European-American communities. It should be remembered that Ola's permission to speak on behalf of the San Carlos Apache Tribe was never revoked. Her style, mannerisms, and speech made her both endearing and effective among many audiences. She also "deployed effective skills as [a] culture broker . . . by forming potent and enduring partnerships based on common interests and candid communication across significant social boundaries." She networked with and promoted communication between her organization and, for example, Apaches for Cultural Preservation, the Mount Graham Coalition, Scientists for the Preservation of Mount Graham, Catholics for Ethics and Justice, Earth First!, National Congress of American Indians, San Carlos Apache Tribe, White Mountain Apache Tribe, various tribes and scholars, and nearly every major environmental organization. Indeed, she "created and sustained networks of individuals and groups who shared [her] goals and perspectives and made specific commitments to desired futures." Her efforts were not one-sided. For example, she worked well with environmentalists and they had great respect for her. When the universities of Minnesota and Virginia planned to join the telescope project in 2001–2002, she made numerous visits to Minneapolis and Charlottesville to educate, lobby, and protest.[89] But she also had the ability to spur people to take action, as was the case when she met with Eddie Vedder from Pearl Jam or novelist Tony Hillerman. She "inspired others—including many with whom they had little or no contact—to pursue heritage stewardship."[90] In 1998, Ola was nominated as an "Inspirational Woman in Preservation for 'her mighty efforts to protect the Apache peoples' sacred lands, ceremonies and coming generations.'"[91]

"In the face of uncertainty and [occasionally] even jeopardy," Ola emerged as an effective leader. Like a person that Welch et al., highlight in their study, Ola "was cruising through [her] retirement when duty and conscience summoned [her] to service."[92] Despite the naysayers—biochemist Michael Cusanovich, who was UA vice president for research from 1988–1998; George Coyne, head of the Vatican Observatory; journalist Bordewich; John Wilson for the U.S. Forest Service; Catholic priest and scholar Charles Polzer; and many male astronomers—she effectively navigated and worked against the implied violence in the coercive force of male and racial domination, various bureaucracies, colonial endeavors, mythmaking and historical revisionism, and disinformation.[93] She made a number of key advances, most significantly regarding the many universities and research institutions that dropped the project.[94] She educated and networked with people on both sides of the Atlantic. Ola also played a important role and was part of the protests to have UA rename the "Columbus" project the Large Binocular Telescope (LBT).

What is most significant and difficult to argue against is that in 2002, after an exhaustive process and a heap of evidence, the entire mountain range was determined eligible for listing on the National Register of Historic Places as a Traditional Cultural Property of the Western Apache people—proof of both Ola's words and the broader Apache tribal claims regarding Mount Graham.[95] Simultaneously, Max Planck Institute abandoned its Mount Graham telescope in June 2002. Although Max Planck cited the mountain as an unsuitable location for astronomy, something that no UA astronomer could deny, the Apaches knew that the supernatural *gaan*, the "Mountain Spirits" who live in the mountain, had yet again protected this sacred place.[96]

Although three telescopes remain on the mountain, Ola's efforts have brought success. The LBT is still not working, which she and other Apaches would argue is because of the *gaan* protecting the place. In fact, in July 2013 it was noted that "only 60 percent of the [Large Binocular Telescope's] observing time is given to astronomers, with the rest devoted to getting its instruments to work." Moreover, "the number of peer-reviewed publications coming from the LBT has barely risen." Since the 1980s, the telescopes have also been plagued by funding and technological difficulties, engineering and manufacturing setbacks, and less-than-ideal site selections on the mountain.[97] The mountain persists, the squirrels are still there, and plenty of people—native and nonnative—are continuing the work that Ola helped to start.[98]

Ola represents both cultural persistence and decolonial action among the Apache—indeed, among all Indigenous peoples. She was an example for countless Apaches about how to behave and act, and effectively navigate and use the white, male American and European political systems. As countless Apaches pointed out during the last twenty-three years of her life, she showed Apache people how to resist colonialism and fight against what appear on the surface to be stronger opponents. Her life and her activist work continue to matter not only to Indigenous people throughout the United States and abroad but also to white Americans and Europeans, environmentalists, and Catholics everywhere fighting for human rights and cultural and environmental justice. Through her invaluable humor, she reminded me to never take myself too seriously. She is exactly the type of person who should be remembered and celebrated frequently, as she represents the kind of exceptional person who influenced generations by displaying a form of activism of which we need more examples.

Many Apaches appreciated Ola's forthrightness. Ola's goddaughter, Shera Day, pointed out how successful Ola was as an activist. "She spoke before the National Congress of American Indians, and she had them pass a resolution to stop the additional $10 million funding that the University of Arizona was trying to get to build more telescopes on top of Mount Graham. Sure enough, after that resolution was passed, President Clinton did veto the bill," according to Day.[99]

Although she was in her late sixties when began to speak out, Ola was behaving normally for her age, vigorously fighting in ways similar to various Apaches who resisted U.S. imperialism and colonialism in the nineteenth century. Tribal council members who considered themselves "modern Apache" valued Ola's knowledge, wanted to learn the "old ways" from her, and relied on her.[100] She was also physically vigorous. Her demanding schedule of travel, public speaking, letter writing, radio and television interviews, and nonviolent strong protest kept her busy, but it was her Apache culture in many ways that empowered her to carry out this work.

Sadly for at least two generations of Indigenous peoples, environmentalists, and activists who supported, followed, admired, and were inspired by her strength of conviction, Ola Cassadore Davis died on November 25, 2012, at age eighty-nine in Tucson.[101] This "little bitty lady," as she once referred to herself, was actually a human powerhouse, a female force of energy, and an Apache to be reckoned with. Her humor, such as when she stated, "We don't want any telescopes; we don't want *Star Trek*," but also her honesty and conviction, will be sorely missed.[102] At Ola's funeral, "Wendsler Nosie gave a moving eulogy for her and called her a 'warrior' who woke up Apaches and taught them how to fight for their culture."[103] As Ola regularly stated, "Some day you will see. . . . This mountain will belong to us."[104]

In the process of writing this article, Ola's husband, Mike Davis, died on April 13, 2013. Bioanthropologist Peter Warshall, founder of Scientists for the Preservation of Mount Graham, died on April 26, 2013. Anthropologist Keith Basso died on August 4, 2013. He was a founding board member of the Apache Survival Coalition.

JOEL T. HELFRICH is a visiting assistant professor in environmental studies at Hobart and William Smith Colleges.

Notes

The author thanks Dwight Metzger, Robin Silver, and Bob Witzeman, as well as Betsy Brandt, David Chang, Jason Eden, Susan Hess, Dave Roediger, especially John Welch, and two anonymous NAISA reviewers. Vegan kudos to Valerie Wallace for her encouragement. This essay is dedicated to Irma McLean D'Arienzo (1928–2013).

1. The volume of academic studies regarding this contested mountain is staggering. See Joel T. Helfrich, "A Mountain of Politics: The Struggle for *dził nchaa si'an* (Mount Graham), 1871–2002" (PhD diss., University of Minnesota, 2010). Also see Elizabeth A. Brandt, "Executive Summary of the Preliminary Investigation of Apache Use and Occupancy and Review of Cultural Resource Surveys of the Proposed Mt. Graham Astrophysical Area, Pinaleno Mountains, Arizona," for Apache Survival Coalition, May 28, 1991; Elizabeth A. Brandt, "Response to the Statements of the Vatican Observatory on the Mount Graham International Observatory and American Indian Peoples; and Statement on the Mount Graham International Observatory (MGIO), The Ecology of the Pinaleño Mountains, and Related Political Issues," May 5, 1992; Elizabeth A. Brandt, "The Fight for *dził nchaa si'an*, Mount Graham: Apaches and Astrophysical Development in Arizona," *Cultural Survival Quarterly* (Special Issue guest editor: Alfonso Ortiz) 19, no. 4 (Winter 1996): 50–57; John R. Welch, "White Eyes' Lies and the Battle for *dził nchaa si'an*," *American Indian Quarterly* 21, no. 1 (Winter 1997), Special Issue: "To Hear the Eagles Cry: Contemporary Themes in Native American Spirituality," 75–109; Giovanni B. A. M. Panza, "The Impaling of Apache Holy Ground: No Conflict Resolution on Mt. Graham" (master's thesis, Prescott College, Arizona, 1997), 1–50; Alice Feldman, "Othering Knowledge and Unknowing Law: Colonialist Legacies, Indigenous Pedagogies, and Social Transformation" (PhD diss., Arizona State University, 1998); John R. Welch, Ramon Riley, and Michael V. Nixon, "Discretionary Desecration: *Dził Nchaa Si An* (Mount Graham) and Federal Agency Decisions Affection American Indian Sacred Sites," *American Indian Culture and Research Journal* 33, no. 4 (2009): 29–68; and Debbie Williams, "Speaking Place, Saving Place: Cultural Diversity, Negotiating Place, and Public Discourse" (PhD diss., Arizona State University, 2012). For more on the environmental history of Mount Graham, as well as

relevant biological studies, see Helfrich, "A Mountain of Politics," 118–74, esp. n. 482.

2. Many San Carlos Apaches refer to themselves and their Apache kin in the Western Apache language, Nnee Biyáti', as Nneé (literally, "the people").

3. See Keith Hamilton Basso, "Declaration of Keith Basso in Support of a Preliminary Injunction on 9 April 1992" for *Apache Survival Coalition v. United States of America* 21 F3d 895 (9h Cir 1994), esp. 5. Some Apaches also cite the Superstition Mountains as the western sacred mountain border and include the Mogollon Mountain range in New Mexico with the White Mountain range on the east.

4. See Helfrich, "A Mountain of Politics," esp. 179–80; 227–29; 234–50.

5. Arizona-Idaho Conservation Act, PL 100-696, 102 Stat. 4571 (November 18, 1988).

6. Charles Bowden, "How the University [of Arizona] Knocked Off Mount Graham," *City Magazine* (Tucson), January 1, 1989, 29–30; Jim Erickson, "UA Asks U.S. to Drop Rare Squirrel from Endangered List," *Arizona Daily Star* (Tucson), August 27, 1986; John Dougherty, "Star Whores: The Ruthless Pursuit of Astronomical Sums of Cash and Scientific Excellence," *Phoenix New Times*, June 16–22, 1993, 2–11; Gregory McNamee, "Mountain Under Heavens," *terrain.org: A Journal of the Built and Natural Environments* 8 (Autumn 2000); Frank Graham, "Mt. Graham Makes All Equal," letter, *Eastern Arizona Courier* (Safford, Ariz.), June 5, 2002.

7. Ruth Rogers, letter, "Science on Sacred Site," *Star Tribune* (Minneapolis), July 9, 2002.

8. Gregg Jones, "K-9s Need Constant Training," *Eastern Arizona Courier* (Safford, Ariz.), April 18, 2004, 1A, 7A.

9. John R. Welch, Dana Lepofsky, Megan Caldwell, Georgia Combes, and Craig Rust, "Treasure Bearers: Personal Foundations for Effective Leadership in Northern Coast Salish Heritage Stewardship," *Heritage & Society* 4, no. 1 (Spring 2011): 102.

10. Welch et al., "Treasure Bearers," 83, 102.

11. Ibid., 87.

12. Norma Coile, "Apache May Seek Halt on Graham," *Tucson Citizen*, October 4, 1989, 1A. For excellent articles regarding Ola, see: Sandra Rambler, "A Determined, Strong-Willed Apache Elder Says: 'Save Mount Graham,'" *The Moccasin* (Globe, Ariz.), October 22, 1991; Carol Ann Bassett, "Fighting for the Heavens: Others before Her Have Failed to Stop the Construction of Telescopes on Mount Graham. But San Carlos Apache Ola Cassadore Davis Isn't Giving Up," *Tucson Weekly*, April 22–28, 1992; Karen Lincoln Michel, "Defending the Dream: Apache to Talk at Dallas Conference about Why She Believes Site Sacred," *The Dallas Morning News* (Dallas–Fort Worth), November 20, 1992, 29A, 34A; Mary Anderson, "Apache Woman Fights to Preserve Sacred Site," *Indian Country Today*, January 14, 1993; Charlotte Snow, "Cultivating Common Ground: Charlotte Snow Explores an Emerging National Union between Native Americans and Environmentalists," *N Magazine* (Northwestern U.), March 1, 1993, 16–19; Maggie Trinkle, "Pearl Jam's Eddie Vedder Cries for Mt. Graham: Chairperson of Apache Coalition Wants Her Culture to Stay Alive," *Arizona Daily Wildcat* (U. of Arizona), November 23, 1993; Stephanie Innes, "Apache Woman Won't Give Up Fight vs. Mt. Graham

Telescopes," *Tucson Citizen*, August 3, 1998; Carolina C. Butler to author, "I admire Ola Cassadore Davis," e-mail, March 17, 2002; Stuart Alan Becker, "Seeing on Mount Graham," *Tucson Weekly*, December 5–11, 2002; Bob Zache, "Double Apache Sunrise Dance Exhausting Event for Everyone," *The Moccasin* (Globe, Ariz.), August 10, 2005; Sandra Rambler, "Tribal Elders Mourn Loss of Spiritual Leader," *Eastern Arizona Courier* (Safford, Ariz.), January 2, 2013.

13. Anderson, "Apache Woman Fights to Preserve Sacred Site."

14. Likely East Fork Lutheran Academy, a boarding school for Apaches, began in 1951.

15. Anderson, "Apache Woman Fights to Preserve Sacred Site"; Ola C. Davis, "Davis Seeks Tribal Council Seat," *The Moccasin* (Globe, Ariz.), September 17, 1996.

16. Paul Brinkley-Rogers, "Apache Past He Helped Save Lives in Medicine Man's Funeral," *The Arizona Daily Star* (Tucson), September 2, 1985, A5; "1,000 Mourn Death of Apache Leader," *The Arizona Republic* (Phoenix), September 2, 1985; Steve Emerine, "Senate Asks Pacheco for Graham Project Forums," *Lo Que Pasa: UA Community News/Calendar* (University of Arizona), October 14, 1991; David L. Eppele, "On the Desert: Apache Medicine Man's Ten Commandments Are Timeless," *The Arizona Territorial*, April 28, 1992, 21. See letters to newspapers by Edison Cassadore: "How Can Telescope Benefit Poor, Uneducated Apaches?" *The Arizona Republic* (Phoenix), April 20, 1992; *The Moccasin* (Globe, Ariz.), April 21, 1992; "Cultural Survival," *The Phoenix Gazette*, April 25, 1992; "UA Anthropology Student Says 'Save Mt. Graham,'" *The Navajo-Hopi Observer*, April 29, 1992; "Losing Heritage," *Tempe, Mesa, Chandler Tribunes*, April 30, 1992; "What Will We Inherit?" *Tucson Citizen*, May 20, 1992. See also the music and biography of Philip Cassadore on the following insert: "Apache: Traditional Apache Songs," Canyon Records Vintage Collection, vol. 5 (Phoenix: Canyon Records, 1998), compact disk, CR-6053. See Betsy Brandt to author, e-mail, May 21, 2013.

17. Anderson, "Apache Woman Fights to Preserve Sacred Site." See also, Trinkle, "Pearl Jam's Eddie Vedder Cries for Mt. Graham."

18. Bassett, "Fighting for the Heavens," 7; Anderson, "Apache Woman Fights to Preserve Sacred Site."

19. Ola Cassadore Davis, letter, "Big Mountain-Mount Graham." See Michael J. D'Amico, "Mountain Under Siege!," *Outdoors West*, Winter 1989 (Dec): 2.

20. Rambler, "A Determined, Strong-Willed Apache Elder, Says: 'Save Mount Graham.'"

21. Paul Brinkley-Rogers, "Apache Past He Helped Save Lives in Medicine Man's Funeral," *The Arizona Daily Star* (Tucson), September 2, 1985, A5; "1,000 Mourn Death of Apache Leader," *The Arizona Republic* (Phoenix), September 2, 1985; David L. Eppele, "On the Desert: Apache Medicine Man's Ten Commandments Are Timeless," *The Arizona Territorial*, April 28, 1992, 21.

22. Anderson, "Apache Woman Fights to Preserve Sacred Site."

23. Peter Aleshire, "Apache's Dream Inspires Struggle," *The Arizona Republic* (Phoenix), September 29, 1991; Bassett, "Fighting for the Heavens"; Lincoln Michel, "Defending the Dream," 29A.

24. Anderson, "Apache Woman Fights to Preserve Sacred Site."

25. Bassett, "Fighting for the Heavens," 6; Anderson, "Apache Woman Fights to Preserve Sacred Site."

26. Coile, "Apache May Seek Halt on Graham," 1A; "Should Observatory Be Built? Some Apaches Say 'No,'" *The Moccasin* (Globe, Ariz.), December 12, 1989, 1. See also, D'Amico, "Mountain Under Siege!," 2; Brandt to author, May 21, 2013.

27. Coile, "Apache May Seek Halt on Graham."

28. Ibid., 1A; "Should Observatory Be Built? Some Apaches Say 'No,'" 6. See also, Bassett, "Fighting for the Heavens."

29. Anderson, "Apache Woman Fights to Preserve Sacred Site."

30. See David Hoye, "Mountain Long Sacred to Tribe, Newly Found Notes Show: Evidence Jeopardizes Observatory Project," *The Phoenix Gazette*, November 21, 1991.

31. Keith Basso, Testimony, Meeting of the U. Senate, Faculty Senate, and Twin Cities Campus Assembly, University of Minnesota, October 30, 2003.

32. Douglas Kreutz, "Apache Group Opposes Mt. Graham Telescopes," *The Arizona Daily Star* (Tucson), May 30, 1990; "Apache Coalition Will Fight Telescopes," *The Moccasin* (Globe, Ariz.), June 5, 1990; "New Apache Coalition Speaks in Opposition to Scope Project," *Eastern Arizona Courier* (Safford, Ariz.), June 6, 1990; Norma Coile, "San Carlos Tribe Vows to Fight Scopes," *Tucson Citizen*, June 17, 1990.

33. "San Carlos Tribal Council Oposes [sic] Mt. Graham Telescopes," *The Moccasin* (Globe, Ariz.), July 17, 1990; Apache Survival Coalition, News Release, "Holy War: Apaches Return from Washington, D.C. after Battle for Sacred Mountain," June 29, 1990.

34. "San Carlos Tribal Council Oposes [sic] Mt. Graham Telescopes"; "Tribal Council Opposes Telescopes," *The Phoenix Gazette*, July 12, 1990, A7; Kevin Franklin, "Apaches Voice Graham Views," *Arizona Summer Wildcat* (University of Arizona), July 24, 1990, 1, 12.

35. Stan Bindell, "Apaches Continue Their Struggle to Stop the Mount Graham Telescope," *The Navajo-Hopi Observer*, October 9, 1991; Peter La Chapelle, "San Carlos Tribal Council Supports Survival Coalition," *Arizona Daily Wildcat* (University of Arizona), December 11, 1991, 11.

36. Sam Stanton, "Agency May Ask Halt on Scopes: Squirrel Numbers Down, Probe Says," *The Arizona Republic* (Phoenix), June 26, 1990, B1-B2; Associated Press, "Congress Probe Recommends Delaying Observatory," *The Tempe Daily News Tribune*, June 27, 1990, B6; Associated Press, "UA Proceeds with Telescopes; Agency Cites Squirrel Concerns," *Scottsdale Arizona Progress*, June 27, 1990: 5; Anne Hazard, "Doubt Cast on Squirrel Study," *The Arizona Daily Star* (Tucson), June 27, 1990, 1, 4A.

37. Ola Cassadore Davis, "Support Appreciated," letter, *The Moccasin* (Globe, Ariz.), January 14, 1992. See also Ola Cassadore Davis, "Thanks for Support for Survival Coalition," letter, *The Moccasin* (Globe, Ariz.), September 1, 1999.

38. Apache Survival Coalition, "#1 Band PEARL JAM to Perform Benefit Concert to Help Save Mt. Graham," press release, November 6, 1993; "Updates: Mt. Graham," *Honor Digest*, January 1994; Blake Morlock, "Scope of New Mt. Graham

Wrinkle Disputed by U of A and Opponents," *The Moccasin* (Globe, Ariz.), February 1, 1994.

39. Mario R. Dederichs, "Sterngucker gegen Eichhörnchen" [Stargazers versus squirrels], *Stern* (Hamburg, Germany) 49, 30 November 1989, 234–36.

40. David Hoye, "Sacred Ground: Apaches Have Reasons to Oppose Mount Graham Telescopes," *The Phoenix Gazette*, May 2, 1991, B1, B4. See also Tim McCarthy, "Smithsonian Throws Punch—Observatory Sees Stars," *National Catholic Reporter*, May 17, 1991: 5.

41. Jacquelyn Coffin, "Does This Republican Congress Have No Shame?" letter, *Indian Country Today*, June 11–18, 1996; Apache Survival Coalition, "Apaches Hit Congressman Renzi for Spurring Desecration of Sacred Mountain," news release, September 20, 2004.

42. David Hoye, "Apaches Ask Regents to Kill Telescope Project: Tribes Showed Little Concern When Asked, U of A Says," *The Phoenix Gazette*, May 4, 1991, B1, B2.

43. UA worked to undermine tribal sovereignty. See Steve Emerine, "Tribal Views of Mt. Graham Distorted in Editorial," letter, *Arizona Daily Wildcat* (University of Arizona), December 6, 1991, 4. See also letters to various newspapers by Ola: *The Moccasin* (Globe, Ariz.), September 29, 1992; "Apaches Remain Proud as They Continue Struggle," *The Navajo-Hopi Observer*, October 7, 1992; "Says Regents Ignore Duties," *Eastern Arizona Courier* (Stafford, Ariz.), December 16, 1992; "No More Rubber Stamp Regents," *Navajo Times*, November 17, 1992; "Regents Ask Apache Coalition to Stop Correspondence," *The Arizona Republic* (Phoenix), December 17, 1992, A21; "Regents Should Listen," *Tucson Citizen*, December 19, 1992; "Reluctant Regents," *TDN Tribune*, January 2, 1993; "Regents Should Respect Input from the Public," *The Navajo-Hopi Observer*, January 13, 1993.

44. Joel T. Helfrich, "On Being an Active Historian and the Usefulness of History: The Case of the Ongoing Struggle for *dził nchaa si'an* (Mount Graham)," *Left History* 15, no. 1 (2010): 151–52.

45. Booz-Allen & Hamilton, Inc., final report, "University of Arizona: Mount Graham Observatory Review Issues," Tucson, Arizona, October 23, 1991, 1–42. UA's Office of Public Information distributed a packet titled, "Mount Graham International Observatory: Southern Arizona's World-Class Site for Science," n.d. [Fall 1988]. Articles included: Ben Avery, "Squirreling Away Land on Mount Graham Makes No Sense," *The Arizona Republic* (Phoenix), July 22, 1988; "Cut the Red Tape on Telescopes for Mt. Graham," editorial, *Tucson Citizen*, July 27, 1988; John P. Schaefer, "Scientific Preserve Is the Right Choice for Saving Mt. Graham," *Tucson Citizen*, July 28, 1988; "Stop Dragging Feet on Mt. Graham Telescopes," comment, *Green Valley News and Sun* (Green Valley, Ariz.), July 29, 1988; "Time to Move on Mt. Graham," comment, *Tucson Citizen*, August 5, 1988; "Congress Must Act on Scopes," opinion, *Sierra Vista Herald* (Sierra Vista, Ariz.), August 7, 1988; "Ruddy Rodent Celebrities: End Impasses on Squirrels," *The Arizona Republic* (Phoenix), August 9, 1988; Henry Koffler, "Opinion Causes Controversy for UA," *Eastern Arizona Courier* (Safford), August 10, 1988; "Action, Not Reaction Answer to Mountain Woe," editorial, *Eastern Arizona Courier* (Safford), August 10, 1988. See also, James Coates, "Fervent Battle Pits Science against

Nature, and Leaves University Divided," *Chicago Tribune*, July 5, 1990, C6, as well as Peter A. Strittmatter, letter, *The New York Times*, June 5, 1990; Steve Emerine, "Squirrels and Telescopes," letter, *The New York Times*, June 5, 1990; Bruce Walsh, Roger Angel, and Peter Strittmatter, "Endangered Telescopes or Species?" *Nature*, November 17, 1994: 215–16; Conrad A. Istock and Robert S. Hoffmann, eds., *Storm Over a Mountain Island: Conservation Biology and the Mt. Graham Affair* (Tucson: University of Arizona Press, 1995); and Michael A. Cusanovich, "*Dzil Nchaa Si An*, Mount Graham: Fact or Fiction," *Cultural Survival Quarterly* 20, no. 3 (October 31, 1996).

46. Coile, "Apache May Seek Halt on Graham," 1A.

47. Roger Featherstone to author, personal communication, November 27, 2013.

48. Connie Cone Sexton, "Ola Cassadore Davis, 89, Voice for Apaches," *The Arizona Republic* (Phoenix), January 15, 2013, B4.

49. Fergus M. Bordewich, "Predators, Victims, and Mother Earth," *Killing the White Man's Indian: Reinventing Native Americans at the End of the Twentieth Century* (1996; New York: Anchor Books, 1997), 204–39. See comments regarding Bordewich: Helfrich, "On Being an Active Historian and the Usefulness of History," 152–53, fn. 18. See also O. V. Farmby-Harrison, "Starry-Starry Trite," letter, *Tucson Weekly*, May 6, 1992; "Telescope Controversy: And So It Goes," editorial, *Eastern Arizona Courier* (Safford, Ariz.), June 3, 1992: 4A; Guy Lopez, "Angry about Overlooked Facts," letter, *The Cavalier Daily* (University of Virginia), February 5, 2002.

50. Cusanovich, "*Dzil Nchaa Si An*, Mount Graham."

51. Jim Erickson, "Apaches Rescind Opposition to Mount Graham Telescopes," *The Arizona Daily Star* (Tucson), July 22, 1993; "Apache Tribe Neutral on UA Telescope Issue," *The Arizona Republic* (Phoenix), July 23, 1993; "Apache Withdraw Opposition," *Tucson Citizen*, July 22, 1993, 2C; "Tribe Drops Telescope Fight," *The Gallop Independent*, July 26, 1993; "Tribal Council Rescinds Decision: Now Doesn't Support, Oppose Scopes," *Eastern Arizona Courier* (Stafford, Ariz.), July 28, 1993; Sal Salerno, ". . . While San Carlos Tribal Council Retreats," *The Circle* (Minneapolis), August 1993; Sal Salerno, "San Carlos Tribal Council Withdraws Opposition to Mt. Graham Telescope Project," *The Circle* (Minneapolis), September 1993: 14.

52. Peter La Chapelle, "Mt. Graham Not Sacred, Ex-Tribal Chairman Says: Claims Official 'Used' by Environmentalists," *Arizona Daily Wildcat* (University of Arizona), October 29, 1991, 1; "Mt. Graham Forum Reveals Two Tribal Viewpoints," *The Moccasin* (Globe, Ariz.), March 31, 1992; Mel Graham, "Learn to Live in Peace," letter, *Eastern Arizona Courier* (Safford, Ariz.), August 1, 2001.

53. Tim McCarthy, "Protest Delays Debut of Vatican Telescope," *National Catholic Reporter*, October 1, 1993, 7.

54. Peter Warshall, "The Heart of Genuine Sadness: Astronomers, Politicians, and Federal Employees Desecrate the Holiest Mountain of the San Carlos Apache," *Whole Earth* 91 (Winter 1997): 30–36.

55. Sal Salerno, "San Carlos Tribal Council Withdraws Opposition to Mt. Graham Telescope Project," *News from Indian Country*, late September 1993: 9.

56. Ola Cassadore Davis, "Non-Destructive Options Needed at Mt. Graham,"

letter, *Indian Country Today*, October 27, 1993, A5; Native American Smoke Signals, "Apaches Keep Up Telescope Resistance Despite Brush-Off at Sacred Mountain," *Native American Smoke Signals*, November 1993.

57. "Astronomers May Sue Apache," *The Moccasin* (Globe, Ariz.), September 10, 1991.

58. Sandra Rambler, "San Carlos Apaches Condemn Desecration of Mount Graham," *Indian Country Today*, October 30, 1995.

59. Peter La Chapelle, "Week Lauds Contributions: Protestors at Ceremony Focus on Mt. Graham," *Arizona Daily Wildcat* (University of Arizona), September 24, 1991.

60. Innes, "Apache Woman Won't Give Up Fight vs. Mt. Graham Telescopes."

61. John Kamin, "San Carlos Rejects UA Proposal," *Eastern Arizona Courier* (Safford, Ariz.), April 18, 2004; Natasha Bhuyan, "Tribe Rejects Funds, Upset with UA," *Arizona Daily Wildcat* (University of Arizona), April 30, 2004; Brenda Norrell, "Apache Reject Money and Bring Honor to Mount Graham," *Indian Country Today*, May 26, 2004.

62. Brandt to author, May 21, 2013; Apache Survival Coalition, "Apaches Hit Congressman Renzi for Spurring Desecration of Sacred Mountain"; Greg Jones, "Congressional Hearing Focuses on ESA Weaknesses," *Eastern Arizona Courier* (Safford, Ariz.), September 22, 2004; Robert Witzeman, "Renzi Wrong about Mount Graham," letter, *Tucson Citizen*, November 2, 2004.

63. Apache Survival Coalition, "Apaches Hit Congressman Renzi for Spurring Desecration of Sacred Mountain."

64. The United States Department of Justice, Office of Public Affairs, "Former Congressman Richard G. Renzi Convicted of Extortion and Bribery in Illegal Federal Land Swap," June 11, 2013 (http://www.justice.gov/opa/pr/2013/June/13-crm-666.html); Associated Press, "Renzi Convicted on 17 of 32 Counts," *Arizona Daily Sun* (Flagstaff, Ariz.), June 12, 2013; Monica Vendituoli, "Renzi's Decline Reflected in Personal Financial Reports," Center for Responsive Politics, *Open Secrets Blog*, June 12, 2013. (http://www.opensecrets.org/news/2013/06/former-rep-rick-renzis-record.html). See also Associated Press, "FEC Accuses Renzi of Illegal Financing," *Arizona Daily Star* (Tucson), December 20, 2004.

65. Nando Minnella, "Apaches at the Parliament: 'It's a Sacred Place. No More Expenditures.' Meeting with Violante in Rome," *Il Manifesto*, July 24, 1998; House of Deputies Press Office, "Violante Receives Apache Community Delegation," press release, July 23, 1998.

66. Peter La Chapelle, "Group Files Suit over Mt. Graham Telescopes," *Arizona Daily Wildcat* (University of Arizona), August 22, 1991, 3A; Jim Erickson, "Apaches Sue to Halt Mt. Graham Telescopes," *The Arizona Daily Star* (Tucson), August 20, 1991; "Apaches Sue to Stop Mt. Graham Telescopes," *The Moccasin* (Globe, Ariz.), August 27, 1991; Mary Anderson, "Apaches Sue Observatory," *The Lakota Times* (Rapid City, S. D.), August 28, 1991; "Apaches Sue to Stop Monstrous Mt. Graham Telescopes: Law Violations by Columbus Project Threaten Apache Religious Freedom," *The Circle* (Minneapolis), September 1991: 12; "U of A Threatening to Join against Lawsuit along with Forest Service," *The Moccasin* (Globe, Ariz.), October 15, 1991.

67. Jim Erickson, "Indians to Press Mt. Graham Scope Fight," *The Arizona*

Daily Star (Tucson), May 31, 1992; George Hardeen, "Spiritual Leaders Conduct Ceremony atop Mt. Graham," *The Circle* (Minneapolis), July 1992.

68. "Talks Target Sacred Sites of Tribes," *The Arizona Republic* (Phoenix), May 23, 1992, B4; K. J. Scotta, "Scope Ruling Draws Apache Tears," *Tucson Citizen*, May 30, 1992. See also, Lincoln Michel, "Defending the Dream"; Karen Lincoln Michel, "Conference Focuses on Observatory Dispute," *The Dallas Morning News* (Dallas–Fort Worth), November 21, 1992; Michael Davis, "Apache Survival Coalition Members Seek Protection of Sacred Lands," *The Moccasin* (Globe, Ariz.), April 3, 2002.

69. Dee Ralles, "Apache Runners Make 'Sacrifice' for Mt. Graham," *The Arizona Republic* (Phoenix), August 21, 1992; Bridget A. Morrissey, "Native Americans Run as Commemoration: Run Commemorates Indigenous Struggle," *Arizona Daily Wildcat* (University of Arizona), August 21, 1992; Xavier Gallegos, "The Long Run," photograph, *Tucson Weekly*, August 21, 1992; A. E. Aralza, "Long Journey into Mexico," photograph, *The Arizona Daily Star* (Tucson), August 21, 1992; Apache Survival Coalition, "Apache Sacred Run Protests UofAZ/Vatican/German Desecration Of Mount Graham," Press Release, August 24, 1992; "San Carlos Apaches Join Spiritual Runs of Indians from Alaska to Argentina," *Copper Country News*, August 25, 1992; "Apaches Part of America's Run," *The Moccasin* (Globe, Ariz.), August 25, 1992; "Tribal Ways: The Run for the Americas," *The Moccasin* (Globe, Ariz.), September 1, 1992; Sandra Rambler, "Traditionally Speaking" column, *The Moccasin* (Globe, Ariz.), September 13, 2000.

70. Among many examples, see Ola Cassadore Davis, "Museum Is No Celebration of History, Only Wrongs," letter, *The Moccasin* (Globe, Ariz.), February 22, 1994; reprinted with alternative titles in *Navajo-Hopi Observer*, February 23, 1994; *Eastern Arizona Courier*, February 23, 1994. See also, Ola Cassadore Davis, "Reader Says UA Praising the Theft of Indian Lands," letter, *Indian Country Today*, March 2, 1994; Ola Cassadore Davis, "Apaches Appeal: Violation of Their Religious Freedom," *Arizona Wildlife News*, Summer 1994: 1; Ola Cassadore Davis, "Telescope Site at Mount Graham," letter, *Nature*, December 15, 1994: 589; Ola Cassadore Davis, "Education without Ethics," letter, *Indian Times*, November 25, 1998 (reprinted in *Eastern Arizona Courier* and *News from Indian Country*); Ola Cassadore Davis, "Hear Apache Plea," letter, *The Arizona Republic* (Phoenix), December 18, 1998; Ola Cassadore Davis, "Davis Protests Opening of Refugium," letter, *The Moccasin* (Globe, Ariz.), June 28, 2000; Ola Cassadore Davis to Mark Yudof (President, University of Minnesota), letter, December 6, 2001; Ola Cassadore Davis, "Apache Folklore" column, *The Moccasin* (Globe, Ariz.), July 3, 2002, June 4, 2003, September 17, 2003, June 16, 2004, and October 20, 2004; Ola Cassadore Davis, "Stanley Not Informed," letter, *Eastern Arizona Courier* (Safford, Ariz.), December 11, 2002; Ola Cassadore Davis, "Arizona Bias Is Showing," letter, *Arizona Republic* (Phoenix), March 22, 2003. In one prescient comment, see Ola Cassadore Davis, "Keep Beef Donations for Funerals," letter, *The Moccasin* (Globe, Ariz.), April 10, 2002.

71. "Mt. Graham Telescope Site Found to Be Defective," *The Moccasin* (Globe, Ariz.), December 1, 1992; Anderson, "Apache Woman Fights to Preserve Sacred Site"; Mary W. Anderson, "Apaches Make a Sacred Run to Mount Graham," *Indian*

Country Today, July 14, 1993, A3; Jim Nintzel, "Squirmin' on the Mount: Earth First! Meets the Force of Law and Order on Mount Graham," *Tucson Weekly*, July 7–13, 1993, 12; Naomi Mudge, "Pearly Jam, Mt. Graham: Eddie Vedder Tells It on the Mountain," *Threshold*, December 1993; SEAC-Southwest, "Environmental and Native Rights Activists Challenge Astronomy Community over Mt. Graham Travesty," press release, January 10, 1995.

72. "Tribal Members Attend Inauguration," *The Moccasin* (Globe, Ariz.), January 26, 1993; Martha Zaye, "About Time for Another Indian Rights Milestone," letter, *The Phoenix Gazette*, February 18, 1993, A9; Martha Zaye, letter, *The Moccasin* (Globe, Ariz.), February 23, 1993; Martha L. Zaye, "Praise for Those Who Seek Change," letter, *Indian Country Today*, March 31, 1993, A5; "Mt. Graham Sacred Run Draws World Field," *The Moccasin* (Globe, Ariz.), August 25, 1999.

73. Sandra Rambler, "Running Fox Is Modern-Day Geronimo," *Native American Smoke Signals*, September–October 1993: 8.

74. Davis, "Davis Seeks Tribal Council Seat."

75. "Apache Tribe Files to Stop Telescopes," *Eastern Arizona Courier*, August 21, 1991, 1A, 10A.

76. Coile, "Apache May Seek Halt on Graham," 1A; "Should Observatory Be Built? Some Apaches Say 'No,'" 6. Ola and her husband were Democrats. See: Steve Yozwiak, "Environmentalist Put President on Notice," *The Arizona Republic*, August 29, 1996.

77. Steve Yozwiak, "Tribe Goes to Europe to Fight Telescopes," *The Arizona Republic* (Phoenix), May 23, 1992; Associated Press, "Apaches Visit Europe in Bid to Halt Mount Graham Telescope," *Arizona Daily Star* (Tucson), May 24, 1992; Sal Salerno, "Apache Delegation Returns from European Tour of Protest," *The Circle* (Minneapolis) 13, June 6, 1992: 28; Apache Survival Coalition, "Apache Delegation to Germany and Italy Return. Deep Concern over Mt. Graham Shown in Europe," press release, May 18, 1992

78. "Apache Delegation Denied Audience with Pope," *The Moccasin* (Globe, Ariz.) 8, no. 89, May 29, 1992. See also, "German Council Confused on Mt. Graham Project Support," *The Moccasin* (Globe, Ariz.), August 4, 1992.

79. Steve Yozwiak, "Ex-Apache Leader Grounded," *The Arizona Republic* (Tucson), n.d. [June 1991]; "Recall Election Reviewed: Kitcheyan Arraigned on Theft Charges," *Eastern Arizona Courier* (Safford, Ariz.), July 17, 1991, 1A, 5A; Tara Meyer, "Apaches to Lobby without Leader," *Arizona Summer Wildcat* (University of Arizona), June 11, 1992, 1, 2; Tara Meyer, "Apaches Leave for Europe Leaderless," *Arizona Summer Wildcat* (University of Arizona), June 16, 1992; Tara Meyer, "Meeting with Pope Angers Tribal Group," *Arizona Summer Wildcat* (University of Arizona), June 23, 1992. See also, "Kitcheyan Guilty on Fourteen Counts," *The Moccasin* (Globe, Ariz.) 8, no. 16, December 15, 1992; Ann-Eve Pederson, "Former San Carlos Apache Chairman Pleads Guilty to Embezzling $63,312," *Arizona Daily Star* (Tucson), July 8, 1994; "Kitcheyan Pleads Guilty; Sentencing September 19 in Tucson," *The Moccasin* (Globe, Ariz.), July 12, 1994; Chad Unrein, "Former Apache Chairman to Be Jailed," *Indian Country Today*, December 8, 1994.

80. Ola Cassadore Davis, Testimony, Meeting of the University Senate,

Faculty Senate, and Twin Cities Campus Assembly, University of Minnesota, October 30, 2003.

81. Rambler, "A Determined, Strong-Willed Apache Elder Says: 'Save Mount Graham.'"

82. See the Friends of Mount Graham video by Sky Crosby, dir., *International Day of Actions in Defense of Mount Graham* (Tucson: ECO Productions, 1994). See also, Gabrielle Fimbres, "More Protest Arrests Possible: Prosecutors Will Review a Tape Made as Anti-Telescope Demonstrators Clashed with Police at UA," *Tucson Citizen*, October 13, 1992.

83. "Apache Tradition Meets Modern Age in European Documentary," *The Moccasin* (Globe, Ariz.), August 16, 1994; Stéphane Goël, dir., *Le Garçon S'Appelait Apache* [This boy's name was Apache] (Climage and Ardèche Images Production, 1995).

84. "VH-1 Focuses on Native American Sacred Sites with 'World Alerts: Makoce Wakan: Sacred Earth,'" *Indian Country Today*, November 24, 1993, A7; VH-1, "VH-1 Focuses on Native American Sacred Sites with World Alerts: Makoce Wakan: Sacred Earth," press release, January 1, 1994.

85. Bordewich, *Killing the White Man's Indian*, 204–6. See also, Anderson, "Apache Woman Fights to Preserve Sacred Site."

86. Claudia Emilitri, "Ansaldo, Workers Ally Themselves with the Apaches: 'Conscientious Objection' Against the Telescope Headed for the Sacred Mountain," *Diario Della Settimana*, July 8–14, 1998; "'Conscientious Objection' at Ansaldo: No Telescope on Mount Graham," *Giornale di Brescia* (Lombardia, Italy), June 10, 1998; "The Strange Accord between the Ansaldo Workers and the Indians and Now the Workers Ally Themselves with the Apaches," *Visto*, June 26, 1998.

87. Ola Cassadore Davis to United Nations' Sub-Commission on Prevention of Discrimination and Protection of Minorities, Working Group on Indigenous Peoples, letter, July 28, 1999; Helen Sheppard, "Apaches Halt UA Telescope Project," *Indian Country Today*, July 25, 1994, A2; Ola Cassadore Davis, "Apache Intervention at the UNCHR Session, Geneva," e-mail, April 20, 1999.

88. Welch et al., "Treasure Bearers," 103.

89. Helfrich, "A Mountain of Politics," 358–421.

90. Welch et al., "Treasure Bearers," 105.

91. "Morning Star Nominates Ola Davis as Inspirational Woman in Preservation," *Indian Country Today*, May 4, 1998; "For Her Efforts to Protect Mt. Graham, Ola Cassadore Davis Nominated as Inspirational," *Indian Country Today*, mid-May 1998.

92. Welch et al., "Treasure Bearers," 106.

93. Helfrich, "On Being an Active Historian and the Usefulness of History," 151–52, fn. 15–26.

94. Helfrich, "A Mountain of Politics," 209–21.

95. National Park Service, United States Department of Interior, "Determination of Eligibility Notification," April 30, 2002.

96. Ruth Rogers, "Planck Institute Has Quit Telescope," letter, *The Moccasin* (Globe, Ariz.), July 17, 2002; Tom Jackson King, "Scope Loses Partner: Germans

Cut Level in Radiotelescope; Still Back LBT," *Eastern Arizona Courier* (Safford, Ariz.), June 26, 2002, 2A; The Southwest Center for Biological Diversity, "Max Planck Withdrawal from Mt. Graham 'Very Likely,'" news release, January 13, 2000.

97. Alexandra Witze, "Teething Troubles at Huge Telescope: The Large Binocular Telescope Gets Off to a Sluggish Start," *Nature*, July 11, 2013: 133–34; Tom Beal, "University of Arizona Astronomers See More Clearly than Ever," *Arizona Daily Star* (Tucson), August 21, 2013.

98. Sandra Rambler, "Apache Tribes Hold Coming of Age Ceremony on *Dzil Nchaa Si An*," *Eastern Arizona Courier* (Safford, Ariz.), August 5, 2013.

99. Rambler, "Tribal Elders Mourn Loss of Spiritual Leader."

100. Kamin, "San Carlos Rejects UA Proposal."

101. Sexton, "Ola Cassadore Davis, 89, Voice for Apaches."

102. Steve Yozwiak, "Scope Work Defiles Site, UA's Head Told," *Arizona Republic* (Phoenix), December 11, 1991, B2.

103. Brandt to author, May 21, 2013.

104. Erickson, "Indians to Press Mt. Graham Scope Fight"; "Indians Reaffirm Opposition to Mount Graham Telescopes," *The Arizona Republic* (Phoenix), June 1, 1992, B2; *The Native American: A Weekly Publication*, June 5, 1992.

Reviews

KELLY S. McDONOUGH

Nahua and Maya Catholicisms: Texts and Religion in Colonial Central Mexico and Yucatan
by Mark Z. Christensen
Stanford University Press, 2013

IN 1539 Don Carlos Ometochtzin, a native lord of the Nahua *altepetl* of Texcoco, was found guilty by the Spanish Inquisition as a "heretical dogmatizer" and subsequently burned at the stake. Among his missteps, Don Carlos purportedly had the (fatal) audacity to question why, if the Catholic faith exhibited so many variations, could pre-Hispanic religious beliefs and practices not peacefully coexist alongside Christianity? Whereas Indigenous deviation from the supposed "one true faith" was often couched in terms of willful disobedience, or mental and moral deficiencies that rendered natives unable to truly understand and accept Christianity, Don Carlos's line of questioning suggests that a uniform version of Catholicism in colonial Mesoamerica was perhaps a theory but clearly not a practice. In *Nahua and Maya Catholicisms: Texts and Religion in Colonial Central Mexico and Yucatan*, ethnohistorian Mark Z. Christensen demonstrates that this was indeed the case.

Through a skilled comparative analysis of seventy-one published and unpublished Nahuatl- and Maya-language sources representing more than three hundred years (1546–1855), Christensen successfully provides definitive documentary evidence of not only the existence of various Catholicisms, but also the distinct ways in which Nahuas, Mayas, and Spaniards created, prescribed, and reflected the Christian message(s) at local and regional levels. The sources include a wide variety of native-language ecclesiastical texts—books of Christian doctrine, confessional manuals, sermons, religious dramas, testaments, and sacramental manuals—which are organized according to three major categories: Category 1: "published 'official' texts written by ecclesiastic authors and/or their aides intended for a broad readership of both ecclesiastic and native populations"; Category 2: "unpublished texts written by ecclesiastics or their supervised stewards for more local audiences, including religious authorities"; and Category 3: "unpublished, unofficial texts written by natives for natives . . . with minimal or no ecclesiastic supervision" (88). This last category, represented by two Nahuatl-language texts and eight in Maya, is one of the more fascinating aspects of the study. In chapter

6, Christensen analyzes two Category 3 documents, one Nahuatl-language (The Conversion of Paul) and another in Maya (The Creation of Adam) both of which exemplify unique Indigenous understandings of Christianity as well as "the possibility for ecclesiastical texts to contain heretical messages" (211).

Nahua and Maya Catholicisms builds on Louise Burkhart's pioneering research that illuminated the influence of Nahua culture on Catholicism during the colonial period (*Slippery Earth*, 1989). Christensen significantly advances the field through an innovative comparative approach that seeks to understand the same for Maya culture, and to bring Nahuatl and Maya texts into conversation. Here it should be noted that while increasingly scholars are attempting to take on Indigenous language sources, few have worked with two very different Mesoamerican Indigenous languages—Christensen definitely raises the bar. Throughout the book, the juxtaposition of precontact religious and cultural practices of Nahuas and Mayas, their markedly different local and regional contexts, the ideological differences among religious orders, and even individual personalities and skill sets, serve to explain the variations among the religious texts and thus the plurality of the religious messages that circulated. The result is a highly complex picture of the differences and similarities between these two Indigenous groups, not to mention among the religious orders with whom they interacted.

An important outcome of this study is the negation of a particularly pernicious idea about Indigenous peoples in colonial Latin America—that of a singular "Indian" experience with Christianity, one that is more often than not understood (at least by the general public) as the Catholic faith being forced on a passive mass of helpless folk. In Christensen's rendering, however, Indigenous peoples are shown to be active protagonists who both shaped and responded to the colonial religious and social world in creative ways. This last point is one of the stronger aspects of the work: with his ability to navigate multiple languages and cultures, Christensen never loses sight of the integral role of natives in the production of religious texts he examines, whether they served as scribes, anonymous assistants to the priests (which he appropriately terms "ghostwriters"), or authors in their own right.

Eminently readable and impeccably researched, Christensen's book provides a fine entry point for the reader with little or no previous knowledge of the evangelization of Indigenous peoples in colonial Mesoamerica. At the same time, his thorough treatment of some of the better-known canonical texts alongside rare and heretofore unknown archival finds are sure to please the specialist. His close readings also remind us how truly lively and revealing ecclesiastical texts can be in providing a window to the colonial world. One example, among many offered by Christensen, is the Franciscan Alonso de Molina's Nahuatl-language confessional manual which includes a question aimed at ascertaining whether the Indigenous confessee, more than likely a tamale vendor, was deceiving his/her fellows: "miyec yn izhuatl yc ticpiqui, ynic tichhueyliya? ([do] you wrap [tamales] with many leaves so that you enlarge them?)" (163). In this short phrase we can imagine the sights, sounds, and smells of a colonial marketplace in Central Mexico, with all of its potential intrigue.

Nahua and Maya Catholicisms should be in the library of anyone who specializes in colonial Indigenous studies in Mexico or beyond, as well as scholars interested in comparative indigeneities. For both the breadth of sources treated and the methodology employed, this book will undoubtedly find an enduring place in graduate seminars on Colonial Latin American history, religious studies, and critical Indigenous studies. It should be mentioned that upon first read, the book seemed more heavily weighted to Nahuatl texts than Maya (the sources include forty-one Nahuatl and thirty Maya). This is not the author's fault. As Christensen points out, for many reasons there are substantially fewer extant Maya texts than there are Nahuatl (12). In the end, the dominance of Nahuatl-language texts in this work only serves to bolster Christensen's argument that Indigenous peoples experienced—and influenced—the religious landscape of colonial Mesoamerica in distinct ways that deserve more careful attention.

KELLY S. McDONOUGH (White Earth Ojibwe Heritage) is assistant professor of Latin American colonial literatures and Indigenous studies in the Department of Spanish and Portuguese at the University of Texas at Austin.

MARIE SCHNITZLER

Indigeneity: Collected Essays
edited by Guillermo Delgado-P. and John Brown Childs
New Pacific Press, 2012

THESE ESSAYS ABOUT INDIGENEITY emerged after the congress "Beyond Race and Citizenship: Indigenous Identity in the Twenty-First Century," which occurred in 2004 at the University of California–Berkeley. The goal was "to provide a forum for Indigenous scholars . . . to address and to reflect upon the new politics of indigeneity" (xvii). Following the same guidelines, the present book was published ten years after the original congress. The articles induce reflection on the analysis of cultural unity and diversity of Indigenous people combined. This collection does not intend to solve the issues around the definition of the concept of indigeneity; such issues remain unresolved in both the international area and the academic world. Indeed, the idea behind the publication is to overcome the essentialized definition of indigeneity. Escárcega Zamarrón's analysis of the Declaration on the Rights of Indigenous Peoples contributes to this agenda by depicting indigeneity not as a consensus but as a negotiated concept. Indeed, various communities use this notion in the international arena to challenge groups' boundaries and to claim international recognition.

The fact that many of the authors are themselves members of Indigenous communities might explain the strong politicization of their articles. For Escárcega Zamarrón indigeneity is "the construction of identities of active resistance" (214). The challenge for Indigenous people is to enter the "new" world without accepting the "acculturation," "assimilation," or "integration" of Indigenous communities. To do so, Fachin promotes cultural diversity as a new political paradigm and Varese makes claims for overcoming the current neoliberal system and partisan ideologies. Some authors refuse to use negative definitions of Indigenous peoples based on Western standards. Wilson, for instance, explains that "colonialism is not removed from the discussion, but [she is] attempting to disallow it from dictating the parameters of [her] thoughts" (91). On this basis, she argues for Indigenous communities to "consciously indigenize [them]selves and [their] lands" (93). Brown Childs proposes to move beyond the dominant/dominated distinction to analyze the relationships among subaltern groups and their possible associations. However, to resist does not mean to reject all Western insights. Doxtater illustrates this idea with an analysis of the Mohawk warrior flag as an original appropriation of Western tools by Indigenous people which offers a "meeting place for the mind" (281) Mohawk communities.

In the book, the key concept of transcommunality underlines two processes: gathering and keeping a personal identity. Brown Childs define it as a "complexly fluid interaction and cooperation that respects rooted multiple territorial senses of affiliation, while also being aware of and concerned with interactions, mutual understandings, and cooperation in the midst of devastating global pressures that undermine both communities and nature" (xvi–xvii). Consequently, the ways to strengthen Indigenous traits and traditions are also discussed. Alluli Meyer describes a new educational program that will help to develop a new type of sciences based on Indigenous values such as unity, oracy, subjectivity, and sacrality. This idea of a new science is put into practice by Rodolfo Meyer in his reflection about the ethnographic movie, a European tool in essence. Alluli Meyer and Rodolfo Meyer's contributions place the resistance in a new area, the one of knowledge, sciences, and education. In this regard, this book reintroduces the notion of the sacred as well as the relationship with the environment in the debate. Language should also strengthen the feeling of belonging to the community. In his essay about Andean territories, Delgado connects the question of the language with political issues and asks for the democratization of democracy, as well as the recognition of Indigenous languages in order to "decolonize the logocentric authority and, often, the graphomania, that often accompanied Eurocentrism" (179). Fachin also discusses the role of Indigenous intellectuals in the creation of cohesion inside communities.

The argument of these authors might be understood as a claim for some reassertion of Indigenous traditions. If we push Escárcega Zamarrón's ideas to their limits, however, this might be analyzed as a re-essentialization of Indigenous identity. Erai raises these issues when she questions the black American boxer Mike Tyson's legitimacy in wearing a Māori tattoo on his face. She concludes her inquiries into Māori social distinctions with an apology of "chaos" as a source of incertitude and flexibility in social classification. Moreover, Baker's article probes into the consequences of such essentialization of traditions. Her essay deconstructs the fight against the "Occident" and the patriarchal Indian discourse that opposes gender freedom and self-sovereignty in order to highlight the constant reconstruction of tradition.

After the reading, a few questions emerge. First, no African case is discussed, although the minorities of the black continent used the same treaties and rhetoric to ask for particular Indigenous rights. The discussion about the Karen fight also concealed the logics of Asian and African specificity, where the whole population could be called Indigenous. Finally, the political dimension of the book has to be taken carefully. The emphasis put on the notion of resistance makes this publication a kind of "Unidentified Political Object." Although Denis Constant Martin (2002) used it mainly in the domain of the arts, this denomination underlines the presence in the book of implicit representations about what indigeneity should be. This political stand sometimes suffers from a lack of deep empirical data, however, and perhaps may leave unquestioned complex notions of "globalization," "neocapitalism," and so on. For these reasons, the concept of transcommunality seems to belong to a utopian world, and each article presents a possible solution for the described issues faced by Indigenous people today. As such, this publication is an interesting contribution in the debate surrounding the future of Indigenous policies.

MARIE SCHNITZLER is a PhD student at the University of Liege, Belgium, and the University of Bordeaux Victor Segalen, France, and research fellow at the Funds for Scientific Research—F.N.R.S., Belgium.

EVAN J. HABKIRK

Victims of Benevolence: The Dark Legacy of the Williams Lake Residential School
by Elizabeth Furniss
Arsenal Pulp Press, 1995 (reprint 2011)

SINCE THE ANNOUNCEMENT of Canada's Truth and Reconciliation Commission, there has been a boom in publishing related to Canada's residential schools. In 2011, Arsenal Pulp Press released its third printing of Elizabeth Furniss's *Victims of Benevolence: The Dark Legacy of the Williams Lake Residential School*. Although it is a concise primer on the impact residential schools had on Native communities, problematic sourcing and evidence and a lack of updating between its 1995 and 2011 printings plague the book, raising the question of why this book was released without revisions.

The message of this book is simple: although resisted by Native populations, the Williams Lake Residential School experience, for children and parents, was a harrowing tale of abuse and neglect. Furniss chronicles this experience through the escape and subsequent deaths of two students, Duncan Sticks in 1902 and Augustine Allan in 1920. Framing the book around resistance, Furniss tries to create a narrative that gives Native peoples agency in the face of colonialism. A discourse of colonization and victimization, however, subverts this resistance narrative. After explaining the ways the Williams Lake community resisted the Oblate missionaries and their school, Furniss points to the uneven power dynamic between Native communities and administrators of the school, stating that "the church and government maintained their control over Native people not only through legal and bureaucratic power, but by being able to control the meaning of events and protests." Enveloped by colonization and assimilation, the Native community is left at the mercy of the school authorities. Furniss ends her book with an address by Chief Bev Sellars at the First National Conference on Residential Schools in 1991, in which Chief Sellars states that many Native communities "know that all suicides, the alcoholism, the very low self-esteem of our people, the sexual abuse, the loss of language and culture, the family breakdown, the dependency on others, the loss of pride, the loss of parental skills, and other social problems that have plagued our people can be traced directly to residential schools."

Although this overstatement may have been intended to raise awareness about residential schools and the problems they caused, Sellars's statement creates a discourse where all problems facing Native communities begin and end with the residential schools. Although many of these long-term intergenerational problems can be linked to the residential school experience, nevertheless, due to differences of school staff and programming, students, and communities the schools were supposed to serve, the true meaning of the residential school experience is composed of many stories. Pinning all social problems on residential schools, while negating other acts of colonization, leaves the federal government and Canadian society able to claim that once the Truth and Reconciliation Commission's mandate is finished, all the problems of colonialism are no longer a governmental issue.

The biggest problem with the book's 2011 printing is the lack of updating since its 1995 release. Although authors and publishers are not required to update books between printings, many important developments regarding residential schools have occurred during this time, including court cases, the Royal Commission on Aboriginal People, and the creation of the Truth and Reconciliation Commission. Most of Furniss's research ends in 1992, leaving many areas where the book could be expanded, especially the 1991 criminal proceedings against Bishop Hubert O'Connor for sexual misconduct. By 1994, the trial was renewed and in 1996, O'Conner was found guilty of the charges. Considering that this is one of the most prominent legal cases regarding the Williams Lake School, and considering that Furniss wanted to provide her readers with a current understanding of residential school issues, this information would have been an important addition to the book.

Although writing about residential schools is a hard road to navigate in Canada's current political climate, some updating should have been done for the reader. Following the success of J. R. Miller's *Shingwauk's Vision* and John S. Milloy's *A National Crime,* one has to wonder if Arsenal Pulp Press released the book's third printing to capture the markets stemming from the sale of these cornerstone works. Whatever the publisher's or author's reasons for not updating content, Furniss's book continues to be a good primer for learning about Canadian residential schools and their legacies. A more experienced reader, however, may want to look elsewhere for an in-depth study of the roles Native peoples, churches, and the Canadian government played in Canada's residential school system.

EVAN J. HABKIRK is a PhD candidate in the history department at the University of Western Ontario.

GINA STARBLANKET

Mark My Words: Native Women Mapping Our Nations
by Mishuana Goeman
University of Minnesota Press, 2013

INDIGENOUS WOMEN'S WRITINGS have received increased attention in recent years beyond the realm of literary studies for their important role in the deconstruction of gendered and colonial relations of power and for their contribution to Indigenous politics of self-determination. With her monograph *Mark My Words: Native Women Mapping Our Nations,* Tonowanda Seneca author Mishuana Goeman offers a unique contribution to this emergent field through an examination of the spatial dimensions of decolonization that exist within the literary works of Indigenous women. With this book, Goeman draws out the ways that settler and Indigenous conceptions of space collide with one another to implicate Indigenous women. At the same time, she also brings to light the discursive techniques through which these tensions are exposed and challenged by Indigenous women's narratives.

Goeman's analysis is deployed through four chapters that take up the writings of Indigenous women from across the United States and Canada, including E. Pauline Johnson (Mohawk), Esther Belin (Diné), Joy Harjo (Creek), Leslie Marmon Silko (Laguna Pueblo) and others. Her review of various literary works elucidates the range of methods and terms that each author uses to foreground Indigenous conceptions of space, relationship, and autonomy. In conducting this study, Goeman's aim is to reveal the political underpinnings and potency of Indigenous women's writings. She does so by emphasizing the ways that these narratives function to disrupt gendered settler geographies and boundaries with the particular objective of Indigenous liberation from colonizing orders.

Throughout the book, Goeman focuses her vision on the process of writing as activism, the revolutionary power of relationships, and the possibilities of confronting spatialized injustice in ways that transcend colonial models of territory, jurisdiction, and race. Through careful review of each author's engagement with different temporal periods, spatialities, and colonial premises, Goeman paints a comprehensive picture of the violence inherent in settler conceptualizations of geography and space. Her analysis exposes the realities of oppression that occur as colonizing forces continuously attempt to narrate relationships to the land and one another by defining borders between human beings through narrow categories based on race, sexuality, gender, and nation. Goeman demonstrates how each of the authors have produced alternative mappings to colonial classifications by remembering, articulating, and sharing Indigenous discourses that function to counter the monolithic histories erected by colonial forces.

Goeman's engagement with the contributions of each author is conducted against the backdrop of U.S. and Canadian law and policy while simultaneously, and seemingly effortlessly, illuminating its global context and applicability. While authors such as Harjo and others place themselves in local sites, invoking embodied geographies and places, their writings speak broadly to the colonial and gendered violence of globalization while illustrating the multiple spatial scales available to Indigenous writers. Goeman demonstrates how Harjo's articulated strategies guide readers toward a discourse that locates each of us "within the world, not just engaging it from the periphery or margin" (120). While Goeman's collective analysis primarily invokes the works of four authors, she constructs an analytical frame that is applicable to the literary works of any Indigenous speaker or writer and identifies techniques useful for anyone seeking to deconstruct the spatialized dimensions of colonialism.

A particular strength of this book involves Goeman's recognition of the value inherent in multiple perspectives on the concept of decolonization. While the author spends most time with writings that are not predicated on the terms established by colonizing systems, she also acknowledges the importance of approaches that choose to engage with those terms to expose their logic of oppression. An example of this can be seen in Goeman's analysis of Johnson's efforts to highlight the barriers that liberal discourses present for gender equity and Indigenous rights (44). Rather than seeking to unsettle the liberal nation-state, Johnson's stories elucidate its ideology and engage in processes of remapping the national terrain through the main characters' struggles to make space for gender equity and equal rights for Indigenous nations within it. This approach allows Johnson to reconceptualize the colonial notions of gender, race, individualism, and property that seek to define abject spaces ranging from Indigenous women's bodies to Indigenous nations. Goeman reveals to the reader the ways in which Johnson's writings function to challenge the liberal logics that shape relationships between intimate couples, providing alternatives to the discourses of the Indian Act (84). Though Goeman is clearly knowledgeable about Indigenous literary activism, she does not use this proficiency to prove her own expertise or to dwell on the limitations of the authors' approaches. Instead, she skillfully draws out the possibilities and strengths in the various conceptions of resistance articulated in this collection of writings.

Mark My Words is an eloquent, compelling, and unique examination of the various ways in which Indigenous women's writings and creative works function to disrupt the gendered and spatialized violence that occurs within processes of settler colonialism while simultaneously advancing Indigenous conceptions of relationship and space. Goeman's specific emphasis on the processes of decolonization and self-determination at play in the work of each contributor, and on the imaginative and productive possibilities that they hold for confronting spatial injustice, represents an innovative contribution to analyses of the emancipatory potential of Indigenous women's literature and creative works. Her conceptualization of gendered spatial geographies is particularly crucial in understanding the range of impacts that colonialism, globalization, neoliberalism, and nationalism continue to have in Indigenous peoples' lives and communities. *Mark My Words* is an outstanding study that should be read by anyone interested in political studies, law, literary analysis, geography, and Indigenous studies. By drawing out the gendered and spatialized nature of colonial structures of oppression and violence, Goeman convincingly demonstrates the pressing need to understand the role of women as central to processes of resistance, self-determination, and mapping of our futures.

GINA STARBLANKET (Cree/Saulteaux-Star Blanket Cree Nation) is working on a PhD in the University of Victoria's Department of Political Science.

SETH SCHERMERHORN

At the Border of Empires: The Tohono O'odham, Gender, and Assimilation, 1880–1934
by Andrae M. Marak and Laura Tuennerman
University of Arizona Press, 2013

IN ADDITION TO WRITING Tohono O'odham history into more nuanced and theoretically sophisticated interpretations of Native American history than has previously been available, Andrae M. Marak and Laura Teunnerman's *At the Border of Empires* masterfully tells "the story of an uncompleted quest for full assimilation" of the Tohono O'odham, a transnational Indigenous people who live along the U.S.–Mexico border that arbitrarily cut Tohono O'odham homelands in half in 1853. Highlighting the themes of imperialism, gender, and Indigenous agency, Marak and Teunnerman deftly illustrate the unintended consequences of gendered assimilation efforts in which U.S. assimilation efforts occurred not in spite of, but rather because of, the peripheral location of the Tohono O'odham. Like other Native American peoples who were often seen as weak, corruptible "proto-citizens," imperial eyes saw the Tohono O'odham as requiring protection from influences of the "wrong sort." Indeed, the perceived need to protect Tohono O'odham from "vices" was part of the rationale for the creation of the Papago Indian Reservation, today called the Tohono O'odham Nation, in 1916 on the U.S. side of the international border.

The key theoretical category of this study is "negotiation," which, much like Gilbert Joseph's "encounter," focuses on "the deployment and contestation of power" (1–2). Crucially, because of this process of negotiation in the differential assimilation of Tohono O'odham in the United States and Mexico, assimilation (in a Gramscian key) is necessarily incomplete. As the authors state in their conclusion, "Negotiation—defined to include everything from exchange and borrowing to circumvention and passive resistance—resulted in efforts at assimilation that were incomplete, complicated, and sometimes unexpected in their application and outcomes" (143).

The book is topically organized. The introduction presents the category of negotiation and situates the book in relation to previous historical scholarship. The first chapter provides a brief historical and cultural background on the Tohono O'odham. Chapters 2 to 5 constitute the body of the work, each taking on a theme of gendered assimilation efforts: vice, marriage, schools, and vocation. Chapter 2 examines divergent O'odham and non-O'odham views of "vice," particularly focusing on the consumption of alcohol. Given the paucity of O'odham commentaries on alcohol, and the inverse relationship between rivers and wine drinking posited in the chapter's epigraph, the analysis of Tohono O'odham *nawait i'ita* (saguaro cactus) wine drinking ceremonies and attitudes toward drinking more generally in this chapter would benefit substantially from the cultural and historical insights gained from Don Bahr's *How Mockingbirds Are*.[1] Chapter 3 examines sex and marriage as areas of "contestation, assimilation, and resistance" (49). The analysis of the Office of Indian Affairs' (OIA) definition of marriage as "heterosexual, monogamous, lifelong, and sanctioned by law . . . patriarchal, consensual, and Christian," is particularly effective in illustrating how the implementation of colonial policies undermined marriage in an "Indian way" (52). The authors also analyze the ironic situation of OIA field matrons promoting marriage for O'odham women, though not for themselves, as a crucial part of the assimilation process.

Chapter 4 examines the striking failures of education as a means of assimilation. A few items worthy of note include the institutional opposition against Tohono O'odham pilgrimages to Magdalena, a student hunger strike against a harsh English-only rule in 1920 at the Santa Rosa day school, and the written observations of Antonia Garcia, a Tohono O'odham student at Topawa, on the "Holy Week Devils" in Cowlic in the 1930s, which is a valuable, though previously unutilized, O'odham contribution to the intriguing literature on O'odham *jejawul*, or "devils." Chapter 5 focuses on the highly gendered, strategic entrance of the Tohono O'odham into the cash economy. The chapter especially examines the roles of field matrons from the 1890s through 1920s, and their intention to transform Tohono O'odham women into "good housewives" who are dependent on wage-earning husbands. Trained as laundresses and housekeepers, many O'odham women continued working in Tucson even after starting a family; thus, the primary connection to the cash economy for many O'odham families was through women who became the family breadwinners—nearly the opposite of what the OIA had hoped the outing system would accomplish.

Chapter 6 offers a comparative counterexample to the Americanization of Tohono O'odham in the United States by focusing instead on the Mexicanization of O'odham in Mexico. Ironically, the Mexican government accomplished most of what the American government could not—the assimilation of Tohono O'odham —through neglect rather than paternalistic government intervention. "Perhaps even more ironic than the weak postrevolutionary Mexican government achieving what the much stronger U.S. government could not," the authors conclude, "is the fact that the Tohono O'odham Nation today fights not only for its own continued political and cultural survival, but also [for] that of the Sonoran Tohono O'odham" (142).

The greatest accomplishment of *At the Border of Empires* lies in its remarkable and original contribution to the study of an understudied period in the history of an understudied people, while it rigorously underscores gender issues that have often been neglected in Tohono O'odham studies. The authors strive to highlight Indigenous agency and Tohono O'odham voices by making significant use of archival resources in both the United States and Mexico. Although Marak and Teunnerman are both archive-based historians, the study would benefit greatly from a more extensive use of Tohono O'odham oral histories. While it is perhaps understandable that archive-based historians would avoid the toils of conducting oral history research within an Indigenous nation, neglecting published oral histories is less excusable. Although this study makes good use of several published oral histories, the published life stories of Juan Dolores, Theodore Rios, and Frances Manuel could aid the authors in their attempt to highlight Tohono O'odham voices and agency.

Overall, this is an important and readable book, suitable for undergraduate classrooms and graduate seminars across the disciplines of history, Native American and Indigenous studies, women's and gender studies, borderlands studies, religious studies, and anthropology. This book should be widely read and discussed, for although it is a single case study about a transnational people along the U.S.—Mexico international border, this book speaks powerfully to the more sweeping histories and transformations of gendered assimilation efforts across Native American and Indigenous communities globally.

SETH SCHERMERHORN is assistant professor of religious studies at Hamilton College.

CAMIE AUGUSTUS

Telling It to the Judge: Taking Native History to Court
by Arthur J. Ray
McGill-Queen's University Press, 2011

SINCE THE LANDMARK CALDER DECISION was handed down in 1973, there has been no shortage of literature on Aboriginal rights and the courts. Most of it, however, has been written by legal scholars. More recently, we have witnessed a growing body of commentary from other scholars, especially historians, anthropologists, and geographers. It is particularly those who have been directly involved in the process of claims as expert witnesses who are slowly uncovering another perspective on Aboriginal law.

Arthur Ray's *Telling It to the Judge: Taking Native History to Court* is one such example. A well-respected historical geographer with a long academic career and author of numerous fur-trade histories, Ray's experience as an academic expert to the courts on significant cases such as *Horseman*, *Delgamuukw*, and the more recent *Powley* makes him the ideal candidate for this task.

A foreword by lawyer Jean Teillet and introduction by legal scholar Peter W. Hutchins outline some of the problems with the Canadian legal system as the venue for settling Aboriginal claims. Ray goes on to detail these very challenges throughout the book—indeed, one of its strengths—while also providing a narrative of his experiences. He shows how, in case after case, the problem of the courts is a problem of historical interpretation. It demands more than the strict legal interpretation of documents: it demands the inclusion and contribution of non-legal scholars, namely historians.

The book's chapters are organized thematically: all revolve around a central issue in Aboriginal law and a specific case. Chapter 1 begins with Ray's first experience as an expert witness in the 1986 *Horseman* case, told in the context of the Aboriginal commercial right to trap. Chapter 2 focuses on *Delgamuukw* and the problems of interpreting evidence. Chapter 3 considers fisheries and harvesting rights through the Ontario case *Wassaykessic*, while chapter 4 examines treaty interpretation in *Victor Buffalo*. Chapters 5 and 6 examine Métis rights and identity from the *Powley* case in Ontario, while chapter 7 examines Métis harvesting rights cases that followed. Chapter 8 rounds off the book with some closing commentary regarding the challenges of expert witness work—one of the most analytical (and interesting) chapters of the book.

Throughout *Telling It to the Judge*, Ray makes a strong and convincing argument for the importance of historical context to law as it applies to Aboriginal rights. He brings a historical perspective to the interpretation of law—something that is still underappreciated in the courts. Indeed, it is in the historical interpretation of legal issues where the greatest potential of the book lies; we might have seen more here. The writing sometimes tends toward a description of events rather than an analytical critique of the process—perhaps this reflects the difficulty of transitioning to semi-autobiographical writing. But the meaning and intent of such detailed description without the larger context of analysis can be lost on the less-versed reader. There are times when Ray seems almost hesitant to offer his own interpretations, and he qualifies them when he does. But it is this much-needed historical interpretation of law that has the potential to bridge the culture gap between the practice of Aboriginal rights by Aboriginal people and the interpretation of them by the courts.

Ray does well to explain the challenges of the mere logistics of the court process. Aboriginal rights cases tend to constitute seemingly endless streams of paper evidence, "sometimes presented . . . without the benefit of any context" (16). He also points to the differences that documentary evidence holds for the courts and for academics: the courts see documents as positive evidence—evidence that is submitted to demonstrate the truth. Indeed, documents are taken literally, at their face value (33). Academics, on the other hand, use documents to support their arguments—and often refute the face value of those documents. Documents are meant to be interpreted, not simply read, and cannot always be believed. Indeed, this difference in the use of documents illuminates one of the fundamental epistemological differences between non-legal and legal experts and demonstrates the heart of the problem of historical interpretation in a court setting.

While most readers will need more background in Aboriginal case law to fully appreciate the finer points of Ray's message, the book will find a place among a wide range of readers. It would make an excellent companion to an undergraduate or graduate course on Aboriginal rights and the courts. It would also be of value to lawyers (and lawyers in training) who could benefit from an understanding of a specifically historical perspective on case law, Aboriginal rights, and legal interpretation. And it would, of course, appeal to the more specialized academics whose interests lie in Aboriginal rights and the courts—legal and non-legal scholars alike.

CAMIE AUGUSTUS is a postdoctoral fellow at the University of Ottawa.

JESSICA BARDILL

Native American DNA: Tribal Belonging and the False Promise of Genetic Science
by Kim TallBear
University of Minnesota Press, 2013

IN THIS FOUNDATIONAL MONOGRAPH, TallBear builds on her previous and ongoing cultural anthropological work about the concept of "Native American DNA" and the applications of that concept within scientific and genetic genealogy communities, as well as what the concept may mean for tribal communities and their sovereign determinations of citizenship. TallBear refuses aspects of anthropological inquiry that would make tribes and their citizens the subjects of her work. This refusal then allows TallBear to focus on the scientists actively creating and utilizing the concept of "Native American DNA" in their work and within larger relations of power.

TallBear delineates the "co-constitution" of Native American DNA as a concept created by science and culture, nature and society. Using Donna Haraway's idea of "partial knowledges," TallBear questions the empirical gaze that would pretend to both be nonsituated and contain the possibility of complete knowledge. She then demonstrates how that gaze guides scientific inquiry and interpretation. One important contribution and critique offered in this text is the clarification of anachronistic misapplications of the terms "genetics" and "DNA" to understand historical uses of "blood" in various sources. Here TallBear encourages Native American and Indigenous studies scholars specifically to recognize that genetics as the basic unit of heredity comprised of DNA (and literal and figurative ideas stemming from that foundation) only emerged after 1953, and thus conflating "blood" with genes in earlier texts is a modern confusion, not an accurate representation. Her warning also responds to scientists who use modern and ancient samples of DNA to examine human migration patterns through comparisons of changes in small regions of the genome. By inferring that these small differences in genes correlate to particular movements of peoples over time, the scientists contribute to what TallBear names "genetic fetishism" in both the scientific and lay communities. TallBear shows that this reliance on, and desire for, genetic information helps to perpetuate older racial and scientific thinking.

TallBear also shows how the conceptual construction of Native American

DNA emerges from centuries-old racial scientific thinking that grouped humans into particular distinguishable categories that had varying relationships to continents. The division (such as Europe and Asia) and collapse (such as the Americas) of these continents into familiar references undergirds the newer but continuous notion of biogeographical ancestry, used in reference to both modern and ancient humans. While TallBear's previous work forcefully asserted the difference between tribe and race, *Native American DNA: Tribal Belonging and the False Promise of Genetic Science* engages with arguments that conceive of Indigenous peoples as tribal as well as racially constructed, and thereby expands on her previous contributions by thinking about the turn to genealogical criteria for tribal citizenship with the support of Kristi Gover's work on tribal constitutions.

For both Native and non-Native scholars entering the field, the Introduction provides a clear overview of "Native American DNA" as a specific constructed concept, as well as how one's entry into both a disciplinary field and the field site itself are already constituted through particular knowledges. Helpfully, the Introduction reviews the situated nature of knowledge for TallBear and others, including credit to her interlocutors and theoretical touchstones across various disciplines. The strongest chapters in the text are "Racial Science, Blood, and DNA" and "The Genographic Project: The Business of Research and Representation." In the former, TallBear sets the stage for readers to understand her particular work but also to interrogate their own spaces of knowledge production. She further demonstrates how her case studies differ from similar work by Alondra Nelson and Sandra Soo-Jin Lee. The chapter on the Genographic Project explores the evolving ethical, rhetorical, and problematic storytelling of a large project that brings together issues of capitalism, scientific pursuit of particular questions of identity and migration, and Indigenous peoples. The conclusion offers hope in the face of these valuable lessons about questionable corporate representation, astutely critical genetic genealogists, and research focused on spin and pursuing a particular history in order to perpetuate power through a racial hierarchy. Here TallBear turns to genetic projects involving Indigenous peoples that are building capacity in tribal nations and challenging the narratives produced by Western scientific projects by offering up their own alternative interrogations and interpretations.

Throughout the text, TallBear works to make sure her readers follow information that may be new to them, such as the science of genetic testing and the intricacies of tribal belonging, both of which have shifted over time and continue to change. This text will be valuable to many scholars engaged in disciplinary and especially interdisciplinary work, from anthropologists and genealogists to genetic scientists and ethicists. It is also useful for tribal community leaders and members who may be considering using genetic testing themselves or who want a better overall understanding of Western science and scientists, thereby inverting the imperial and empirical gazes.

JESSICA BARDILL (Cherokee descent) is assistant professor in the Department of English at East Carolina University.

KATRINA PHILLIPS

Indians and Wannabes: Native American Powwow Dancing in the Northeast and Beyond
by Ann M. Axtmann
University Press of Florida, 2013

AMERICAN INDIAN DANCES are integral political, religious, and cultural elements, and they have long been subjects of non-Native fascination—and fear. Native delegations to Washington, D.C., staged performances near the White House in the 1820s, but the federal government intensified its efforts to eradicate Indian dances in the late nineteenth and early twentieth centuries. Non-Natives in the United States and Europe leapt at the chance to see American Indian performers in Wild West shows, and historians have argued that promoters like Buffalo Bill Cody hired Indians *because* they could dance. Today, Indians continue to dance—and the powwow circuit is a common stage.

According to Clyde Ellis and Luke Eric Lassiter, powwows are a dynamic source of American Indian expression "anchored in deeply respected traditions but clearly modified over the years by the shifting tides of identity and belief that have appeared in every Indian community." The dances themselves are a central component, but powwows serve as spaces to find old friends and make new ones, share songs and dances, and reaffirm "shared experiences" (see Clyde Ellis, Luke Eric Lassiter, and Gary H. Dunham, *Powwow,* 2005).

Indians, however, are not the only ones traveling to and participating in powwows. In *Indians and Wannabes,* independent scholar Ann M. Axtmann examines powwow history, details specific dances and their use of time and space, and attempts to highlight the issues of race, belonging, and the problematics of those who wish to "play Indian." The book is an excellent primer for those interested in the differences in styles and regalia, as well as the nuances of individual powwows; while Axtmann's work on the more difficult aspects is well intentioned, the analysis is somewhat lacking.

This interdisciplinary work seeks to reach an audience interested in dance and an audience interested in American Indian studies, but the disparate nature of these disciplines may lead to confusion. Those unfamiliar with the vocabulary of dancers and choreographers may struggle with some sections, but Axtmann's vivid descriptions of how powwow dancers use their bodies and the space around them provide an intriguing account: "As [contemporary grass] dancers coordinate roach, bells, fringe, and body movement, they exude an intense visceral dexterity that is demonstrated by how they integrate movement, music, and regalia while performing repetitive movements on the right and the left" (35).

Axtmann provides what might be considered a CliffsNotes version for those unfamiliar with the politics of American Indian history, which is necessary, but the nuances of federal Indian policy and the numerous Native responses to these policies are not fully explained. While it is true that Native performers were often constrained by the boundaries of Wild West shows and world's fairs that were produced by and consumed by whites, as well as working under constraints imposed by missionaries, reservation Indians, and sundry government officials, scholars such as L. G. Moses, Clyde Ellis, John Troutman, and Paige Raibmon, among others, have shown that Native performers had a significant amount of agency in terms of their performances and their contractual obligations to employers.

Axtmann is keenly aware of her position as a non-Native and places herself squarely outside the powwow circle, but this distance is, at times, nearly insurmountable. The voices of Native powwow organizers, vendors, and dancers are not nearly as present as they could—and perhaps should—be, and this silence is telling, since Axtmann spent fourteen years traveling to powwows in Connecticut, Maine, Massachusetts, Montana, New Jersey, New York, North Dakota, and Washington, D.C. The incorporation of more Native voices would have produced an incredibly compelling narrative, particularly in her connections between traditional dances, contemporary dancers, and American Indian history. She notes, for instance, that traditional women dancers move along the periphery of the circle at many powwows: "By facing inward toward the sacred center of the circle, they also turn away from the outside—from the nation-state, mainstream U.S. society, capitalism, Anglo-American values, racism, and perhaps other factors that Indian women might want to exclude from their consciousness as they protect their community" (103). This is a beautiful sentiment, but it is one that would be strengthened through the voices of these women who were taught these dances by those who danced before them, those who knew and believed in the purpose of these dances.

The questions of race, "playing Indian," and intellectual ownership are the book's most complex topics, but these subjects require a more in-depth investigation than the book allows. The lines separating authenticity, appropriation, and appreciation become increasingly blurred as non-Natives attempt to join the ranks of powwow dancers, and debates over race and identity remain at the forefront for many American Indians.

Axtmann notes that it is often hard to distinguish hobbyists, mixed-blood participants, or wannabes—those she deems "non-Indians who dance in the arena circle 'as if' they were Indians or 'as if' they were performing Native

American traditional dances" (14, 108). However, she describes several young dancers on the sidelines at a powwow who "were Caucasian in outward appearance" and whose movements "approximated the grass dance style, but their movements were not as full-bodied or as vigorous as the hundreds of Native grass dancers I have observed" (133). Whether these dancers were Native or not, this assessment raises problematic assumptions about what Indians should look like versus what they do look like and brings intermarriage and blood quantum into play. Similarly, ascribing race onto a performer is a significant problem, particularly when one recalls the government practice of allowing officials—not American Indians—to determine who was Indian and who was not based solely on artificially constructed notions of Indianness.

Axtmann also addresses the issue of wannabes, whose dogged desire for what they deem authentic creates a narrow viewpoint of Indians and Indian dancers. Some seem subdued, "as if they are aware they are in the wrong place," while others move "as if in a trance . . . oblivious to the drum or the other dancers in the arena circle" (129). Their presence at powwows provokes "questions of meaning, authenticity, appropriation, and race" and, while Axtmann's effort is noteworthy, these questions are not fully answered.

KATRINA PHILLIPS is a PhD candidate in the Department of History at the University of Minnesota.

KYLE T. MAYS

Our Fires Still Burn: The Native American Experience
by Audrey Geyer
DVD distributed by Audrey Geyer/Visions, 2013

THE DOCUMENTARY *Our Fires Still Burn: The Native American Experience* (2013) is a one-hour film produced by independent media artist Audrey Geyer. This compelling picture tells of the resilience of Native communities in Michigan, with a particular focus on the Saginaw Chippewa Indian Tribe, located approximately 155 miles (249 km) northwest of Detroit, and about 70 miles (112 km) north of the capital, Lansing. In thirteen chapters, the author recounts the deep losses and trauma of Native American peoples at large, and the resurgence of the Saginaw Chippewa Tribe in particular, fueled by traditional ceremonies and modern economic enterprises. *Our Fires Still Burn* centers on two themes: trauma and resilience.

The first few chapters explain the trauma of the boarding school era, such as the experience of Native youth at the Mt. Pleasant Industrial Boarding School. This was a time when Indigenous communities experienced a cultural and familial genocide throughout the United States: young people were kidnapped from their homes and, as a result, almost an entire generation of youth were cut off from their cultures, languages, and peoples. It also shows how some Indigenous peoples lived in "two-worlds," living within mainstream U.S. society, or avoiding giving their children an Indigenous identity in order to avoid cultural/racial discrimination.

Although the documentary suffers from an illogical structure (meaning it jumps from topic to topic), it does point to three issues that are becoming increasingly important topics in Indigenous communities and studies: language revitalization; the state of Indigenous men, or masculinity; and youth. It mentions that, although Indigenous women suffer from domestic and sexual abuse, most tribal communities lack *well-briety* (the combination of well-being and sobriety) programs for men. Although the documentary doesn't spend a lot of time on this subject (and the others), the mention of these important topics might spark a deeper interest by viewers.

Michigan's Indigenous communities are healing their peoples through a myriad of means. From the use of the Sacred Fire and sweat lodges, to art and journalism, Indigenous peoples are able to positively affect not only Indigenous communities but also non-Native communities. From a discussion with Anishinaabe elder and spiritual leader Bruce Hardwick leading people in prayer and sweat lodges to Native News Network founder and editor Levi

Rickert (Prairie Brand Potawatomi), to Yakima artist Bunky Echo-Hawk, Native peoples use a variety of methods to heal and pass on teachings to Native communities. Perhaps the greatest strength of *Our Fires Still Burn* is the desire of all Indigenous elders to pass on teachings to the Seventh Generation: Native youth.

While properly showcasing the survival of the Saginaw Chippewa Tribe, the documentary fails to provide historical context for the development of this particular tribal community. Instead, the audience is left with important questions. Who are they? Where did they come from? How did they end up on the reservation? Without broaching these questions and others, it is assumed that the Saginaw Chippewa simply lived on the reservation. There is no discussion of the Treaties of 1855 or 1864, which essentially created the Isabella Reservation, combining the Saginaw, Swan Creek, and Black River bands into the present Saginaw Chippewa community.

Despite its lack of historical depth, *Our Fires Still Burn* would be great for all ages, from young adolescents to adults with little to no knowledge of contemporary Indigenous realities. It could also be used in an introduction to a Native American Studies course and lower-level Midwestern history courses at the college level. The documentary may lack depth, but it does make at least one major point for non-Indigenous peoples: that Native peoples have survived, are still here, and can blend modern and traditional ways of knowing to make a better life for their children, as Native Americans have been doing for centuries.

KYLE T. MAYS (Saginaw Chippewa) is a PhD candidate in the Department of History at the University of Illinois, Urbana–Champaign.

New from **DUKE UNIVERSITY PRESS**

A Nation Rising
Hawaiian Movements for
Life, Land, and Sovereignty
NOELANI GOODYEAR-KA'OPUA, IKAIKA HUSSEY
& ERIN KAHUNAWAIKA'ALA WRIGHT, EDITORS
Photographs by EDWARD W. GREEVY
Narrating Native Histories
83 photographs, paper, $27.95

"It is history, it is culture, it is wisdom, it is art, and it is an invaluable contribution to the literature of Indigenous resurgence."—***Taiaiake Alfred***

"No other volume has addressed from so many perspectives the struggles involved in the Hawaiian sovereignty movement of the past four decades."
—***Vicente M. Diaz***

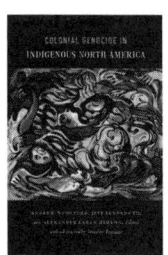

Colonial Genocide in Indigenous North America
ANDREW WOOLFORD,
JEFF BENVENUTO &
ALEXANDER LABAN
HINTON, EDITORS
Foreword by
THEODORE FONTAINE
13 illustrations, paper, $26.95

Rhythms of the Pachakuti
Indigenous Uprising and State
Power in Bolivia
RAQUEL GUTIÉRREZ AGUILAR
Translated by STACEY ALBA D. SKAR
Foreword by SINCLAIR THOMSON
New Ecologies for the Twenty-First Century
Latin America in Translation
paper, $25.95

Formations of United States Colonialism
ALYOSHA GOLDSTEIN, EDITOR
14 illustrations, paper, $27.95

@DUKEpress

DUKE
UNIVERSITY PRESS
www.dukeupress.edu

To order, please call
888-651-0122

REMEMBERING THE MODOC WAR
Redemptive Violence and the Making of American Innocence
Boyd Cothran
"Cothran's brilliant book will change the way readers think about Western history, Native American studies, collective memory, and the culture of consumerism."
—**Ari Kelman**, University of California, Davis
264 pages $34.95
A project of First Peoples: New Directions in Indigenous Studies

SEASONS OF CHANGE
Labor, Treaty Rights, and Ojibwe Nationhood
Chantal Norrgard
"Shows us why labor is significant for indigenous history. Norrgard pushes beyond existing work in this burgeoning field to show how culture, environment, treaty rights, and colonialism shaped Indian workers' experience and their demands for social change."
—**Colleen O'Neill**, Utah State University
216 pages $29.95 paper
A project of First Peoples: New Directions in Indigenous Studies

TRADERS AND RAIDERS
The Indigenous World of the Colorado Basin, 1540-1859
Natale A. Zappia
"A major contribution to the fields of Native American history, borderlands history, and early California history."
—**David Igler**, University of California, Irvine
256 pages $39.95

THE GIFT OF THE FACE
Portraiture and Time in Edward S. Curtis's The North American Indian
Shamoon Zamir
"Well researched, convincingly argued, and elegantly written . . . constitutes a remarkable achievement and a highly significant contribution to Native American studies and visual cultural studies."
—**Shari Huhndorf**, University of California, Berkeley
352 pages $39.95

TRIBAL TELEVISION
Viewing Native People in Sitcoms
Dustin Tahmahkera
"Highlighting strange but telling moments in the history of indigenous representation on U.S. and Canadian television, Tahmahkera makes a real contribution to our understanding of television and race. What might seem lighter than a soufflé—take The Brady Bunch, for instance—becomes a serious and interesting subject in the author's hands."
—**Randolph Lewis**, University of Texas at Austin
256 pages $27.95 paper

CHOOSING THE JESUS WAY
American Indian Pentecostals and the Fight for the Indigenous Principle
Angela Tarango
"Brilliantly challenges prevailing assumptions within Native studies, anthropology, and religious studies about the relationship between Native identity and religious/spiritual practice."
—**Andrea Smith**, University of Michigan
240 pages $32.95 paper

THE RED ATLANTIC
American Indigenes and the Making of the Modern World, 1000-1927
Jace Weaver
"An original, learned, and comparative historical narrative of transatlantic cultures and nations . . . will surely inspire and influence future students, research, and writing on the subject."
—**Gerald Vizenor**, University of California, Berkeley
352 pages $29.95

FRAMING CHIEF LESCHI
Narratives and the Politics of Historical Justice
Lisa Blee
"Illustrates in fresh, compelling ways the complex nature and importance of the endeavor we call history. It could be a valuable teaching tool for students of historical method and historical memory, both graduate and undergraduate."
—**Alexandra Harmon**, author of *Rich Indians*
320 pages $32.95 paper
A project of First Peoples: New Directions in Indigenous Studies

eBOOK
Most UNC Press books are also available as E-Books.

UNC Press books are now available through **Books @ JSTOR** and **Project Muse** – and **North Carolina Scholarship Online (NCSO)** on Oxford Scholarship Online.

THE UNIVERSITY of NORTH CAROLINA PRESS
at bookstores or 800-848-6224 • www.uncpress.unc.edu

NEW RELEASES
FROM UNIVERSITY OF MINNESOTA PRESS

Red Skin, White Masks
Rejecting the Colonial Politics of Recognition
Glen Sean Coulthard
Foreword by Taiaiake Alfred

Glen Sean Coulthard fundamentally questions prevailing ideas of settler colonialization and Indigenous resistance.

"A remarkably distinctive and provocative look at issues of power and opposition." —**Joanne Barker**, San Francisco State University

$22.50 paper | $67.50 cloth | 248 pages | Indigenous Americas Series

The Road Back to Sweetgrass
Linda LeGarde Grover

"(A) deeply moving and healing book."
—**Heid E. Erdrich**, author of *Original Local*

$24.95 cloth/jacket | 208 pages

Savage Preservation
The Ethnographic Origins of Modern Media Technology

Brian Hochman

Shows how widespread interest in recording vanishing races and disappearing cultures influenced audiovisual innovation.

"Eye-opening." —**Lisa Gitelman**, New York University

$27.50 paper | $82.50 cloth | 312 pages

Agitating Images
Photography against History in Indigenous Siberia

Craig Campbell

How photographs complicate our understanding of the history between indigenous Siberians and Russian communists.

$27.00 paper | $81.00 cloth | 288 pages
First Peoples Series

The Queerness of Native American Literature

Lisa Tatonetti

"Will change the future of Native American and Indigenous Studies." —**Qwo-Li Driskill**, Oregon State University

$25.00 paper | $75.00 cloth | 304 pages
Indigenous Americas Series

University of Minnesota Press • www.upress.umn.edu • 800-621-2736